Unpayable Debt

ON THE ANTIPOLITICAL

Unpayable Debt

Denise Ferreira da Silva

Sternberg Press

CONTENTS

For
Maria Amélia Ferreira da Silva, my mother
Ilka Maria Carvalho da Silva, my niece

In memoriam
Laureana Araújo da Silva and Erinea Romualdo Ferreira, my grandmothers
Sonia Ferreira da Rocha and Marlene Silva Araújo, my aunts

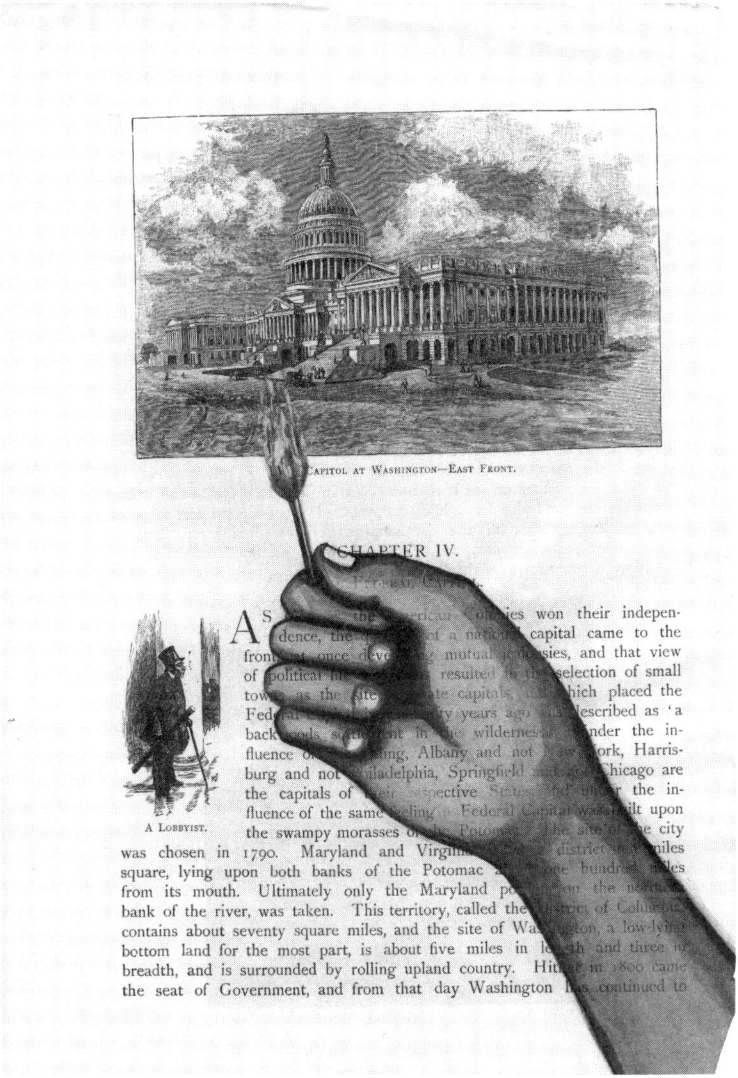

Rajkamal Kahlon
From the series *American History*, 2012
Gouache on book page

Future Perfect

Having had it already happen when approached in the scene of subjugation, her wounded body violates the linearity of space-time. No one had to bother to check if she was dead or alive. Already dead, as she always will have been, before the house was found, before the door was broken open. No one will have to be indicted for killing her—dead, she, someone, everyone. Already interpreted, resolved by/as blackness, the cause and circumstances of her death will not require judicial review, because her wounded body refigures authority (and total and symbolic violence), where equality (the figure of liberty in law and rights) supposedly reigns.

Knowing what happened to her and how it happened does not matter, because the racial event does not take place then/there. An ethical act that unfolds in the scene of nature, it occurs in the moment of justification (for what will have already happened). Each racial event is an instance of the symbolic tools of raciality performing in the juridical moment, fully in the domain of necessity. It does not register the play of representation in which space and time combine and unfold together, which is a distinct ethical scene, namely, the one belonging to the historical (Humanity) and historial (Subjectivity) figurings of the *transparent I*. Instead, because it takes as datum that which is a product of the scene of regulation, that is, of the tools of scientific reason, it is nothing more than the anticipated turning of the scientific and formal categories—a turning that actualizes a juridical authority resting on logical necessity and simultaneously resolves its economic circumstances as ethical occurrences. Effected in each and every deployment of the prevailing explanation for racial subjugation, one operated by blackness, the category, that turning, which I call the racial dialectic, consistently belies the limitations posed by time—both linear (historical) and circular (logical)—as an ontological given, empirical element, and political horizon.

How to break this perverse circuitry that resolves the economic as the ethical as it brings—or perhaps only because it brings—the scientific in support of authority? *Unpayable Debt* is a response to this question; that is, it is not so much an answer as an illustration, a one-off experiment with a tool and a procedure designed to crack the circuitry, to expose, to crack open the racial dialectic and describe how it figures the liberal political architecture in its complexity. This image first came to me as I was trying to make sense of how those who lacked equity had been forced to take on loans with exorbitant (variable) interest rates were blamed for the global economic crisis of 2007–8. Holders of subprime loans, black and Latinx economically dispossessed persons, were presented in explanations for the crisis as profitable (economically) because their anticipated inability to pay them back made the loans more valuable. However, when that inability was realized, and the abstract financial instruments of which they were part vaporized, these black and Latinx persons were found responsible (ethically) for the near collapse of the global economy. In that global-economic-crisis discourse, I found, the tools of raciality performed as perversely as they do in justifications for what is never treated as the juridical crisis it is, namely, police shootings of unarmed black persons—an explanation that attributes the undesirable outcome to a moral failing caused by racial or cultural difference. Considering this similarity, the image of *unpayable debt* seemed most appropriate to capture, in the economic-ethical corner, what the "scene of nature" captures in the juridico-ethical corner: the racial dialectic performs the role of rendering racial subjugation alien to the functionings and structurings of the liberal political architecture.

When I first considered the image of *unpayable debt*, I immediately thought of Dana, the main character in Octavia E. Butler's 1979 novel *Kindred*, and her predicament: to save the life of Rufus, the child of a Slave Owner, who is also her ancestor. That obligation, I found, was perhaps the best rendering of a debt someone owes but is not hers to pay. Not hers to pay because it was not her decision that led to it—to being a descendant of a Slave Owner (and to travel in time to save his life) or to making the profitability of a mortgage-based security be contingent on her lack of equity. However, the debt is hers because her blackness signals both slavery and lack of equity. More importantly, Dana's obligation—the debt that is the condition of possibility for her existence, in which family and slavery are indistinguished but not indistinguishable—has its own violations, in particular of the separations of time and space. Each instantaneous relocation from her house in 1976 Los Angeles to the Weylin plantation in early 1800s Maryland, each time to save Rufus's life, traverses that which is sustained by spacetime delineations, namely, the delimitations of then and now (she meets her long-dead ancestors) and the determination of here and there (she saves the life of a long-dead ancestor). That is, Dana's fulfillment of her obligation violates the linearity that is at the basis of the ontological descriptors (formality and efficacy) and pillars (separability, determinacy, and sequentiality) of post-Enlightenment thinking—for instance, as it breaks the rules of both sequentiality (the future operating in the past) and efficient causality (the effect becoming the condition of possibility for the cause), it is incomprehensible. Until one realizes that the violation does not go unpunished: in the last return trip to her Los Angeles home Dana loses the arm that Rufus grasped as he was dying, after she struck him when he tried to rape her.

That arm stuck in the wall, the incomprehensible evidence of Dana's travels in time, has inspired the black feminist reading tool assembled to carve the image of unpayable debt, which is this book. What this re/de/compositional tool, the figure of the *wounded captive body in the scene of subjugation*, allows is a turning of the grounds of post-Enlightenment thinking. Having been designed to track, explicate, and annihilate the workings of the social-scientific category of blackness, it seeks to undermine its metaphysical basis and theoretical effects in examining the presentations of the ethical and the economic scenes of value. At the same time, this tool, like Dana's travels in time, reads in/through—as she re/de/composes—these scenes an image of the post-Enlightenment political architecture in a way that renders explicit how slavery (as an economic structure) and raciality (as a symbolic arsenal) remain operative in the global present and thus are crucial in the functioning of the state and the accumulation of capital. Throughout these previous moments, Dana signals how violations of spacetime separation are possible if thinking is inspired by materiality instead of necessity; if, instead of unity and necessity, the guiding image of existence presupposed implicancy and infinity; if it is assumed that the *elementa* that enter the composition of everything, anything, that exists in spacetime have always already existed but also include what can, could, and may never come into actual existence.

What lies ahead is, as I warned above, propositional as well as experimental; that is, it does some of the work expected from philosophical and theoretical interventions. Each chapter is also a presentation of the proposed manner of thinking. Each chapter has four moments and performs the same movement, which starts with the incomprehensibility of Dana's impossible charge and closes with an account of existence that obtains its possibility. Any attempt at summarizing each chapter—and the whole book for that matter—will be lacking and most likely misrepresent it, because a description of what is done cannot repeat *how* it is done. What I will do, then, is to give brief descriptions of what is covered in each chapter, knowing that the reader may be disappointed and/or pleased by what she encounters as she reads them. In chapter 1, "Not even by the law here," I assemble and introduce the task performed by the figure of the *wounded captive body in the scene of subjugation*. As a referent of the Slave in the scene of total violence, her tasks include signaling the troublesome distinction between Human (Man, the Subject, Humanity, Subjectivity) and Thing (body, nature, object, world) as well as the scenes featuring them, both the philosophical ones (the scene of representation and the scene of regulation) and the political ones (such as the ethical and the economic scenes of value). In chapter 2, "the most perfect hallucination," the *wounded captive body in the scene of subjugation* confronts the racial dialectic by recalling what is disappeared in the logical circle presupposed and produced by the social-scientific explanation for racial subjugation. Two movements are significant here. First, attending to her leads to the distinction between two moments of post-Enlightenment thinking, namely the determinative (the nineteenth century) and the interpretive (the twentieth century). With this distinction, it is possible to attend to how necessity (operative in determinative statements) remains operative in a social-scientific program governed by liberty (operative in interpretive statements). In the second movement, the activation of the *wounded captive body in the scene of subjugation* as a figurative tool exposes how what the racial dialectic seeks to collapse is precisely what the racial event cannot but evoke—that is, how blackness records the juridical and economic "relation" that has been crucial in the assembling of state and capital. In chapter 3, "a foreign language," I turn to the economic scene of value, where the *wounded captive body in the scene of subjugation* confronts Marx's equation of value by recalling its contingency on an ethico-juridical distinction. However, as she bursts through the equation itself, that is, the formal presentation of value, she does not set up a dialectic or a division, or make related moves, that is, sublation or resolution. Instead, she dissolves the very terms that are positioned in an equivalence, collapsing the distinctions that render the specificity of the liberal polity as well as the ones that render the human body the sole relevant factor in the creation of value. Finally, in chapter 4, "where flesh joined with plaster," the *wounded captive body in the scene of subjugation* gathers the debris of the post-Enlightenment deployments of the Human and the Thing that she confronted in the ethical and the economic scenes of value, in both the determinative and the interpretive moments. Toward the end of this *world*, the *known* world, the *wounded captive body in the scene of subjugation* guides a speculative exercise in which undeterminability directs the outline of both *deep implicancy* as descriptor and *corpus infinitum* as an image of existence that obtains every event and every existent not as one (unity) or as unique (identity) but in their fractality, as each is a singular re/de/composition of that which has always existed.

CHAPTER 1
“Not even by the law here”

> “Do you think the trader took him all the way to New Orleans?” I asked.
>
> “Yeah. He was getting a load together to ship them down there.”
>
> I shook my head. “Poor Luke. Are there cane fields in Louisiana now?”
>
> “Cane, cotton, rice, they grow plenty down there.”
>
> “My father’s parents worked in the cane fields there before they went to California. Luke could be a relative of mine.”
>
> “Just make sure you don’t wind up like him.”
>
> “I haven’t done anything.”
>
> “Don’t go teaching nobody else to read.”
>
> “Oh.”
>
> “Yes, oh. I might not be able to stop Daddy if he decided to sell you.”
>
> “Sell me! He doesn’t own me. Not even by the law here. He doesn’t have any papers saying he owns me.”
>
> “Dana, don’t talk stupid!”
>
> “But …”
>
> “In town, once, I heard a man brag how he and his friends had caught a free black, tore up his papers, and sold him to a trader.”
>
> I said nothing. He was right, of course. I had no rights—not even any papers to be torn up.
>
> “Just be careful,” he said quietly.
>
> […] I would have to be careful, all right, and be ready to run if I seemed to be in any danger of being sold.
>
> —Octavia E. Butler, *Kindred*

“Any papers saying he owns me,” she retorts. As if papers were enough to prove or disprove his father’s right to trade her. No papers. Papers. It would not matter, because then/there, where Dana and Rufus meet and converse, their positions, established by *his* authority (and not a given hierarchy), are given by the color of their skin. He owns her, even if, as it turns out, Rufus (and his father) is her ancestor. What if she had papers? What use would they be if Rufus or his father—or any white person then/there—decided to punish her, to use the lash? Because it is not only that she could be sold—even without papers showing that they owned her, Rufus and his father could beat her, as they did. And yet, they did need papers, even if they were false. They knew that, and so did Dana and their Slaves. They needed papers to prove that an enslaved person (body-mind) was to be expended however they (the Slave Owners) wanted.[1] The title assured this as a legal right, that is, as their *authority* to make decisions about how to expend the enslaved person and whether they were to live or die. That is why she "said nothing." Existing as a black person there and then, she knew that having "not even any papers to be torn up" renders her no-thing before the law and customs of mid-1830s Maryland.

Why should it matter if Dana had papers or not, if she could read or not, even if she could teach someone else to read? What is at stake? With her papers in hand she could do so many things: she could migrate up north and make sure not to be found near a farm or field again; she could decide to stay, to find a free companion and try to make do, as others tried; she could even decide to sell her labor to the Weylins. Why it did matter is precisely because papers would place Dana in a position that was not acceptable back then/over there. Papers, of course, were not enough. Papers could be, as they often were, torn up. The freed woman or man could then be sold by anyone (any white person, that is) who showed papers and/or claimed that they owned them.

Having no papers made no difference there, where/when existing as a black person meant that one's person (body-mind) could be claimed by anyone who looked like they could own her. As would become the law of the land about two decades from the time in which Dana found herself, having been a slave rendered a black person forever subjected to being returned to the position of the captive. A position without ethical significance in a moment when liberty and equality emerged as attributes of Humanity and descriptors of the Human, which was also when

1 Consistent with the argument here being an intervention in political philosophy, my usage of the term *person* (body-mind), as will become more evident in chapter 2, recalls John Locke's rendering of the term, as in this passage: "Thus the limbs of his body are to everyone a part of himself; he sympathizes and is concerned for them. Cut off a hand, and thereby separate it from that consciousness he had of its heat, cold, and other affections, and it is then no longer a part of that which is himself." Locke, *An Essay Concerning Human Understanding* (London: J. M. Dent, 1993), 182.

the initial elements that would enter into the confection of the analytics of raciality were being assembled. Nevertheless, even in that juridical position without ethical significance, the captivity of the laboring body could be proved, ascertained, and secured; but her mind, as Dana learned all too well, of that no one would ever be certain. Not in the market, not in the fields, even as her body-mind is expended in the movements, the gestures, in everything needed to turn soil, water, the horse, or the plow into cotton bolls; no one (not then/there, not here/now) would ever know. Not the songs she chanted to ease the burden, the forced, the expropriated labor under the summer sun or the winter snow—none of that attests that the Owner successfully controlled her mind. And that Dana knew; that had everything to do with not allowing the Slave to learn how to read, that had everything to do with that moment in time, when a person's value was attached to her mind, to what she knew and to what guided her as she went about existing day to day. And while back then/there, she also learned that when a black person appears to try to express such *value*, the lash is released with all its might.

"Not even by the law," Dana says, but she knows that it did not and still does not matter. Whatever the law protects, whatever falls under that mode of equalizing, does not include a black person. Which meant that Dana learns in her last encounter with Rufus that the title, the paper attesting the Owner's authority to dispose of the Slave, was the only paper that mattered. That paper is the only one recognized by the Juridical (the State and the Court) structures—and that force followed Dana back in her last return home, when she lost her arm caught in the wall. Thinking with that wall and the injury it holds opens up a venue for reading the political architecture of the global present as the workings of the Colonial, the Racial, the Juridical (the State and the Patriarch),[2] and Capital. A reading guided not by a question

---

2 Throughout this book, the terms juridical (as the moment of the political) and Juridical (as the general category) also refer to cisheteropatriarchal power. By locating the patriarch in that moment, the argument here stays consistent with early modern political philosophy, in particular Locke's description of the body

driving the assignation of causality (seeking determination) or the attribution of a purpose (aiming at interpretation)—because these tools of the *transparent I* (in the guise of the Knowing Subject) cannot but keep Dana's predicament constrained by the Subject's limited and limiting means for comprehension. Beginning with Dana's wounded body, with that which attests to both the Owner's authority and the occurrence of the scene of total violence (the scene in which killing and/or raping is the goal), this reading immediately locates the encounter in its political context, where it would attend to its juridical, economic, symbolic, and ethical conditions of occurrence.

By addressing the Slave in the scene of total violence, where she troubles the separation between Human and Thing, this reading exposes the *transparent I* (in the guise of the ethical and the economic subject) at work in the impossibility of addressing how the Colonial and the Racial work in/as global capital. For the Negro, insofar as it is a common name for property, a Thing in the economic scene of value did not count as anything deemed unique to the Human, which is considered solely under morality (in the ethical scene of value). However, that total violence is deployed to assure compliance; the Slave, insofar as she is a Human being, is not like any other property, that is, she is a commercial thing but neither natural nor artificial. Everything else, any other existing thing, would fall under the natural or the artificial, and therefore would not be contemplated by the principles of Humanity, namely liberty and equality. For it is precisely this ambiguity, her being a Human that figures fungibility instead of dignity, that makes the possibility thinkable that then/there, as here/now, there was no question that, like the horses, the soil, the rainwater, and the sunrays, the body of the Slave, as well as her mind, transduced into cotton, sugarcane, tobacco, or any other commodity that her labor brought into existence as such.

---

politic as the playroom of the propertied citizens, who retain sovereignty over their households, that is, as patriarchs. See, in particular, John Locke, *The Second Treatise on Civil Government* (Indianapolis, IN: Hackett Publishing, 1980), chap. 6.

"scene of unprotected female flesh"

> A female body strung from a tree limb, or bleeding from the breast on any given day of field work because the "overseer," standing the length of a whip, has popped her flesh open, adds a lexical and living dimension to the narratives of women in culture and society. This materialized scene of unprotected female flesh—of female flesh "ungendered"—offers a praxis and a theory, a text for living and for dying, and a method for reading both through their diverse mediations.
>
> —Hortense J. Spillers, "Mama's Baby, Papa's Maybe"

What did Dana see when she looked at her body and saw that it was missing a piece? What did she think when she saw blood in the plaster? Perhaps the pain was too much at that moment: she was in no condition to contemplate what had just happened to her. Living in Los Angeles, California, in the mid-1970s, she was familiar with that type of injury, the kind of violence that is done but to which no one is assigned blame, responsibility, because it is always already authorized—the violence perpetrated or allowed by the State. For then as now, sixty years after finally obtaining guarantees from the state of basic civil rights, such as voting,[3] every black person in the United States witnesses their federal government challenging their right to protest against police brutality, to demand accountability, to take to the streets and demand justice. No matter how many times police killings

---

3 The Voting Rights Act of 1965 was the third legal act—the other two being the Fourteenth and Fifteenth Amendments to the US Constitution—designed to protect black Americans' exercise of a most basic citizenship right. As it happens, on June 25, 2013, this crucial piece of legal protection was dramatically weakened by the US Supreme Court in the *Shelby County v. Holder* decision, which "struck down a formula [...] that required certain states and localities with a history of discrimination against minority voters to get changes cleared by the federal government before they went into effect." Sam Levine and Ankita Rao, "In 2013 the Supreme Court Gutted Voting Rights—How Has It Changed the US?," *Guardian*, June 25, 2020, https://www.theguardian.com/us-news/2020/jun/25/shelby-county-anniversary-voting-rights-act-consequences.

of unarmed black persons are denounced, no matter how many criminal and civil-rights cases are opened in the wake of such events, each denunciation and every legal case seems to add to the glossary of justifications. Every authorized or unauthorized deployment of symbolic (in the case of subprime loans) or total (mass shooting, police shootings, or arrests) violence against black and Latinx persons has a justification that exceeds modern mechanisms of justice because it shares the same grounds, namely necessity.[4]

What else can be done? To bring down the symbols of hate, to demand the end of the juridical institution whose main task seems to be to deploy racial violence. What else? What is left to say about what no one can even pretend does not take place? How many more explanations, descriptors, must one use—racial profiling, stereotyping, racial codes? Each and every descriptor for that which explains (the efficient or formal cause of) police shootings seems to get it right, but none exposes how necessity authorizes these decisions to shoot—this exercise of the State's right to kill—because necessity also operates within them. Since this is the case, all that is left, then, is to do the work of re/de/composition—that is, simultaneously disunifying, disfiguring, and redesigning that which necessity sustains. Where to begin? More adequately, how to begin, once again? Both my reading strategy and my tool this time around, the *wounded captive body in the scene of subjugation*,[5] occurred to me as I tracked Hortense

---

4 I have developed the argument on how necessity operates in the authorization of police brutality (as in numerous shootings of unarmed black and Latinx persons in the United States, for instance) and other deployments of total violence against black persons and in black territories in a few articles, most recently Denise Ferreira da Silva, "No-Bodies: Law, Raciality and Violence," *Griffith Law Review* 18, no. 2 (2009): 212–36; and Ferreira da Silva, "Scene of Nature," in *Searching for Contemporary Legal Thought*, ed. Justin Desautels-Stein and Christopher Tomlins (Cambridge: Cambridge University Press, 2017), 275–89.

5 Although it does not perform in the same way, or perform the same task, Spivak's "native informant" has certainly inspired the assembling of the *wounded captive body in the scene of subjugation*. See generally Gayatri Chakravorty Spivak, *A Critique of*

Spillers's distinctions between "the captive body," "skin color," and "flesh."[6] When attending to the terms and turns of Spillers's argument rather than its content,[7] I find in operation something

Postcolonial Reason: Toward a History of the Vanishing Present (Cambridge, MA: Harvard University Press, 1999). After reading an earlier draft of this manuscript, Fred Moten asked me if I knew of Joy James's "captive maternal." Since I did not, he sent me a couple of different pieces by James, one of them on Octavia Butler's *Kindred*. Reading James's writings on the captive maternal, I found similarities and differences with the *wounded captive body in the scene of subjugation*. The similarities are many; they are, I think, also expected, because the captive maternal and the *wounded captive body in the scene of subjugation* are referents of the female slave. Thus, because both recall the female in the scene of violence, they can also be read as referents of the black woman. Here, I think, is the most important distinction. The wounded captive body in the scene of subjugation is a female, but she is not a woman. She is nobody's mother and no one's wife or lover. She does not reflect the white European cisheteropatriarchal male position as a political position, because she stands outside and against precisely that form of enunciation as she targets its constitutive moments (ethical, juridical, symbolic, economic). James's captive maternal is, in my understanding, a political figure, a powerful and necessary one, which bears both the brunt of racial domination and a unique capacity to resist and undermine it. The *wounded captive body in the scene of subjugation* is a poethical tool, that is, a reading device, which has been designed to take apart that which is the condition of possibility for the text, discourse, and liberal (white European cisheteropatriarchal male) position of domination. For distinct deployment of the captive maternal, see Joy James, "Captive Maternal Love: Octavia Butler and Sci-Fi Family Values," in *Literature and the Development of Feminist Theory*, ed. R. Goodman (Cambridge: Cambridge University Press, 2015), 185–99; and James, "The Womb of Western Theory: Trauma, Time, Theft, and the Captive Maternal," *Carceral Notebooks* 12 (2016): 253–96.

6 These terms are developed throughout her landmark 1987 text, Hortense J. Spillers, "Mama's Baby, Papa's Maybe: An American Grammar Book," *Diacritics* 17, no. 2 (Summer 1987): 64–81.

7 As I have done before, I take liberties when borrowing from Spillers, while doing my best to remain close to her approach. When appropriating these terms, however, I am not concerned with getting at her "meanings," as I am not taking these terms as concepts, which would presume both that they do comprehend (whatever they are applied to describe) and that their usage

that recalls *blacklight*,[8] as each of its movements dissembles and disorganizes accounts of both racial and cisheteropatriarchal subjugation. While the turns of her argument retrieve significations of blackness buried within its constitution as a social-scientific tool (an onto-epistemological construct), each of her terms, I find, figures a political dimension that I map onto one of the many moments of the post-Enlightenment political architecture—namely, the juridical and the economic (the captive body) and the ethical (flesh) through the workings of the symbolic (skin color). Framed after Spillers's method, and tasked with rendering Dana's charge both comprehensible and something to be accounted for, the *wounded captive body in the scene of subjugation* performs the task that blackness alone can, which is to re/de/compose the post-Enlightenment onto-epistemological *intrastructure* and political architecture by exposing how the former works within the latter to support the arrangement of the Colonial, the Racial, the Juridical (the State and Cisheteropatriarchy), and Capital at work in the global present.[9]

Targeting the circularity of sociologist Daniel Patrick Moynihan's thesis on the "Negro family," Spillers's threefold argument—tracking the workings of skin color, retrieving the captive body in the scene of total violence, and recalling the wounded unprotected female slave body—exposes how the prevailing account of racial subjugation, the racial dialectic,

---

assures comprehensibility. This does not mean that they are not or could not be appropriated in this way.

8 For a description/deployment of blacklight as a black feminist poethical tool, see Denise Ferreira da Silva, "Blacklight," in *Otobong Nkanga: Luster and Lucre*, ed. Clare Molloy, Philippe Pirotte, and Fabian Schöneich (Berlin: Sternberg Press, 2017), 245–52.

9 I devised the term *intrastructure*—inspired by Karen Barad's notion of intra-action—to capture and comment on the microforms (pillars and descriptors) that compose modern thought, those that enter into the constitution of concepts and categories and are presupposed (as the operative element) in its formulations. See Barad, *Meeting the Universe Halfway: Quantum Physics and the Entanglement of Matter and Meaning* (Durham, NC: Duke University Press, 2007).

operates as a mechanism of racial power, that is, how it transfers and shifts the registers of racial subjugation. Moynihan's 1965 report is a typical articulation of the racial dialectic. After recalling centuries of slavery and decades of segregation, and registering how dispossession (income, standards of living) characterizes black US Americans' economic situation,[10] he concludes that the "fundamental problem" is their "family structure," the fact that it is "crumbling," and argues that as "long as this situation persists, the cycle of poverty and disadvantage will continue to repeat itself."[11]

Spillers's first maneuver is to track the symbolic workings of skin color in Moynihan's report, how the concept of ethnicity comprehends the economic and juridical situation of black males and females as an effect of an affectable (pathological) family arrangement (female-headed households).[12] In particular, she distills how his statement on the black family does no more

---

10 Though the phrase is not without its merits, I do not think that "blaming the victim" sufficiently captures the effects of the sociological account of racial subjugation. As I have said many times before, the perverse effect of this explanation is that it renders the markers of racial subjugation an effect of the "laws of nature" presented in social-scientific signification. This is not a matter of blame; it is about truth.

11 Daniel P. Moynihan, *The Negro Family: The Case for National Action* (Washington, DC: Office of Policy Planning and Research, United States Department of Labor, March 1965), accessed July 15, 2020, https://web.stanford.edu/~mrosenfe/Moynihan%27s%20The%20Negro%20Family.pdf.

12 "Under the Moynihan rule," she argues, "'ethnicity' itself identifies a total objectification of human and cultural motives—the 'white' family, by implication, and the 'Negro Family,' by outright assertion, in a constant opposition of binary meanings. Apparently spontaneous, these 'actants' are wholly generated, with neither past nor future, as tribal currents moving out of time. Moynihan's 'Families' are pure present and always tense." Further, she notices how, in Moynihan's account, this social-scientific tool "freezes in meaning, takes on constancy, assumes the look and the affects of the Eternal. We could say, then, that in its powerful stillness, 'ethnicity,' from the point of view of the 'Report,' embodies nothing more than a mode of memorial time." Spillers, "Mama's Baby, Papa's Maybe," 66.

than rehearse the logical circle characteristic of accounts of racial subjugation.

A crucial aspect of her analysis of ethnicity is to refer its fixing effect, which she calls "mythical," back to its form, highlighting how it presupposes the principle of identity and, along with it, carries the force of necessity. By showing how the sociological construct "Negro family" is one side of a given binary, Spillers exposes how force of necessity accounts for the violent (productive) effect of signification of ethnicity and other social-scientific tools of racial knowledge that have been deployed in the past hundred years or so, such as the notion of race relations.[13] This effect of signification has ethical implications, as ethnicity's ("mythical") time—in its staged (both hidden and explicit) comparison of "white" (patriarchal) and "black" (matriarchal) families, the former being both the measure and expression of what is *valued*—hides an account of why patriarchy names the *proper* family arrangement and how black families have become headed by females.[14] Exactly this hiding of the comparison that exposes the operation of necessity through the principle of identity and the devaluing of blackness figured in the binary of white family/black family provides both onto-epistemological descriptors, namely *formality* and *efficacy*, that warranted ethnicity's effectiveness as a tool for comprehensibility: (a) *formality* as a strategy of engulfment, a concept that comprehends as it produces (taxonomically) categories of human collectives and carries in itself an intrinsic comparison among them; and (b)

13 For what Moynihan suggests, she proceeds, is "that black males should reign because that is the way the majority culture carries things out [...]. Those persons living according to the perceived 'matriarchal' pattern are, therefore, caught in a state of social 'pathology.'" Spillers, 66.

14 For instance, this is the point of departure of a later study that Moynihan coauthored with the sociologist Nathan Glazer, in which they state that "white Anglo-Saxon Protestant culture [...] is still the norm in American life" in spite of the significant number of immigrants in the country. Glazer and Moynihan, *Beyond the Melting Pot: The Negroes, Puerto Ricans, Jews, Italians, and Irish of New York City* (Cambridge, MA: MIT Press, 1970), 10.

efficacy as a sociological concept that renders the *ethical* moment (figured as moral or cultural traits) the locus of causation of juridical domination and economic dispossession. When, in the mid-twentieth century, ethnicity replaced race as the proper concept in the investigation of multiracial social spaces,[15] it effectively excluded any consideration of the juridical and economic dimensions of racial subjugation.[16]

---

15 The word ethnicity (and related ones such as ethnic) has been around for centuries, like the term race. Ethnicity as a sociological concept was deployed in the early twentieth century in a manner consistent with the interpretive regime and, usually, in rejections of the nineteenth-century (determinative) notion of race. For instance, in a text probably written in the decade that preceded his death in 1920, Max Weber joins in the rejection of the biological (“inherited and inheritable traits that actually derive from common descent”). Instead, he advances the notion of “ethnic groups”—“human groups that entertained a subjective belief in their common descent because of similarities of physical type or of customs or both.” Weber, *Economy and Society: An Outline of Interpretive Sociology*, ed. Guenther Roth and Claus Wittich, vol. 1 (Berkeley: University of California Press, 1978), 385, 389.

16 Let me comment further on how ethnicity realizes *efficacy*. Ethnicity was deemed preferable precisely because it presupposes, as the context of investigation, a “heterogenous” *moral* (social) context composed by ethnic groups who both differ from and relate to each other through their “cultural differences” (see Glazer and Moynihan, *Beyond the Melting Pot*, 10). Ethnicity’s ethical advantages consist in explaining a group’s economic and juridical situation as a necessary effect of its *moral/cultural* (anthropological or historical) specificity, that is, its cultural identity. This indistinction between the social, the cultural, and the moral can be explained by how the concept of the cultural, in the early twentieth century, appears in interpretive versions of sociology. Though they privilege consciousness (that is, the mind and not the body) as the locus of social phenomena, Émile Durkheim and Max Weber, for instance, advance different accounts of the source of the contents of consciousness. For Durkheim, these would be exterior, that is, the material (economic and juridical) conditions of existence, which, in turn, also express the contents of the collective consciousness; see, for instance, Durkheim, *The Elementary Forms of the Religious Life*, trans. Joseph Ward Swain (Mineola, NY: Dover, 2008). For Weber, on the other hand, the sources are *interior*, that is, the “subjective meaning” that orients (“insofar as [it] takes account of the behavior of others”)

After this first and effective move—the short-circuiting of Moynihan's argument, which is basically an unpacking of how ethnicity operates as a determinative tool—Spillers aptly avoids falling prisoner to the limits of the interpretive episteme.[17] This is accomplished in her second move, which introduces the

individual action and inform social institutions and organizations (Weber, *Economy and Society*, 4). In their study, Glazer and Moynihan highlight an aspect of ethnicity (and other concepts that refer to collectives as moral units, such as nationality) that would be challenged many years later, which is the idea of "ethnic identity" (that is, individuals' identification as members of a culturally defined group). "The ethnic group in American society became not a survival from the age of mass immigration but a new social form," they argue, which, in addition to "distinctive language, customs, and culture"—which may even have been lost—is "continually recreated by new experiences in America," and these groups "are also interest groups" (Glazer and Moynihan, *Beyond the Melting Pot*, 16–17).

17 These passages from Moynihan's preface to *The Negro Family* give a sense of Spillers's point of departure:

> The United States is approaching a new crisis in race relations.
>
> In the decade that began with the school desegregation decision of the Supreme Court, and ended with the passage of the Civil Rights Act of 1964, the demand of Negro Americans for full recognition of their civil rights was finally met.
>
> [...]
>
> In this new period the expectations of the Negro Americans will go beyond civil rights. Being Americans, they will now expect that in the near future equal opportunities for them as a group will produce roughly equal results, as compared with other groups. This is not going to happen. Nor will it happen for generations to come unless a new and special effort is made.
>
> There are two reasons. First, the racist virus in the American blood stream still afflicts us: Negroes will encounter serious personal prejudice for at least another generation. Second, three centuries of sometimes unimaginable mistreatment have taken their toll on the Negro people. The harsh fact is that as a group, at the present time, in terms of ability to win out in the competitions of American life, they are not equal to most of those groups with which they are competing. Individually, Negro Americans reach the highest peaks of achievement. But collectively, in the spectrum of American ethnic and religious and regional groups, [...] Negroes are the weakest.
>
> [...]

terms—the captive body, skin color, and wounded flesh—I borrow from her analysis.[18] By focusing on black and Indigenous bodies and colonial (juridico-economic) conditions, she returns to the scene of total violence, the colonies ("that order, with its human sequence written in blood"), and blackness as a referent of slave labor.[19] Recalling the colonial (Slavery and Conquest) "past" as the scene of total violence, as the site of the production of the Slave (captive) and the Native, she short-circuits the logic of ethnicity in a way that renders blackness, instead of a signifier of cultural difference, a mark(er) of a juridico-economic structure that yields a symbolic order mapped onto the captive body.

Spillers's second maneuver clears the path for my retrieval of that referent of blackness, the removal of which allows the logical inference to hold, namely Slavery's particular form of juridical domination and economic dispossession. The pairing of *skin color* and *the captive body* dissipates the circularity of

---

> Indices of dollars of income, standards of living, and years of education deceive. The gap between the Negro and most other groups in the American society is widening.
>
> The fundamental problem, in which this is most clearly the case, is that of family structure.

18 Spillers, "Mama's Baby, Papa's Maybe," 67.

19 The full quote:

> That order, with its human sequence written in blood, *represents* for its African and Indigenous peoples a scene of *actual* mutilation, dismemberment, and exile. First of all, their New-World, diasporic plight marked a *theft of the body*—a willful and violent (and unimaginable from this distance) severing of the captive body from its motive will, its active desire. [...] This profound intimacy of interlocking detail is disrupted, however, by externally imposed meanings and uses: 1) the captive body becomes the source of an irresistible, destructive sensuality; 2) at the same time—in stunning contradiction—the captive body reduces to a thing, becoming *being for* the captor; 3) in this absence *from* a subject position, the captured sexualities provide a physical and biological expression of "otherness"; 4) as a category of "otherness," the captive body translates into a potential for pornotroping and embodies sheer physical powerlessness that slides into a more general "powerlessness," resonating through various centers of human and social meaning. (Spillers, 67; italics in original)

ethnicity. And this occurs precisely because Spillers does not take the (social) scientific descriptor of cultural difference onto the historical stage, but rather seeks to explain the current situation of black families as an effect of the history of expropriation. By introducing the captive body and flesh in parallel with the symbolic apprehension of skin color and its symbolic apprehension of the captive body, Spillers immediately preempts an interpretive reading of her account of coloniality and slavery, which would have made it a tale of the origin of the United States' historico-cultural identity ("An American Grammar Book," the subtitle reads). Had she done that, Spillers would have mapped the circularity of "mythical" time onto the linearity of historical time—a move that would result in raciality's hijacking of the economic-juridical significance of captive labor, thereby explaining slavery away (in the relay operated by scientific universality). In short, skin color would signal that which is being explained, namely that the "female-headed household" is a family configuration specific to/productive of the black social subject conceived historically, that is, interpretively. By allowing this removal of the black body from the register of the concept of the cultural (in both its anthropological and historical versions), which presupposes but does not examine the writing of the black subject as an effect of its organic arrangement and the mental (intellectual and moral) functions it signifies, Spillers also invites a recalling of the Slave's (the captive body's) violent (juridico-economic) context of existence.

Let me turn to her third term, *wounded flesh*, before I describe to what effect I borrow and repurpose all three terms. Her juxtaposing of skin color, the captive body, and wounded flesh draws attention to total violence, inviting a thinking that moves with and through the captive body and (wounded) flesh.[20] A

---

20 In a 2006 conversation with Saidiya Hartman, Farah Jasmine Griffin, Shelly Eversley, and Jennifer L. Morgan, Spillers comments on the publication context of this field-founding work: "What I was trying to do when I wrote that essay many years ago was to find a vocabulary that would make it possible, and not all by myself, to make a contribution to a larger project. I was looking

radical reversal becomes possible because her presentation of the flesh invites a figural and not merely propositional move. More particularly, in her proposal I find that we attend to the flesh's gift of a "praxis and a theory, a text for living and for dying, and a method for reading," a "vocabulary," and, especially, a proper theme for ethical consideration.[21] Flesh is imaged through/as/

---

for my generation of black women who were so active in other ways, to open a conversation with feminists. Because my idea about where we found ourselves in the late 1970s and the mid-1980s, was that we were really out of the conversation that we had, in some ways, historically initiated. In other words, the women's movement and the black movement have always been in tandem, but what I saw happening was black people being treated as a kind of raw material." Spillers, in "'Whatcha Gonna Do?' Revisiting 'Mama's Baby, Papa's Maybe: An American Grammar Book,'" *Women's Studies Quarterly* 35, nos. 1/2 (Spring–Summer 2007): 300.

There is no question that what she set out to do has been accomplished. Probably not so much in feminist and gender theorizing, because if it had, these practices would have moved to places where liberal feminism would not be able to follow. Black studies, and not only black feminist theorizing and practice, on the other hand, has benefitted greatly from thinking with Spillers's female flesh ungendered (I, of course, include my own work here). Among these are two relatively recent works: Nahum Dimitri Chandler, *X—The Problem of the Negro as a Problem for Thought* (New York: Fordham University Press, 2013); and Alexander G. Weheliye, *Habeas Viscus: Racializing Assemblages, Biopolitics, and Black Feminist Theories of the Human* (Durham, NC: Duke University Press, 2014). I mention these two engagements with Spillers's theorizing because of how differently we take her figure. This, I find, is an indication of its generosity. How my misappropriation of Spillers's figure both is inspired by and greatly differs from Chandler is spelled out in Denise Ferreira da Silva, "Hacking the Subject: Black Feminism and Refusal beyond the Limits of Critique," *philoSOPHIA* 8, no. 1 (2018): 19–41. I find that the main difference with Weheliye is that I probably read *flesh* as an ethical device and take off with it into a speculative exercise; Weheliye, on the other hand, takes flesh's force as a political and ethical concept deep into a critique of post-Enlightenment thought. Very different takes, definitely, and both generative.

21 Spillers, "Mama's Baby, Papa's Maybe," 68. For an interesting recent take on this offer—the violated wounded flesh as a "necessary space of love"—see Roberto Montero, "Love in the Flesh,

in the wound, which comes between (mediates) skin color and the captive body. That is, the juridical position of captivity (total domination) authorizes total violence, which the flesh exposes, as it comes through the skin that signifies unprotection, black skin, which authorizes the use of coercive force to curb the "will" of the enslaved. That mark, the signal of the Owner's authority, imprinted on the Slave, secures the latter as an ethico-juridical figure, that is, a person whose mind the Owner has the authority (right) to violently nullify and whose body the Owner has the right to confine and kill. Furthermore, Spillers's proposal that the distinction between body and flesh be superimposed onto "the captive" and the "liberated position" renders the captive body as a person, that is, an ethical figure whose referent is not liberty but physical integrity (of life and limb) and, as such, one who immediately recalls how the threat of total violence lies at the core of the modern political program.[22]

From the terms and movements of Spillers's analysis I gather a function—as a correspondence involving presumably separate domains, that is, the symbolic and juridical and the ethical and economic—of the *wounded captive body in the scene of subjugation*, which I call *negativation*. Explicitly presented as a disruption of the intrastructure of post-Enlightenment thinking (the principle of identity, the thesis of necessity, as well as the onto-epistemological descriptors and pillars these constitute), its principal capacity is to expose how necessity operates in all moments of the post-Enlightenment political architecture

Toni Morrison and Hortense Spillers 30 Years after Beloved and Mama's Baby, Papa's Maybe," *Alpenglow: Binghamton University Undergraduate Journal of Research and Creative Activity* 4, no. 1 (2018): 2.

22 "Even though the European hegemonies stole bodies—some of them female—out of West African communities in concert with the African 'middleman,' we regard this human and social irreparability as high crimes against the flesh, as the person of African females and African males registered the wounding. If we think of the 'flesh' as a primary narrative, then we mean its seared, divided, ripped-apartness, riveted to the ship's hole, fallen, or 'escaped' overboard." Spillers, "Mama's Baby, Papa's Maybe," 67.

because its main role has been to support transparency, the ontological descriptor that sustains the writing of modern existence as the actualization of the ethical principle of liberty. For the most part, my task in this book is to expose, describe, and unsettle this arrangement, and to articulate an invitation to an image of existence that is not supported by force of necessity or the mechanisms of symbolic and total violence it sustains.

Let me now return to Spillers's terms and movements to render explicit how the *wounded captive body in the scene of subjugation* operates. The first and definitive movement is, as noted above, explicating the effects of signification of ethnicity. What her analysis of ethnicity highlights is the crucial move, or should I say removal, registered by the term *black*, which is that *skin color* becomes once again the privileged signifier of cultural (moral) difference. More specifically, in Moynihan's report blackness becomes a *natural* (empirical) trait that corresponds to a *moral* (collective mental) *form*, which is actualized/expressed as a high number of female-headed households. This enters into social-scientific studies as datum—that is, studies of ethnicity incorporate, as an assumption, the correspondence between skin color and moral traits that was produced in nineteenth-century anthropological versions of racial knowledge. When ethnicity becomes the guiding concept in studies of 1960s social conditions in the United States, it explains black subjugation as an effect of racial difference, since the corresponding *moral* attributes—captured by the concept of the cultural—are interpreted as the cause for the observed economic dispossession and juridical domination (exclusion, segregation, high rates of incarceration, etc.). My point is: if ethnicity explains the black social (economic and juridical) situation, it is only because the racial Category of Blackness already encompasses the *necessary* connection (produced by the analytics of raciality) between skin color and moral attributes.[23] Or, in other words, it is the determinative

23 Quantitative studies usually, but not only, rely on this association, as if skin color somehow assures the "objectivity" of ethnic (self-)

tool (as produced in nineteenth-century anthropology and the twentieth-century sociology of race relations), as indexed by skin color, that renders Moynihan's account of the causes and consequences of "black pathology" comprehensible. *Necessity*, as I elaborate in chapter 2, sustains this immediate connection that supports and hides the circularity of the explanation because it both presupposes previous explanations that make the linkage and replaces them. The conclusion that having such a family structure consists in a pathological condition presumes a logical inference:[24] if whiteness identifies the dominant racial group, and this group has predominantly male-headed households, then the male-headed household is the norm; hence, if black folks have female-headed households, then their family arrangement deviates from the norm, that

---

identification. For instance, an article on approaches to measuring ethnicity comments on the use of the "mutually exclusive category approach" to study "patterns of social inequalities" in the United Kingdom. It is designed to "place individuals into the most appropriate ethnic group category" based on characteristics such as "skin colour and nationality." Skin color also figures into the other approach mentioned (the multiple characteristics approach) both directly and indirectly. Regardless of the approach, however, ethnicity always entails circularity, which is rendered in explicit comparisons ("in the United Kingdom and in many other nations, some ethnic minority groups exhibit sustained differences in patterns of family formation and living arrangements in comparison with other groups") or in implicit ones ("compared with other areas of the United Kingdom, some urban areas in London, the North West of England and the English Midlands have much higher ethnic minority populations. Ethnic minority groups are often clustered in areas of high deprivation, and this may be particularly relevant to studies of social networks and neighbourhood effects"). Roxanne Connelly, Vernon Gayle, and Paul S. Lambert, "Ethnicity and Ethnic Group Measures in Social Survey Research," *Methodological Innovations* (January 2016), https://doi.org/10.1177/2059799116642885.

24 Let me reproduce a quote from the Moynihan report that Spillers uses in her article: "Ours is a society which presumes male leadership in private and public affairs. ... A sub-culture, such as that of the Negro American, in which this is not the pattern, is placed at a distinct disadvantage." Spillers, "Mama's Baby, Papa's Maybe," 66.

is, it is pathological.[25] What is not considered is that before their family arrangement is termed pathological (in sociological studies), the economic and juridical situation of black persons has already been determined (scientifically explained) as pathological—as the expression and actualization of their affectable mental (intellectual and moral) attributes; that is, black "skin color" had been written as an index of (moral and intellectual) pathology.[26]

By retrieving blackness as a referent of the captive body, Spillers troubles the prevailing account of racial subjugation by exposing its juridical, economic, and ethical dimensions. This second move is also crucial because it targets the principle of identity as it operates within these social-scientific constructs. The captive body dislodges the grounds (skin color) onto which the neat dichotomy between white family (normal) and black family (pathological) rests. What is presupposed here is that it is possible to classify racially any given human body (empirically or as a Thing), that blackness and whiteness referring to racial types are categories (formal or categorial) applicable to bodies that are Human (universal or a biological or historical concept)—that is, each duality, each distinction presupposes a common (empirical, formal, or final) ground, or an identity shared by both. When the captive body figures blackness, the juridical aspect enters the scene and disrupts its symbolic (historical and scientific) setup. It does so because it recalls all that is disappeared in the logical inference that explains racial subjugation.

---

25 This aspect has been highlighted by Roderick Ferguson, who notes how in the Moynihan report "equality of outcome and indeed peace [...] depended on the gender and sexual compliance of African American culture." The report, Ferguson writes, "suggests the African American's distance from the normative ideals of American citizenship." Ferguson, *Aberrations in Black: Toward a Queer of Color Critique* (Minneapolis: University of Minnesota Press, 2004), 121.

26 A fuller elaboration of this argument has been published elsewhere; see Denise Ferreira da Silva, *Toward a Global Idea of Race* (Minneapolis: University of Minnesota Press, 2007).

Let me spell out the disruptive force of the captive body —how it recalls necessity (in the guise of juridical authority) at work in the very assembling of transparency, the modern ontological descriptor, which is reproduced in symbolic (social-scientific and historical) tools and formulations. More specifically, let me show how attending to her disturbs what has become the main account of the scene of subjugation: Hegel's famous lord-and-bondsman passage. When the captive body replaces skin color as a referent of blackness, the neat dichotomy presupposed and reproduced by the tools of raciality, like ethnicity, cannot hold. For one, because their positions do not postulate *equality*, the Slave and her Owner figure a duality (Human and Thing) that does not set up a Hegelian dialectic, that is, a linear movement (of the positing of, and the sublating of difference by, sameness). No sublation takes place here, as Hegel's "movement" of recognizing—not in the description of the "pure Notion of recognition" but in how it appears for self-consciousness, that is, as the scene of the life-and-death struggle—sets up a dichotomy and hierarchy between the two initially self-sufficient and equal self-consciousnesses: each enjoying a presumed *identity* (Kant's pure universality) given by their immediate *liberty* and postulated *equality*—in the moment of the encounter, in which one is "only recognized" and the other "only recognizes" that which remains in its aftermath.[27] There is no movement here for two reasons that expose the correspondence of moments considered unrelated—namely, the juridical, the symbolic, the ethical, and the economic—and, in doing so, their political role. First, because they are not mediated by each other—as they do not meet as equally independent (free) entities—this apparent duality (Human and Thing) is mediated by a third element, the Slave Owner's *authority* (given by the juridical mechanisms of the colony) to use physical force over the resources (including the body's productive capacity, that is, labor) and the residents

27 G. W. F. Hegel, *Phenomenology of Spirit*, trans. A. V. Miller (Oxford: Oxford University Press, 1977), 112.

of a conquered land. In the scene of racial subjugation, I find at work, resolved in the symbolic moment, the logic of obliteration (the social-scientific rendering of the necessity of total violence), which, as refigured in raciality, requests the annihilation of the racial "other" (and the unbecoming ideas and practices it arouses) for the return to the *proper* functioning of the liberal polity.[28] As I said above, the Owner and the Slave meet outside the post-Enlightenment ethical moment. In the market where the Slave is bought, the Owner is on the same footing—as indicated by the juridical form of property and the economic form of money—as the Trader (or former Owner). There, as well as in the field or the Owner's household, the Slave has only economic (use) value. Put differently, as a juridically mediated relation, the Slave/Owner pair troubles the onto-epistemological presumption of identity that grounds social-scientific and historical accounts of racial subjugation.

Second, the lack of movement also refers to an ethical departure when the Slave and the Owner are considered economically. Though they meet in the Market, the Slave and the Owner do not stand there on equal terms, as in the moment before the encounter in Hegel's passage, on an empty stage where they play as "pure universality," or immediate being-for-itself, at

28 For an explication of the logic of obliteration, see Ferreira da Silva, *Toward a Global Idea of Race*. As Frantz Fanon described, the colonial context has no need for superstructure—that is, cultural, ideological, or other representational mechanisms. "In the capitalist countries a multitude of moral teachers, counselors and 'bewilderers' separate the exploited from those in power. In the colonial countries, on the contrary, the policeman and the soldier, by their immediate presence and their frequent and direct action, maintain contact with the native and advise him by means of rifle butts and napalm not to budge. It is obvious here that the agents of government speak the language of pure force." Fanon, *The Wretched of the Earth*, trans. Constance Farrington (New York: Grove Press, 1963), 38. This aspect of the colonial context has also been theorized by Patrick Wolfe, who describes the operating element as the "logic of elimination." See Wolfe, "Settler Colonialism and the Elimination of the Native," *Journal of Genocide Research* 8, no. 4 (2006): 387–409.

the threshold of the scene of representation (or what Hegel terms the "movement of recognizing"). For it is only in the aftermath that Hegel's two self-consciousnesses emerge in a not-yet-ethical relation, in a hierarchy mediated by things, from where self-consciousness proceeds toward Ethical Life, "submerged in the Spirit of its people," the place "of abstract universality, of pure thought, which disembodies them and imparts to the spiritless Self, to the individual person, a being that is in and for itself."[29] From the moment the captured person arrives—on the slave ship or through time travel, like Dana—or is born, she is caught in a juridico-economic context in which she becomes a Slave, that is, a living and thinking thing (a body-mind) whose productive capacity (labor) is to be extracted and can be exchanged. Fully unfolded in the scene of regulation, the moment of "abstract universality," juridically rendered, and still under the ethical rule of the divine author and ruler,[30] the Slave/Owner relation

29 The full passage: "In the ethical life, the Self is submerged in the Spirit of its people, it is the universality that is *filled*. But *simple individuality* raises itself out of this content, and its levity refines it into a 'person,' into the abstract universality of right or law. In this, the *reality* of the ethical Spirit is lost, and having lost all content, the Spirits of national individuals are gathered into a single pantheon, not into a pantheon of picture-thought whose powerless form lets each Spirit go its own way, but into the pantheon of abstract universality, of pure thought, which disembodies them and imparts to the spiritless Self, to the individual person, a being that is in and for itself." Hegel, *Phenomenology of Spirit*, 454 (italics in original).

30 Here I am making a distinction between two articulations of the juridical in modernity: on the one hand, the one found in the political-philosophy writings of Locke and Hobbes (pre-Enlightenment philosophers), for whom the ethical moment remains under the divine ruler and author, and on the other, the one found in Kant and post-Enlightenment philosophers who, like Hegel, embarked on projects that design the ethical scene of value on some version of transcendental reason. I locate the Owner and the Slave in the former—for historical reasons, that is, because slavery in the modern world is implanted under it, but also because, even in the post-Enlightenment period, the task of justifying slavery was taken over by the scientists of Man, even though religious arguments did not fully disappear.

is staged in a political (juridical, economic, ethical, symbolic) context, in which the captive is not a modern person (an ethico-juridical thing) but property (an economic-juridical thing). Put differently, the captive body (one of the referents of blackness) does not play in the ethical scene of representation because she is fundamentally a juridico-economic thing.

The Slave is not the Other of the (title holder) Owner.[31] The Slave is his/her property. Juridically, the captive body, defined by its use value, is one with the land upon which she is forced to apply her labor while occupying the same juridical position—namely, a title. (Understandably, nineteenth-century abolitionist discourse focused primarily on asserting or proving the Slave's humanity.)[32] The Slave does not stand on the same ethical terrain as the Owner. Hers is not the "pure universality" ("self-sufficiency")—of liberty or immediate self-determination—that self-consciousness enjoys prior to the moment of ethical life, but that ethical terrain shared with the things to which she applies her labor, her negation. Because she plays not in the scene of representation (of the moral) but in the scene of regulation (of the natural or artificial), negation is not an apt descriptor for

31 Here again it is important to recall that, unlike Hegel's self-consciousnesses facing each other in the life-and-death struggle, after which one becomes the slave, with actual slavery the two enter into unequal positions. What you have then is not a one-off event in which subjugation is achieved once and for all but the repetition of the scene of violence, precisely because the owner could never be sure that the person standing before him or her already enslaved has relinquished her will.

32 I return to the antislavery discourse in the following chapter by way of Saidiya Hartman's reading of it; see Hartman, *Scenes of Subjection: Terror, Slavery, and Self-Making in Nineteenth-Century America* (New York: Oxford University Press, 1997). For now, I just want to highlight how antislavery statements did charge defenders of slavery with violating the post-Enlightenment ethical program and the ethical figure of humanity it assembled. However, that did not prevent Scientists of Man from assembling a notion of racial difference that writes European bodies and territories as expressions of humanity—its onto-epistemological descriptors (universality, historicity) and its distinguishing ethical principles (liberty, equality, and dignity).

how she stands before the Owner—because she is already his possession, because she is owned like an animal or thing while at the same time having a *will* (when total violence is deployed, her possession of this exclusively human mental trait is exposed), that is, her capacity to refuse (to work, to laugh, to dance, to cry).

For this reason, I find that, as the captive body, her task is that of *negativation* (in particular its obsolete meaning, that is, as refusal) and, as an ethico-economic-juridical referent of blackness, she recalls something that its historical and social-scientific (symbolic) renderings consistently try to undermine.[33] Both person (the assumption that the enslaved has a will renders the Owner's right to deploy total violence acceptable and necessary) and thing (a captive body much like that of the horse, as Marx highlights when describing the specificity of slave labor), because she refers simultaneously to both, the captive body has the capacity to fracture the distinction between the symbolic, the juridical, the economic, and the ethical moments. And in doing so, she generates an image that shows all four operating, in tandem, in the constitution of the post-Enlightenment political architecture.

For the most part, my task here is to describe her function and make it available for thinking. In chapters 2 and 3, I activate the negative capacity that the captive body has gifted blackness, which is to bring out the juridical to disarrange the symbolic and its constructs, such as Nature and *world*, and to bring the ethical into the figuring of the economic that informs our critiques of State and Capital. In both, my re/de/composition of the racial dialectic (chapter 2) and of Marx's equation of value (chapter 3) activates the captive body to release blackness from

33 Lest we fall back on some kind of essentialism, it is important to recall that "being" negative is not an intrinsic trait of black persons. Negativation is a capacity that blackness, as a Category, acquires precisely because it had to be assembled—along with other tools of raciality—in the post-Enlightenment moment, when the notions of universal liberty and equality enter the description of the proper modern (social) configuration and its (human) subjects.

the socio-logics that cannot but explain racial (economic and juridical) subjugation as an effect of racial (moral and intellectual) difference, which consists of a datum (that demands theoretical accommodation) or residuum (that signals incomplete modernization). Though this activation has many unanticipated consequences, it suffices for my purposes here that it exposes how social-scientific comprehension of the black person (through skin color) rests on a logic that can only be sustained through the disregard of the juridico-economic position enslaved African persons and their descendants would occupy in the Americas and the Caribbean.

When performing this function, the wounded captive body in the scene of subjugation also facilitates consideration of thinking without necessity and the intrastructure it sustains. What Spillers offers is a thinking that begins with violence but goes beyond a remembrance of violence done. By replacing a conceptual descriptor (juridical liberty) of the early liberal ethical figure of the person with a material one (physical integrity), attending to the flesh (that is, "the concentration of 'ethnicity'") shows how skin color supports ethnicity's hold on comprehensibility.[34] For what skin color does not do—which is an effect of the nineteenth-century version of racial knowledge—and the attention to the flesh cannot but do, is register total violence, each and every daily act that held the captive and the captor in relation. What is it that the wounded (broken skin/exposed) flesh does? First, it displaces as well as exposes coloniality as the mode of governance that defines the figure of the captive, which is characterized by authorized total violence, and it hosts (because its exposure signals the demand for it) the Slave's creative capacity as well as the extractive and expropriative character of the juridical relation that is enslavement. Second, it shows blackness and its signified emerging in the context of total violence, thereby immediately—along the lines Fanon describes—recalling an ethical context governed by self-preservation (in the register of the natural), as it appears in Locke's and Hobbes's writings;

34 Spillers, "Mama's Baby, Papa's Maybe," 67.

it signals a divide between those whose physical integrity is protected by the juridical authority and those whose physical integrity is violated because, like other natural things, their juridical status is property.[35] Third and finally, it makes one wonder whether the wounding and the marking, as inscriptions of colonial (juridico-economic) power, remain in later juridico-economic formations and tools, such as subprime loans, coffee, cotton, sugar, and commodities that become money, but also in the soil, the waters, the forests, and the air—in transformed *elementa* (the most basic components) of mass energy of each and every drop of blood and each and every scream of pain.

What I am suggesting here is that when the flesh fractures and stains the proclaimed *transparent* post-Enlightenment ethical moment, when it figures that which can be violated and that which must be protected, skin color (and its capacity to explain liberty and its signifiers, such as right and property) is not the only casualty. The whole grammar of modern thought—and not only, but definitely also, the "American grammar" that Spillers explains so powerfully—and the forms and ends that secure it, may not resist the onslaught of materiality, in particular if it does not rely on the forms of the body but instead takes the flesh, thought of as unformed, that is, the *elemental* (as opposed to the physical) moment of matter, as the point of departure for thinking.[36] Thinking with the flesh, one can contemplate the possibility of traversing spatiotemporal boundaries, as the "transfer" Spillers invites us to wonder about definitely recalls

35 Perhaps crucially missing when Foucault wrote about race in terms of a contraposition of the "discourse on race" and "state racism" is how, in the colonial context, racial difference (in its biological and sociological renderings) would consistently refer to and activate a juridical authority associated with property (title) and not sovereignty. See Michel Foucault, *"Society Must Be Defended": Lectures at the Collège de France, 1975–1976*, trans. David Macey (New York: Picador, 2003), 43–64.

36 My appropriation of the quantum-physics figuring of matter resembles Judith Butler's but differs from it in important ways. See Butler, *Bodies That Matter: On the Discursive Limits of Sex* (New York: Routledge, 1993), 31–49; and Barad, *Meeting the Universe Halfway*.

that slave labor did occur, that the transfer of potential energy (flesh, bones, blood, etc.) of the enslaved person's body did result in the creation of value (both use and exchange value, as I discuss in chapter 3).[37] And thus when finally placed at the beginning of thinking, the untapped ethical demand of the flesh, of Spillers's wounded captive body, opens up a channel, an onto-epistemological wormhole, through which an image of existence without separability, determinacy, and sequentially can be contemplated.

Foregrounding total violence, the *wounded captive body in the scene of subjugation* tracks how the force of necessity is the operational element in the post-Enlightenment philosophical infrastructure and political (juridic, economic, ethic, and symbolic) architecture. Each of these features corresponds to a mode of deployment of *necessity* while approaching what exists. On the one hand, juridically, *necessity* sustains the modern privileging of *production* and dependence on *extraction* to authorize (through Law or the State) and justify (ethically) certain practices toward that which is named *natural*. On the other hand, scientifically, it also authorizes and justifies coercive and expropriative practices and infrastructure that violate prevailing conceptions of what properly constitutes the *moral* in post-Enlightenment thinking. Several things can be said through this distinction. Here I am particularly interested in how it exposes how (a) in the colonial juridico-economic context, the *natural* authorizes the use of lethal force in moves that are extractive (toward the land) and expropriative (toward the colonial [political] figures of the Natives and Slaves), and (b) the *moral*, which works within the Racial political/symbolic apparatus, occludes

37 In the previously cited conversation with Saidiya Hartman and others (see note 20), Spillers talks about how "Mama's Baby, Papa's Maybe" was a response to how blackness was treated at that moment as raw material but not as the basis for thinking. It is not lost on me—though I didn't know about this conversation when I started thinking about this topic—that I begin and stay with blackness as a referent to raw material. I do not know what Spillers will think of it when she reads these words; I hope it will be the beginning of another conversation and more collaborative thinking.

the workings of the colonial juridical modality and prevents an appreciation of the productive character of that which has been obtained through extraction and expropriation precisely because it constructs the Colonial figures of the Native and the Slave as nonproductive according to the determinative (scientific) and dominative (juridical) laws. In both cases, necessity provides the metaphysical grounds for modern thought, which supports the distinction between the natural and the moral, because the latter is the distinguishing quality of those existents capable of noticing its operations, while the former is applied to those whose existence is controlled by them.

From Spillers's presentation of her argument, which dislodges the then prevailing accounts of both racial and patriarchal subjugation, I derive two simultaneous movements, both of which destabilize the neat (stable/fixed) onto-epistemological arrangement and make explicit the fourfold arrangement that is the post-Enlightenment political (juridic, economic, ethic, and symbolic) moment. On the one hand, the *wounded captive body in the scene of subjugation* exposes and disrupts the movement of signification (the logic circuitry) that supports the seemingly stable/fixed social-scientific construct—namely, the racial dialectic—properly assembled with onto-epistemological descriptors: a causal movement, in which bodily *forms* (racial difference) *effect* unbecoming mental traits that, in turn, *effect* juridical domination and economic dispossession.[38] Targeting how this prevailing explanation for racial subjugation substitutes the ethical for the economic and juridical, the wounded captive body in the scene of subjugation confronts the symbolic with the juridical and, muddling the ethical moment, opens the question of whether and how to depict existence without rendering something like *world* or Nature as (transparent) mirrors. On

38 What I am presenting in this book is an expanded description of the racial dialectic, which I have described elsewhere; see, for instance, Denise Ferreira da Silva, "The Racial Limits of Social Justice: The Ruse of Equality of Opportunity and the Global Affirmative Action Mandate," *Critical Ethnic Studies* 2, no. 2 (2016): 191.

the other hand, she exposes and interrupts the movement of signification (determination) that supports the also seemingly stable/fixed social-scientific construct, namely Marx's formalization of his law of value, which remains at the core of leftist descriptions of today's political architecture.[39] Targeting how this descriptor relies on an ethico-juridical distinction to circumscribe the proper mechanism of capital accumulation, the wounded captive body in the scene of subjugation confronts the economic with the ethical and tears the symbolic membrane that protects the economic scene of value, and in doing so, releases the laboring body to an image of existence that neither presumes nor predicates the separations that render value itself. In sum, Spillers's exposition—the composition in which skin color, captive body, and flesh render the wound, the flesh exposed, the torn black skin—does more than trouble the grammar of (and which also separates) racial and cisheteropatriarchal (gender-sexual) subjugation.

Without the cooperation of *liberty* and *necessity* in the onto-epistemological operations of the principle of *identity/equality*, which obtains transparency as an ontological descriptor, none of the attributes post-Enlightenment thought postulated to the Human and Humanity, the scientific projects it supports, or the political architecture built around it would hold. This is a gift of the *wounded captive body in the scene of subjugation*; as she stands unprotected, she exposes the metaphysical and onto-epistemological threads that constitute and separate the many moments through which raciality governs the political architecture of the global present. Through the operation of mechanisms that will be described later, this crucial element

39 Here I am developing an argument that was introduced in Denise Ferreira da Silva, "Unpayable Debt: Reading Scenes of Value against the Arrow of Time," in *The documenta 14 Reader*, ed. Quinn Latimer and Adam Szymczyk (Munich: Prestel, 2017), 81–112; and Ferreira da Silva, "Reading the Dead: A Black Feminist Poethical Reading of Global Capital," in *Otherwise Worlds: Against Settler Colonialism and Anti-Blackness*, ed. Tiffany Lethabo King, Jenell Navarro, and Andrea Smith (Durham, NC: Duke University Press, 2020), 38–51.

for critical thinking remains incomprehensible. Why? Because any consideration of *comprehensibility* requires as a first step an account of how necessity operating through, between, and within the *natural* and the *moral* renders the conditions that generate Dana's unpayable debt incomprehensible. Among other things, I bet, such an account will render the distinction untenable. And, I hope, it might even help in the more radical project, which is to dismantle the empire of transcendental reason through a re/de/composition of everything that finds its grounds in necessity.

"the ongoing present of a common refusal"

> This open collective being is blackness—(racial) difference mobilized against the racist determination it calls into existence in every moment of the ongoing endangerment of 'actual being,' of subjects who are supposed to know and own. [...] 'To consent not to be a single being,' which is the anoriginal, anoriginary constitution of blackness as radical force—as historical, paraontological totality—is, for Robinson, the existential and logical necessity that turns the history of racial capitalism, which is also to say the Marxist tradition, inside out. What cannot be understood within, or as a function of, the deprivation that is the context of its genesis, can only be understood as the ongoing present of a common refusal.
>
> —Fred Moten, "The Subprime and the Beautiful"

Exposing the protective range of the presumption of liberty, the *wounded captive body in the scene of subjugation* recalls how, in post-Enlightenment thought, necessity's operations are made evident where the symbolic and the juridical moments are more likely to meet, that is, in statements, practices, and decisions that involve killing or letting die.[40] My interest is in the way this reflects how the political/symbolic operation of racial knowledge, when dedicated to explaining instead of eliminating racial

40 For a discussion of how necessity operates in scientific and juridical universality, see Ferreira da Silva, "No-Bodies"; and Ferreira da Silva, "Scene of Nature."

subjugation, has been added to the glossary of justifications for the use of lethal force—that is, state officials' display of otherwise unacceptable indifference toward, and its creation and sanction of economic mechanisms that further dispossess, black persons and populations. Put differently, much of the political work that necessity has done in the post-Enlightenment period—which gives the force of the symbolic as a political moment—concerns how it operates through raciality both as a common ground of and basis for deciding among what is ethically, juridically, and economically *proper*.

From this consideration, that is, from attending to how *necessity* establishes that which is deemed "valid," "right," "specific," "real," or "worthy," it is possible to trace its workings in the post-Enlightenment versions of the economic and ethical as scenes of values in the moment of determination or judgment. Not, I propose, by making further distinctions, but by attending to how these various meanings of *proper* operate in these political moments—that is, how necessity is what establishes a statement as accurate, resolved, or true (scientific), what makes an action worthy or good or not (ethical), the undesirable that drives production/accumulation (economic), and what makes something right or legal (at the juridical level). Furthermore, all four moments (ethical, economic, juridical, and scientific) are simultaneously traversed by the distinction between Human/Humanity and Thing,[41] that is, the *moral* and the *natural*: (a) the scientific level refers to the *natural* while (b) the ethico-juridical moment refers to the *moral*, (c) the scientific and the juridical are sites of operations of (*natural*) laws and rules (dominative force) and the ethical is the site of operation of (*moral*) principles (productive force), and (d) the economic refers to labor as both applied physical ability (*moral*) and inherent material capacity (*natural*) to transform that to which it is applied (*natural*).

41 As noted earlier, I use the term Thing (*das Ding*) as a referent to the Kantian concept of nature (ordered whole) and the phenomenological writing of the world.

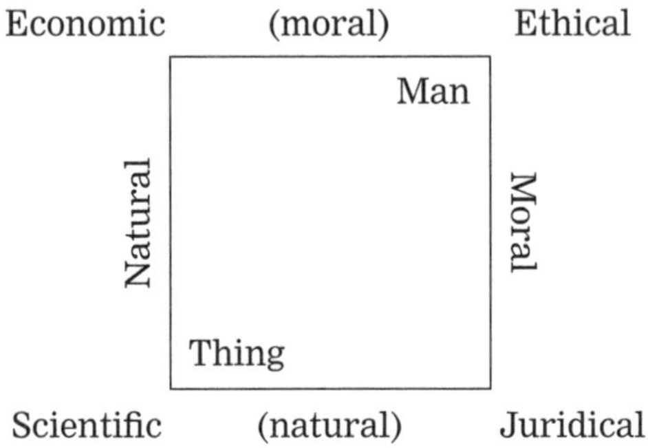

A characteristic of the Racial and its tools is that they operate with/in and conjugate the two moments that stand on opposite sides, namely (a) the scientific, which corresponds to the Thing (natural), and (b) the ethical, which corresponds to Man/Humanity. Though facing each other, the metaphysical line separating Human/Humanity and Thing renders it troublesome to consider both jointly. To be sure, much of the difficulty in accounting for racial subjugation as proper to the design and mode of inhabitation of the post-Enlightenment political architecture has to do with how raciality disarranges these correspondences. It does so because racial difference continues to operate even after the early twentieth-century turn that disavowed the scientific as the proper moment for establishing the what and the why delimiting Man and its successors—the Human (scientific), Humanity (historico-transcendental), and Subjectivity (historico-phenomenological). A move that does not reach far enough and results in that necessity continues to operate underground or, perhaps better, inwardly (intrastructurally, so to speak), that is, as the sine qua non for the scientific and unmentionable ground of the historical text.[42] From there, the entrails of modern thinking in the Classical

42 As I discuss in chapter 3, Marx's critical move was to foreground necessity in the moment of the *natural* (as survival)—attributing to labor a role that Johann Gottfried Herder attributed to Language—as the distinctive Human trait that explains juridical and economic formations that appeared throughout History,

and post-Enlightenment epistemic regimes, comes the basis for the attribution of incomprehensibility to anything that violates *necessity* in any of these moments or in any statement on the Human or Humanity that fails to keep apart the scientific and the ethical.

Not surprisingly, when the wounded captive body in the scene of subjugation confronts the social-scientific (determinative) Category of Blackness (as skin color), since it is a referent of the conjugation of the ethical and the scientific—not in its interpretive rendering but as a product of the Science of Man, that is, the knowledge project that assembled the modern notion of racial difference—it exposes necessity doing its political work through the ethical, economic, and juridical moments. That move, I contend, brings about the collapse of the separation between these moments of the post-Enlightenment political architecture. Not because it hosts something that has yet to come under the scrutiny of knowledge, but because Blackness (the category) is the product of knowledge that most ostensibly displays how necessity designs the post-Enlightenment political architecture. It does so, I argue, because the very philosophical statements that postulated the principles and described what would be the properties of modern ethical and juridical moments—here I have in mind Kant's and Hegel's in particular—had to deal with the fact that, unlike in the case of Indigenous Americans, whom they presumed would disappear, early industrial capital's reliance on slave labor made its disappearance both improbable and undesirable. For this reason, the most these philosophers could do was to posit, without spending much time on details, the Negro's incapacity to comprehend or enact the principles and procedures that distinguish the modern ethical and scientific program. What they did not and could not do, because doing so would suggest another metaphysics, another image of the Human and the Thing, was provided when the human as such (an existent among others) could be safely included among the objects of

---

which, in turn, becomes a site of operation of the scientific laws of nature.

knowledge, which rendered all and any descriptors for Human existence an effect of necessity. Incomprehensibility, then, refers to this metaphysical relay (opening/closure to another image of existence) that blackness activates when recalled by the wounded captive body in the scene of subjugation, namely, a political entity that refers to both the domain of the Thing and the domain of the Human/Humanity, and exposes necessity (juridical and economic) supporting the (ethical) reign of liberty. The fundamental *separation* the Category of Blackness has been produced to signify—the Negro, as Thing, Hegel's object of no value—could never be articulated positively without risking the ethical principle that sustains the modern program, namely liberty. Unless, of course, it also included an account of how the subject of liberty had its conditions of existence as Owner secured by the *necessary* (juridically authorized) deployment of total violence on persons (body-mind composites) conceived as without (ethical and economic) value, namely, the wounded captive body in the scene of subjugation. Had that been the case, had necessity's support not operated in the entrails of modern thought, liberty itself would become an attribute of a thing—Man as he existed in the colonial context, that is, the Conqueror (of Native lands), the Settler, and the Owner (of Slaves), and the practices and instruments of total violence used to secure his lethal authority.

As the common name given to Humans who are nothing, objects without value, the Category of Blackness signals but does not express—because it is itself a product of modern thought—a metaphysics without necessity. For, as Fred Moten states, "what cannot be understood within, or as a function of, the deprivation that is the context of its genesis, can only be understood as the ongoing present of a common refusal."[43] Another articulation of

---

43 Fred Moten, "The Subprime and the Beautiful," *African Identities* 11, no. 2 (2013): 238. Because the black (American) subject, Frank B. Wilderson III reminds us, "is in a structurally impossible position," the whole of modern grammar is under the ongoing threat of "incoherence"—if it were only inward-looking, it would be incomprehensible. Wilderson, "The Prison Slave as Hegemony's

this potential, one that is key to this effort to dissolve the forms that keep the radical disruption that is blackness from being unleashed, is what I read in Moten's rendering of blackness, which, like Spillers, also presents a *negativ(e activ)ation*—the "ante-analog" or "the anticipatory project of celebration" that is both anti-ontological (as a claim) and ante-ontological, that is, what is against and (at the same time) what stands before spatially (as non).[44] For blackness, the ante- (position) that is first and foremost an anti- (disposition) already houses the kind of reversal of thinking necessary for rendering Dana's charge in such a way that it not only stands before (and beyond) comprehension but also invites (as against or anti-ontological) thinking that can dissolve value, in both its economic and ethical scenes.

Reading with the wounded captive body in the scene of subjugation, it is possible to delineate the how of this dissolution, of the *negative*—not of *negation* because of the non-Hegelian pairings this figure recalls.[45] She holds the Human and the Thing in extreme tension: Human, a person with all the physical traits of Man but not that which is given in the juridical structures of the body politic, namely liberty; and Thing, property that can be sold and bought to work on other things, but only owing to the threat of total violence. Because it is both at once, the captive body (that is, the Slave), as a colonial (juridico-economic) existent, figures the refusal of resolution; that is, her economic position promptly signals (and troubles the separation of) the ethical and

---

(Silent) Scandal," in *Warfare in the American Homeland: Policing and Prison in a Penal Democracy*, ed. Joy James (Durham, NC: Duke University Press, 2007), 31.

44 Moten, "The Subprime and the Beautiful," 240.

45 Incidentally, it is possible to read this as negation—by reading this moment from the perspective of the "I," as in Hegel's tale of lord and bondsman. Instead, I choose to situate this scene in the context of Spillers's deployment of skin color and flesh because, owing to the lack of movement in the encounter in Hegel's scene, there remains the impossibility of writing the encounter as a moment of confrontation (of equally free self-consciousnesses) in the unfolding (ethical) scene of representation. Why this is unavoidable will become more and more evident as my argument in this book unfolds.

economic moment of the post-Enlightenment political architecture. Ethically, this tension signals a conflation—as Slave, she exists as Human (a person with will and productive capacity that can be expropriated or exploited) and as an instrument of production (a thing whose capacity to work can be extracted). That ethical tension, as I discuss in chapter 2, which signals how the total violence that holds the Slave's Humanness and Thingness is never sure of its effectivity, sutures the racial dialectic and is key to its unraveling. Juridically, this tension yields an inversion: a Human that is property, that exists as a thing (with productive capacity).[46] That juridical distinction, as we will see in chapter 3, is crucial to Marx's assembling of capital as the descriptor of the post-Enlightenment economic scene since it is specified with the argument that, because the worker is not free to sell her labor power, the Slave Owner–Slave Labor relation, unlike the Property Owner–Wage Labor relation, is *not equal before the law*. To be sure, this tension concerns post-Enlightenment thinking because, early in the classical order, it was settled that the Slave did not figure among those the divine ruler and author created in his likeness. Or, put differently, the captive body does not participate, as Sylvia Wynter reminds us, in the ethical whole composed of those who had been saved, those created by God.[47]

Through the wounded captive body in the scene of subjugation and the singular manner in which, as a referent of the juridical, she presents the post-Enlightenment political architecture, it is possible to contemplate and appreciate the in/distinction between the economic and the ethical scenes of value. An in/distinction, it is important to say explicitly again,

---

46 Here and in later pages I employ the categories of historical materialism in the description of the Slave as a colonial (juridico-economic) subject, that is, as labor. Later, in chapter 3, I make the move that abandons this formulation of labor. Unfortunately I cannot anticipate it here. I am just warning the reader not to hold on to these familiar terms too tightly.

47 Sylvia Wynter, "Unsettling the Coloniality of Being/Power/Truth/Freedom: Towards the Human, after Man, Its Overrepresentation—An Argument," *CR: The New Centennial Review* 3, no. 3 (2003): 257–337.

that exposes how the presumed separation—but only because of the erasure of the (*moral*) line that links them—relies on that which makes both comprehension and valuation possible and is also that which supplements (because it substitutes for) the juridical moment. What I am referring to here is the role of the symbolic in the modern political architecture and in particular the arsenal of raciality, which was assembled when the tools of scientific reason were applied to produce the truth of the Human and its conditions of existence, and which, when doing so, addressed *him* as Thing. The in/distinction between the two scenes of value was articulated in a moment of the philosophical conversation that rendered *knowing* and *being* inseparable and, under the imperative that the Human (like Man before) enjoys ontological and epistemological supremacy, demanded accounts of *existing* premised on the fundamental separation between the Human and the Thing.

For centuries now, necessity (as expressed in the armature of logic) has remained the abhorred and celebrated ground for modern knowledge claims. Through the laws of logic (the principle of identity/equality and the correlated law of noncontradiction and principle of the excluded middle) and the onto-epistemological descriptors and pillars they sustain, necessity has supported the reign of Man/the Human, including its writing as *the* thing of liberty.

From Galileo, Descartes, and Kant to Deleuze and Badiou, European philosophers have rendered necessity through mathematical procedures that carry the same force of necessity as that of the Aristotelian orthodoxy against which these self-named modern philosophers rebelled—namely, syllogism. What is not usually discussed is how, as early modern philosophers reclaimed the laws of logic—the principle of noncontradiction (propositions *a* and *not-a* cannot both be true), the law of the excluded middle (either *a* or *not-a* is true, there is no mediating proposition between them) and the principle of identity ($a=a$)—as unique to the rational mind, they did so in the process of transforming every existent and event into appearances, as *nature* (the scientific) and *world* (the phenomenological). Furthermore, necessity, as it is derived from formal (logical) principles, sustains early modern philosophers' formulation of the onto-epistemological pillars (separability, determinacy, and sequentiality) and fundamental descriptors for what exists (formality) and happens in the world (efficacy). In sum, necessity constitutes the most basic component of the intrastructure of post-Enlightenment thinking.[48]

How this happens becomes evident when one traces the operations of necessity and the laws of logic in the Kantian and Hegelian versions of transcendental reason.[49] Key to this accomplishment is the force of *necessity*, that is, the fact that constructs and statements internally held by the laws of logic do not need to take into account what it is made of. Put simply, whatever is said about events and existents, in accordance with these laws, derives its *truth* status from *how* it is constructed (*a priori*) and not from whether or not it corresponds to *what* it is about (*a posteriori*). For Kant, this *a priori* ground consists of the (*formal*) transcendental tools of the rational mind; for Hegel, it consists of the transcendental self-actualizing force, the (*final*) spirit; for both, this productive tool or force is Thought.

In both the descriptors (formality and efficacy) and the pillars (separability, determinacy, and sequentiality) that enter into the composition of post-Enlightenment onto-epistemological constructs and statements, necessity works intuitively, that is, abstractly, through an image of existence as *linearly* ordered. Though linearity was introduced earlier in the trajectory of modern philosophy by philosophers such as Galileo and Francis Bacon, its pervasiveness in post-Enlightenment thinking can be attributed to Kant's assembling of the transcendental and to how it remained, though modified, in Hegel's version of the

48 For a discussion of these terms, see Denise Ferreira da Silva, "On Difference without Separability," in *32nd Bienal de São Paulo: Incerteza Viva*, ed. Jochen Volz and Júlia Rebouças (São Paulo: Fundação Bienal de São Paulo, 2016), 57–66.

49 A more elaborate discussion of their versions of transcendental reason—Kant's productive nomos (productive and controlling form) and Hegel's transcendental poiesis (self-producing force)—can be found in the first part of Ferreira da Silva, *Toward a Global Idea of Race*.

transcendental. Later, in chapter 2, I elaborate on this argument regarding the Kantian program. For now, let me make two general comments regarding the significance of linearity to the confection of post-Enlightenment descriptors and pillars.

Linearity operates within the following Kantian presuppositions—which function to sustain them—regarding knowledge statements about existents and events that carry necessity. On the one hand, it is the guiding image for the onto-epistemological descriptors: (a) *separability*—that what is to be known is exteriorly or interiorly distinguished/distinguishable from everything else, that is, separable spatially (with a location in a grid); (b) *determinacy*—that knowing consists principally in identifying the (interior or exterior) cause of the observable effect and subsuming phenomena under concepts or categories, which are displayable as a grid or table; (c) *sequentiality*—that existents and events are separable temporally, with a position in a sequence (imaged as an ascending line).[50] On the other hand, it is intrinsic to the onto-epistemological descriptors, formality and efficacy, which derive from how the Kantian program limits the scope of scientific knowledge to the form (as opposed to content or matter) of things and their relations. These are aspects that would resolve the scenes of reason, the scientific and the historical, to constitute the onto-epistemological bases that distinguish post-Enlightenment thought; they comprise the most general conditions of comprehensibility.[51] Of relevance here is how the laws of logic (in particular, the principle of identity/equality) that obtain necessity operate through these pillars and descriptors as constructs, statements, and formulations that describe Human (collective) existence

50 The centrality of discovery is foregrounded in classical texts such as Galileo’s major works, *The Two New Sciences* (Toronto: Wall & Emerson, 2000) and *Dialogue Concerning the Two Chief World Systems* (New York: Modern Library, 2001), and Bacon’s *Advancement of Learning*, in *Selected Philosophical Works*, ed. Rose Mary Sargent (Indianapolis, IN: Hackett Publishing, 1999).

51 For descriptions of the scenes of reason, see Ferreira da Silva, *Toward a Global Idea of Race*.

produced in the nineteenth century's determinative regime (in the scientific scene of reason) and the twentieth century's interpretive regime (in the historical scene of reason). In particular, I am interested in how they assemble the concept of the social—under these distinct regimes of the post-Enlightenment episteme. Two aspects are of special interest: on the one hand, how the writing of the social, across different scenes of reasons, yields issues such as how to reconcile the natural and the moral, that is, how the scientific rendering of the Human as *object* under certain *relations* reconciles with the ethical notion of Humanity; and on the other hand, how to conciliate two distinct operators of *unity*—the foremost logical principle in terms of *identity* (qualitative) and the same principle presented as *equality* (quantitative). Both yield the social as a *totality* of sorts, an *ordered* (quantitatively or qualitatively) unit or circumscription, but the qualitative (historical) totality abhors necessity (for it is the limit of liberty), while the quantitative (scientific) totality cannot hold without it. Things become complicated, of course, when the attempt at conciliation involves constructs of the Human—as *objects* and *relations*—produced under different regimes.

When the *wounded captive body in the scene of subjugation*, the object without the ethical (because partly Thing) and economic (because not a productive Human) scenes of value, is activated in chapters 2 and 3, *she* exposes and releases the terms and movements that facilitated the reconciliation of the moral and the natural (in the sociological account of racial subjugation) and of the historical and the scientific (in the historical-materialist account of capital accumulation), respectively. In chapter 2, *she* disarranges the racial dialectic when she shines as a juridical figure and pierces through this scientific construct, which is governed by the ethical moment. In chapter 3, *she* implodes Marx's formalization of the general law of value when she shines as an ethical figure and dissolves the outer membrane (historical) and inner sutures (scientific) that gather capital as a totality. Enacting how our *ongoing present* retains that which can only be met with common refusal, the *wounded captive body in the scene of subjugation*'s movement is one of *traversion*. Not the expected itinerary, the unfolding, the progress that is the substratum of historical and biographical accounts, *hers* is the *negativating* work needed to render comprehensible Dana's fulfillment of her charge, for it to be seen for what it could have been had not linearity prevailed in the modern image of existence. Turning attention away from the objects and relations that both explain and reinstitute racial subjugation enables the defying gesture—that is, *common refusal*. That which activates the very impossibility of the "black subject"—its incomprehensibility—allows the contemplation of how blackness (unleashed from within its categorial confines, that is, lowercase "b" blackness, as the common name for existents both human and nonhuman) describes a mode of existing that exposes how the world as we know it—that is, as Nature and *world*—is also, and perhaps more fundamentally, a site of operation of total violence or the theater of necessity, the one in which the two crucial nineteenth-century emancipatory concepts equality and identity (both ethical proxies for the juridical notion of liberty) reveal the perversity of modern thinking.

"the cause is the consequence"

> When you examine at close quarters the colonial context, it is evident that what parcels out the world is to begin with the fact of belonging to or not belonging to a given race, a given species. In the colonies the economic substructure is also a superstructure. The cause is the consequence; you are rich because you are white, you are white because you are rich. This is why Marxist analysis should always be slightly stretched every time we have to do with the colonial problem.
>
> —Frantz Fanon, *The Wretched of the Earth*

Theorizing from battlegrounds located on opposite margins of the Mediterranean (Algeria and southern Italy, respectively), Frantz Fanon and Antonio Gramsci dealt with the challenge of rewriting the historical-materialist text or, more precisely, the challenge of rendering its presentation of determinative unity adequate to the interpretive version of the modern political architecture, in which the ethico-symbolic pair appears more relevant than the juridico-economic in the assembling of political subjects. From within the parameters of the interpretive episteme, their versions rewrite, in different ways of course, the *transparent I* as a hybrid of *homo historicus* and *homo laborans*.[52] Each, in a different way, participated in a redesign of the historical-materialist text that neither advanced an adequate critique of its own version of *homo scientificus* nor attended to how the latter entered into the composition of the twentieth-century global political architecture.[53] Unsurprisingly, however, each version is consistent with its global position: Gramsci identified the cultural-historical as a terrain for political struggle, while Fanon derived a racial-historical account that instituted a dialectic that, instead of leading to a further stage of development of the Human, would lead to a not-yet-conceived Humanity. Expectedly, Gramsci would have a greater influence than Fanon on later theories and analyses of the relationships between the racial and capital.[54]

---

52 My reference for *homo laborans* here is Hannah Arendt's discussion of Marx, labor, and the human as "*animal laborans*." See Arendt, *The Human Condition* (Chicago: University of Chicago Press, 1958), 124 (italics in original). For a different (from Arendt's) take on Marx's deployment of the term, see Sarah Vitale, "Beyond *Homo Laborans*: Marx's Dialectical Account of Human Essence," *Social Theory and Practice* 46, no. 3 (July 2020): 633–55.

53 Certainly, they are relevant both to how descendants of Indigenous and enslaved populations would fare in the independent postcolonies of the Americas and South Africa and to how European colonial incursions in Africa and the Middle East had to respond to the political principle of self-determination, which was also articulated through various combinations of raciality and the nationality principle.

54 Though it might be because the analysis of racial subjugation has inherited a sociological framework and its particular deployment of the concept of the cultural, a possible explanation for this development may be due to other causes—such as the intellectual circumstances of the post–Second World War world and the Cold War, which from the critical point of view would respond to a certain avoidance of historical materialism, in the United States in particular, which has been the center of racial theorizing.

Of relevance to my task here, however, is how both Fanon and Gramsci, in different ways, dealt with what has been an intractable demand on the twentieth-century versions of the historical-materialist text, which is the need to reconcile its original determinative presentation of unity with the interpretive refiguring of the modern liberal political architecture and the elevation of the *homo historicus* (in the concept of the nation) as a criterion for validating claims to sovereignty (political self-determination).[55] They had to deal with how to adapt the original version of historical materialism, which, as I discuss in chapter 3,[56] formulates labor according to the Kantian rules of scientific signification—that is, as the category that determines capital as a totality, a unity established through the articulation of the logical principle of identity as it is operationalized by mathematical tools (as equality). For Gramsci, the challenge was not one of accommodating another scientific concept but one of integrating the interpretive (historical) rendering of the concept of the cultural. Fanon, however, moved to integrate the concept of the racial, once considered scientifically sound, at a moment in which it had been displaced by the concept of the cultural as the proper descriptor of the Human as a unity of multiplicity. Hence, his challenge resulted from the interpretive

55 Writings on “the national question” and “the Negro question” by figures from Lenin to C. L. R. James indicate that the theorizing and organizing of the revolution require the integration of historicity—through the concepts of the cultural and the nation—in a theoretical-political program designed under the terms of the nineteenth-century determinative episteme.

56 My use of the phrase “historical materialism” gives away my inhabitation of an intellectual field flavored by structuralism/post-structuralism—in particular as it was presented in Rio de Janeiro in the 1980s, where Althusser and his students had some influence, even as Foucault was breaking through; see, for instance, Louis Althusser et al., *Reading Capital* (London: Verso, 2016). I am using a term that prevailed in the early twentieth century, well aware that it already situates the Marxist program within the interpretive episteme. However, I find it useful because, though a determinative program, Marx and Engels situate it in the historical, as will be discussed in chapter 3.

moment, where racial difference reads as datum or residuum, which means that it could be included, but only as a new empirical dimension that would lead to a further development of a proper theoretical or analytical framework. Nevertheless, it would never acquire determinative (analytical or causal) or interpretive relevance because the racial is not seen as a proper modern political ((juridic, economic, ethic, and symbolic)) concept. In any event, both had to deal with the challenge of keeping intact Marx's assembling of capital as a totality—as the (determinative) unity of multiplicity designed as a system assembled on the basis of the mathematical notion of equality—under an epistemic regime governed by the historical rendering of the *transparent I*.[57]

Framing a particular geo-historical context, each presents the capitalist mode of production as a fractured whole (well, as a duality, in properly Marxist terms); each proposes an analytical approach that attends to how the cultural (Gramsci) and the racial (Fanon) feature in its constitution. Early twentieth-century Italy's political context demanded that Gramsci picture contending parts that are geographically and culturally divided. He attends to the modalities of subjugation, identifying two modes of deployment of force: physical domination and ideological apprehension. Hence the answer for the guiding question imposed by the notion of totality (a presentation of unity in an image of the "social" that foregrounds an agonistic plurality)—the question of how unity is maintained, that is, one that requests efficacy or identity as the form of the response—is also the key for the revolution, which would lead to a different kind of unity, sustained by the subaltern's particular (ideological

57 In chapter 3, I discuss the distinction between Kant's and Hegel's versions of totality. There I also provide an account of why this discussion does not fall in with the classical Marxist debates on totality, as animated by Lukács's and Althusser's renderings of the notion, as presented, respectively, in Georg Lukács, *History and Class Consciousness: Studies in Marxist Dialectics*, trans. Rodney Livingstone (Cambridge, MA: MIT Press, 1972); and Louis Althusser, "Contradiction and Overdetermination," *New Left Review* 1, no. 41 (January/February 1967): 15–35.

or cultural) principle. That is, the focus of the analysis is the superstructural moment. In Gramsci, the reader recognizes the expected operations of a divided social configuration—along economic, cultural, and political (domination/subordination) lines—that are pieces of the same juridico-economic cloth. For this reason, the very possibility of ideological domination, the configuration presents a totality divided within itself but still self-transparent.

Less than twenty years after Gramsci’s death, Fanon described the colonial context as violently constituted and ordered; that is, he described it as the product of total violence in various guises—land dispossession, labor expropriation, humiliation, and police and military repression. Total violence, he argues, maintains its unity, and it alone will bring an end to that racially divided world and the parts (the colonizer and the colonized) that constitute it. What I find generative in Fanon’s description of the colonial context is how it neither yields nor presupposes a universal (it is not immediately applicable to all colonial situations), nor does it identify a particular case among others of the same kind (all colonial situations are governed by total violence)—though the case could be made that he proposes the colonial as a site that (only a revised version of the original presentation of) the historical-materialist text could explain. More significantly, whereas Gramsci’s version fully belongs to the post-Enlightenment context, Fanon’s is only a comprehensible description of the political context under the interpretive episteme if understood as the tale of the production of pathological (mentally ill) political subjects. Otherwise, it is incomprehensible because, for one, while he remains faithful to Marx’s eschatological version of the dialectic, Fanon sets up an anti-Hegelian dialectic that is not adequate to the interpretive regime or to determinative (social-scientific) signification. On the one hand, it stages a confrontation that, like Marx’s version of the dialectic, has no possibility of sublation; that is, it does not presume that the negation of negation will lead to a further development of self-consciousness. On the other hand, because it does set up a confrontation, Fanon’s account of colonial/racial subjugation departs from sociological accounts of racial subjugation since it does not preserve whiteness as transparency, and instead, as an explicit departure from Phenomenology, in writing the colonizer and the colonized as products of coloniality, it announces the disappearance of both (and the concomitant transubstantiation of the Settler and the Native into "a new Man") as the cleansing effect of anti-colonial total violence.[58] To be sure, Fanon's version of the racial dialectic contains elements, which he did not explore, that permit the dissolving of the logical circuitry produced by sociological accounts—though that may account for why his version has not been as successful in historical-materialist quarters of the critical field.[59] In chapter 3, I elaborate the argument, advanced above, that Gramsci's interpretive version of historical materialism has had more takers than Fanon's. Before doing so, however, it is necessary to take a closer look at how the Colonial and the Racial enter contemporary analyses of Capital that recognize their import as mechanisms of global subjugation.

Perhaps the greatest feat of the racial dialectic has been how effectively it renders the operations of the Racial (through the racial and cultural difference of the "others of Europe") irrelevant to the analysis of Capital, even in this moment when the practices of coloniality and the significations of raciality play such a crucial role in support of global state capital. Though it manifests at different levels and in various ways, contemporary critiques of global capital deal with racial difference as a matter already organized by separability as it works with/in sequentiality and determinacy. Let me briefly situate the argument, which I develop in chapter 3, in a commentary on Aníbal Quijano's and Sylvia Wynter's writings on the coloniality of power. Departing from conventional historical-materialist analyses, both thinkers tackle the triad of the Colonial, the Racial, and Capital from different perspectives. To a certain extent, my own take on this trio

---

58 Fanon, *Wretched of the Earth*, 316.

59 A telling exception is Glen Sean Coulthard's deployment of Fanon's framework in theorizing colonial relations in *Red Skin, White Masks: Rejecting the Colonial Politics of Recognition* (Minneapolis: University of Minnesota Press, 2014).

resonates with both: like Quijano, I find that the Racial refigures the Colonial at the political/symbolic level; like Wynter, I find that it does so in combination with the notion of the Human.[60] The similarities in our analyses stop here for reasons that may already be obvious to the reader, which are related to my inclusion of the Juridical (the State) in the equation.

What I identify in Quijano's and Wynter's critical accounts is still a certain investment in maintaining intact historical materialism (Quijano) as the foremost critique of Capital as an economic form and the Human (Winter) as an ethical concept. Because blackness threatens the very basis that makes both cohere, its activation cannot but dissipate the forms (secured by the laws of logic) on which their force relies, which I think is a necessary step toward an ethico-political program that does not reproduce the total violence, the ferity, at the core of modern thinking and the political (juridic, economic, ethic, and symbolic) architecture it supports. Introducing the argument presented in chapter 3 vis-à-vis Quijano's and Wynter's propositions might give a better idea of the extent of the disarranging of the critical grounds enacted by thinking the political through blackness.

Framing Quijano's thesis about the relationship between race (racial difference), colonialism, and Capital is the classic sociological (interpretive) separation between structure and culture (or ideology), or between the economic and the social. This allows the thesis that race emerges as a colonial "mechanism of domination," a "principle of social classification," which distinguishes between two kinds of labor: paid (white/European) and unpaid (non-white/non-European). According to Quijano, race—or the coloniality of power—operates in global capital by

60 Aníbal Quijano, "Coloniality of Power, Eurocentrism, and Latin America," *Nepantla: Views from South* 1, no. 3 (2000): 533–80; and Wynter, "Unsettling the Coloniality." For an extended engagement with Wynter's thought, see Denise Ferreira da Silva, "Before *Man*: Sylvia Wynter's Rewriting of the Modern Episteme," in *Sylvia Wynter: On Being Human as Praxis*, ed. Katherine McKittrick (Durham, NC: Duke University Press, 2015), 90–105.

guiding the distinction between paid and unpaid ("colonized races") labor. From this results a heterogeneous totality, that is, a "global capitalist coloniality of power" constituted through articulations of all "historical forms of labor control around the capitalist wage-labor relation" that takes the form of assigning "all forms of unpaid labor to colonial races" and "salaried labor to the colonizing whites."[61] Without violating the classic historical-materialist notion that wage labor distinguishes capital, Quijano introduces a "particularism" (an abnormal kind of labor) to correct world-systems theory with the argument that race—which emerges under colonialism as a mechanism for controlling wage (surplus-value generating) labor—now organizes global capital, as it introduces a hierarchy in the category of labor that facilitates the exploitation of non-white/non-European people all over the world. Throughout the analysis, race does not figure as an economic category; it remains a (symbolic) datum, a social (moral) matter, which, when taken into account, allows for a reconceptualization of the economic concept of capital that can comprehend its newest configuration, namely a "global capitalist coloniality of power."[62] This happens through the acknowledgment of capital's dependence on an "improper"—from the point of view of the post-Enlightenment ethical program—kind of labor, as a means for the domination of universal (proper) labor.[63]

Conversely, Wynter's contribution to the theme of the coloniality of power is framed by a distinction between science and culture—also an interpretive take—that promises a separation between truth and ideology. With the help of a vast list of anthropological works, she introduces a universalism—the

61 Quijano, "Coloniality of Power," 539.

62 "Insofar as the social relations that were being configured were relations of domination, such identities were considered constitutive of the hierarchies, places, and corresponding social roles, and consequently of the model of colonial domination that was being imposed. In other words, race and racial identity were established as instruments of basic social classification." Quijano, 534.

63 In chapter 3, I return to this idea of totality in a discussion of Stuart Hall's thesis on societies structured in dominance.

Human's capacity to produce and hide from itself both its collective existence and accounts of it, or "descriptive statements"—which explains and promises to transcend modern cultural hierarchies. For Wynter, the coloniality of power, or race, is the hierarchical descriptor that governs modern European answers to the ontological question of who we are, while also answering the ethical question of how we ought to live and act, in a way that renders white Europeans' mode of being human the only true presentation of what is, in fact, Human. Modern European "descriptive statements," she argues, reproduce earlier hierarchies (such as the medieval perfect heaven versus fallen earth) and construct European Man to represent all that is truly human. Meanwhile, other peoples' modes of being and of describing humans represent nonhuman "Others." Locally significant (invented by Europeans) and culturally specific, "race," she writes, "was therefore to be, in effect, the nonsupernatural but no less extrahuman ground (in the reoccupied place of the traditional ancestors/gods, God, ground)."[64] Race, according to Wynter, is a modern "descriptive statement," the primary effect of which is to sustain "systemic stigmatization, social inferiorization, and dynamically produced material deprivation," in particular of black populations everywhere in the world.[65]

For Quijano and Wynter, ever since Europeans' conquest and occupation of the Americas and the Caribbean, racial difference's role (as a symbolic, ideological tool) has been to facilitate the appropriation of labor and land in the Americas and elsewhere in the global space. The difference is that for Quijano, racial classification establishes *proper* (white/European) Labor, and for Wynter, it establishes the *proper* (white/European) Human. When thinking through the relationship of the Colonial, the Racial, and Capital, their approaches offer little, however. Indeed, for both, racial difference as a datum operates as a principle for classification that creates hierarchies that are *exterior* (a) economically, as to the proper capitalist production of value,

64 Wynter, "Unsettling the Coloniality," 264.
65 Wynter, 266.

which necessitates paid labor, per Quijano; and (b) ethically, to properly modern (universalist or "transcultural" or "acultural") thinking, because it relies on "extrahuman" grounds, per Wynter. For this reason, neither thinker provides a satisfactory account of the Colonial/Racial/Capital triad. More importantly, linear temporality forces a starting point in which the racial, as a colonial mechanism, is *anterior* to state capital properly constituted. And here, too, blackness figured as skin color performs its social-scientific role, which is to circumscribe, delimit, and separate what is properly modern from what is not.

With the guidance of the *wounded captive body in the scene of subjugation*, in chapter 3 I return to one of Marx's presentations of the equation of value. There *she* recomposes it, in a movement that recalls blackness at the intersection of the juridical and ethical moments, from where it pierces the totality that is Capital from within, and in doing so vacates anteriority and exteriority. Ignoring the onto-epistemological descriptors and pillars that support the racial dialectic, which remains the prevailing account of racial subjugation and the historical-materialist account of capitalist production, my task is preoccupied with two simple questions: First, how does one inherit such an obligation? And second, why is it not one's to pay? As I take these questions seriously as referents to an unpayable debt, I assemble a fractal figuring of the Colonial, the Racial, the Juridical, and Capital that, violating separability, collapses its effects (anteriority and exteriority), which is so crucial in the delimitation and determination of Capital. Now, this is just one moment of the unleashing of blackness's capacity—negativation—within the modern political architecture. The second, less accepted move is the dissolution of the stage on which the economic and the ethical scenes of value unfold. For it shifts the precondition for the intelligibility of—the image of existence that sustains—modern thinking. It describes existence not as a relationship but as a context marked by singularity and implicancy in which everything retains its dis/similarity, that is, everything exists as deeply implicated in/as/with each and every other existing thing.

"was morally lawful to deal in as article of property"

> 4. A free negro of the African race, whose ancestors were brought to this country and sold as slaves, is not a "citizen" within the meaning of the Constitution of the United States.
> 5. When the Constitution was adopted, they were not regarded in any of the States as members of the community which constituted the State, and were not numbered among its "people or citizens." Consequently, the special rights and immunities guarantied to citizens do not apply to them. And not being "citizens" within the meaning of the Constitution, they are not entitled to sue in that character in a court of the United States, and the Circuit Court has not jurisdiction in such a suit.
> 6. The only two clauses in the Constitution which point to this race, treat them as persons whom it was morally lawful to deal in as articles of property and to hold as slaves.
>
> —*Dred Scott v. Sanford*

If what was then/there "morally lawful" has yet to be extricated from the Category of Blackness, and is in fact relentlessly actualized by it, the crucial question becomes how to approach existence from the scene of total violence without rewriting blackness as, in Fred Moten's words, a function, or how to unleash blackness from within its categorial holdings, where it is more apt to dismantle the modern grammar. This is not an easy task, for several reasons. Two of them are evident in Dana's charge, in the very description of her predicament. The first reason, which relates to what Moten calls the "ongoing present," has an implication for how one describes the ethical and the economic scenes of value. On the one hand, her obligation to save her ancestor-Owner, even if only to preserve her own existence, carries a particular rendering of materiality into a domain, the ethical, in which it should not play a role. Forget for a moment how hers is an obligation that—as is the case with anything that becomes a signifier of the kind of condition blackness identifies—immediately displaces the two major items in the modern ethical grammar, namely liberty and equality. Forget, in other words, that slavery is a juridico-economic relation in which Dana is property (like Dred Scott) and Rufus has a claim on her (when she is back in antebellum Maryland). Now try and consider Dana's obligation ethically, merely in terms of moral principles—such as "Thou shalt not kill" or "Act as if your maxim is a universal law." It is nonsensical because these refer, respectively, to authority (of God) or universality (of the Moral Law); her obligation does not belong to these registers.

Having to protect on the basis of a blood relation is a demand that recalls a different ethical register, one that is a referent to the family—with obvious links to patriarchy—but that in this context (of slavery) refers to the *elemental*. Her body—or rather the code (DNA) that guides its constitution—is the only link between her and Rufus. In her family history, he is an Owner who took a Slave (being black then/there, Alice is always a Slave),[66] Dana's ancestor, as a lover, and without a statement from the woman as to whether or not theirs was a romantic liaison—even if it was one, because he is her Owner, theirs is not a relation between equals, the juridical relation in the form of title overrides that—the sentimental aspect that presumably accompanies family relations is not there. Furthermore, there is no possibility for a claim based on identity between her and Rufus. (It does not matter whether the opposite would be the case between her and her "several times" great-grandmother, because Dana's charge is to save Rufus's life, not Alice's.)

My point here is to recall that Dana saves Rufus's life several times not because of affect, inclination, sentiment, belief, or desire.[67] None of the motives Kant dismisses in *Critique of Practical Reason*—because they are linked to previous conceptions of morality—matter to her. Nor does it matter to her that Rufus is Human (as in a being with intrinsic value, that is, Humanity), because she has no choice (with regard to self-interest

66 It does not matter that Alice was a freed woman. Like Dred Scott, a white person could claim her as a slave.

67 In case the reader does not take it for granted, this does not mean that affect, sentiment, or inclination did not operate in regard to relations (familial or not) among enslaved persons "across the landscape to others, often sold from hand to hand, of the same and different blood in a common fabric of memory and inspiration." Spillers, "Mama's Baby, Papa's Maybe," 75.

or self-determination) whether or not to travel in time to save his life. None of this matters because, as the principle of liberty directs, as a Slave she is not (ethically) Human but Thing (to which someone has a juridical claim). All that connects them, which is also the *ongoing present* Dana shares with Alice and Rufus's other Slaves, is her flesh, organs, cells, molecules, atoms, protons, phonons, electrons, nucleons.

For this reason, Dana's charge allows us to ask a question that does not have any significance in an ethical moment governed and devised by Humanity, its principles (liberty and dignity) and the tools of raciality: What if ethical descriptions had at their core a commonality that is not mediated by identity (as a shared particularity that is familial, national, historical) or by liberty (general equality) established through the universality of shared (rational, formal, transcendental) ideas? What if ethical descriptors did not presume substantive or formal commonality (identity or equality) figured as atemporal or aspatial and yet fundamentally immanent? Directly asked: What if the basis of our ethical program was simply that everything that exists, has existed, or may come to exist is made of the same raw material, the *elementa*, the quantic things (particle-wave emanations) whose re/de/composition allows us to say anything about their existence? If we begin, as I do, by concurring with this question, such a point of departure for thinking troubles the very notion of value.

On the other hand, then, Dana's charge—saving her Owner-ancestor's life—exposes a breach in the play of value, which again is activated by her body's travels across different moments (spatiotemporal) of her ongoing present. The breach, to be sure, occurs because of the tearing of the symbolic membrane that separates the ethical and the economic scenes of value. This is not the register of measures and principles. Without an economic aspect that can be monetized, Dana's obligation has an economic significance that cannot be calculated (in an extension to the future or the past), operationalized (through arithmetic), or computed (with algorithms). Her obligation cannot be formalized or translated into mathematical formats (geometry, algebra, arithmetic, calculus) through which it could then be equated with the money form. Nonetheless, Dana's moral obligation is incomprehensible because it is instituted by slavery (a colonial juridico-economic structure) and secured by its juridical form and method of governance (title and total violence, respectively), and related rendering of authority. Here the correspondence (which always works across time) is between the physicality of the relation (which was not a familial one) and the fact that Dana had to protect the physical integrity of someone who could kill, rape, maim her, in order to ensure her own physical existence.

Lacking papers that would verify (but not protect) her condition as a freed or born-free black person, Dana occupies a troubling position in the colonial context, one that reveals it as a fundamentally cisheteropatriarchal political context: a black woman who had never been enslaved, traded, or freed. Troublesome but not uncommon, not dissimilar to other black persons existing in the same spatiotemporal moment. Not having papers that could be torn up, Dana exists in antebellum Maryland similarly to how Dred Scott (and all other enslaved persons) lived in Missouri. Their juridical positions are incomprehensible: in Dana's case, there is no person who is black without having ever been property; in Dred Scott's case, there is no person who is black and no longer property. Focusing on "papers," that is, on the captive body as the object of a title, I attend to the various moments and modalities of the deployment of force to uncover how necessity works, through skin color, with the social-scientific categories that, like ethnicity, refigure total violence in the political/symbolic moment. Foregrounding the Juridical, I begin with the moment of the decision/determination, in which the Slave Owner refers to authority as figured in Slavery and Patriarchy. Why? Think of those occasions when, as in the US Supreme Court's decision in the *Dred Scott v. Sanford* case, the juridical is exposed as a site of operation of necessity and not liberty: whatever the phrase "morally lawful" does in paragraph 6 may be relevant, but here I focus on what it does in terms of signaling an exception within the ethico-juridical category of the person—the persons "of the African race." The key to this improper juridical standing is obviously the equivalence of blackness and property, which results in the black person occupying—even with papers—the juridical position of Slave;[68] that is, the equivalence of skin color and property registers black persons' lack of protection (hence the otherwise oxymoronic phrase "morally lawful") afforded by the law to the citizenry, which is the necessity that justifies juridical authority.[69] At the same time, however, this very juridical form of property holds the key to unraveling the equivalence, because having a title over a person's body does not alone assure the use of her capacities. For it is the authority to deploy physical (including total) violence that institutes the position of the Owner who extracts and expropriates slave labor.[70]

What comes to the fore here is precisely how the category of property functions as a relay when it performs as a juridical mediator between the economic and the ethical scenes of value. Lindon Barrett's analysis of value as form and force touches on this in/distinction. Value, he recalls, signals juridical mediation in two moments: on the one hand, as originary force, and on the other hand, as the form(alizing) moment that covers the originary violence. It "introduces itself by way of a violent agency that it subsequently seeks to deny," and Barrett terms that inaugural moment of violence the "forcible disrupting and altering of

68 Among the earlier juridical codifications that equated skin color and property status were the slave deeds of the late 1600s. See Cheryl Harris, "Whiteness and Property," *Harvard Law Review* 106, no. 8 (June 1993): 1718.

69 Let me share David Lloyd's comment on this passage when he read an early version of the manuscript: "Is this oxymoron not also a moment in which the separation of the legal and moral/ethical collapses, as you've argued, making a kind of non-sense. It's an oxymoron because of the separation, by which the functioning of the law must disregard ethical claims where they conflict with the letter of the law. It's a tautology in the transcendental register in which the legal is supposed/held to be the statutory articulation of the ethical, the universal law. The Justice's incoherence manifests in this antithetical figure, at once tautology and oxymoron, that troubles the division of spheres."

70 This too is addressed in the Dred Scott decision, when the court finds that Sanford had the right to apply coercive force against Dred Scott and his family.

otherwise established forms."[71] I read this phrase as a description of physical and not only representational (symbolic) violence—though I am convinced that when using this phrase, Barrett is referring to both. Read through the Dred Scott decision—in other words, by attending to juridical mediation, the property/title that justifies and authorizes the citizen ("morally lawful") to employ (coercive) physical violence against persons—blackness, treated not as skin color (signifier of racial and cultural difference) but as that which identifies the "captive body" (as was evident to Dred Scott and Dana), also indexes how the possibility of negativation resides in necessity, that is, the fact that necessity (force and form) upholds liberty. Liberty, the foremost modern ethical principle, directly or indirectly figured as equality, can only render violence here; that is, Dana's charge is a breach of the ethical program because it signals that the presupposed exclusive attribute of the proper modern economic subject is contingent upon its opposite, that is, the Slave's captivity.

Related to Moten's *common refusal* is the challenge to any thinking that fails to relinquish the post-Enlightenment onto-epistemological pillars and descriptors. Here is where the present text seeks to intervene more directly, which is to register the *ongoing present* of slavery in/as global capital. What it takes, as we know, is nothing short of collapsing the formal (categorial) boundaries—which impose descriptors such as anteriority and exteriority—between Capital, the Racial, and the Colonial. Regarding the ethical scene of value, Dana's charge allows a moving away from its principles and inspires questions that prefigure yet-to-be-entertained images of existence, of what happens and what exists. Regarding the economic scene of value, Dana's charge has a subtler but no less damaging effect, which is that it allows one to image yesterday's Slave coexisting with today's descendants. Not so much its *elementa*, but the singular composition itself—a whole body that travels through time/across a way, and the arm that gets stuck in the last trip back.

---

71 Lindon Barrett, *Blackness and Value: Seeing Double* (Cambridge: Cambridge University Press, 2009), 28.

Precisely because, even though it is incomprehensible, such a trip is imaginable, or more importantly to modern thinkers, visualizable—it inspires "what if" questions that target the core of economic explanations, in particular the Marxist postulate that labor time is the determining factor in exchange value. These questions include how the conceptual frameworks devised for the analysis of capital presupposed onto-epistemological descriptors and pillars designed to make it impossible for the forms (concepts and categories) they underwrite to establish any connections between the Colonial, the Racial, and Capital. An important part of the task here is to dissipate these symbolic tools in order to do both: to expose their workings and to find how they can be used to re/compose the account of racial subjugation in a way that interrupts its unfolding.

The parallel track signaled by the *wounded captive body in the scene of subjugation* is what is exposed by its repetition, or what the black Brazilian writer Conceição Evaristo captures nicely with the phrase: "We agreed not to die."[72] From there it is impossible to avoid the problem of staying with total violence without reproducing its effects, which results from how the tools of raciality (and the inherently perverse dialectic they set up) fail to comprehend as political the refusal to comply to the logic of obliteration. All they can do is rewrite an "impossible" (black) subject, under the assumption that Subjecthood/Subjectivity is the sine qua non for existence. Hence, the only possible move here is to bring about the dissolution of the tools of raciality (hitting the form constituting them), of the onto-epistemological pillars and descriptors that account for their intelligibility (their capacity to comprehend), and of the metaphysics that underwrites them. Dana's charge—her own submission to a formidable obligation—is itself an instance of such refusal: she kept her Owner-father alive in the past to ensure her own existence in her present and, in doing so, she honored her Slave ancestors' refusal to die. More importantly, the fact that

72 Conceição Evaristo, *Olhos d'água* (Rio de Janeiro: Pala Mini, 2018), 117 (my translation).

she did not perform her charge unscathed is a reminder of the ongoing operation of total violence, of the ferity, that ensured the expropriation of the labor (matter's capacity to transfer as potential energy) of enslaved persons. Nevertheless, this very mark of physical violation registers the continuation of the juridical relation and the total violence it authorizes, now operating through the political/symbolic tools of raciality, such as the notions of racial and cultural difference, the Category of Blackness, as well as through juridico-economic terms and relations, such as property or equity.[73]

Two moves become necessary for dealing with these difficulties. Both take place at the level of thinking; more particularly, they are designed to take advantage of the opening afforded by a contemplation of Dana's charge in light of Hortense Spillers's question, which anticipates both of Moten's phrases: on the one hand, the possibility of thinking the *ongoing present* from a "raw material" (*elemental*) perspective, one that refuses to reduce existence to the forms and functions of the living body or "social condition"; on the other hand, the recognition that the violence that characterized slavery as a colonial juridico-economic structure has been met with an insistence not to perish, a refusal of the logic of obliteration. Notably, this intervention targets the very bases of the incomprehensibility of Dana's charge through a double movement of dispersion and negativation, both designed to dismantle the core of the racial dialectic and unleash blackness to perform the critical (ethico-political) task C. L. R. James and Cedric Robinson claim it alone can,[74] which is to dismount modern thinking from within.

---

73 Here I have in mind the financial meaning of equity, that is, ownership of houses, cars, and other assets, which is measured for accounting purposes by subtracting liabilities from the value of an asset. For example, if someone owns a car worth $29,000 and still has to pay off $10,000, she has $19,000 of equity.

74 Cedric Robinson, "Capitalism, Marxism, and the Black Radical Tradition," interview by Chuck Morse, *Perspectives on Anarchist Theory* 3, no. 1 (Spring 1999), http://www.hartford-hwp.com/archives/45a/568.html.

***

Lacking value (in the ethical scene) only because of its capacity to yield value (in the economic scene), the body of the captive person does not refer to the excluded (which gives coherence to) or the constitutive outside (which delimits the borders) of the Subject. Exhibiting the marks of violence that tell the indistinction between liberty and property, the wounded captive body in the scene of subjugation turns attention to the physicality of the system and demands that the question of violence be raised anew. What the authority to deploy total violence for using this peculiar property exposes is the operation of the (force of) Law and the State in the daily workings of slavery—through mechanisms that preserve/protect the citizen's (Owner's) right to property. In the in/distinction between protection and preservation, which is precisely where *necessity* sustains and protects *liberty*, resides the place of the juridical in the economic relationship that is slavery.

Here the apparent incomprehensibility of slavery in the theorizing of the post-Enlightenment political architecture is also resolved. For liberty is that which the juridical structures of the liberal polity are said to protect, but only by ensuring that the citizenry preserve its property. In other words, the indistinction between liberty and property is the kernel of the liberal framework, that which accounts for the relay at work in the racial dialectic. It is also that which can be dismounted in the movement of negativation, as the marks of violence on the flesh of the captive expose that what defines the Owner is not liberty but the juridically protected *right* to deploy total violence in order to extract from his or her property.

At that moment, the scene of violence (the life-and-death struggle) does not join two self-determined entities enjoying unrestricted liberty in a struggle out of which one, the weaker, emerges as Slave. In this juridically framed scene of total violence, the Owner has unrestricted authority, given by the juridical form of title that is protected by the State, and the Slave (the already caught, sold, enslaved) is twice removed from juridical protection: as someone's (a citizen's) property—a right that the State has the obligation to protect—and as such, the Slave has no claim to the protections available to citizens. Owner and Slave do not enter the scene as equals with attributes that are the *negation* of the other's similar attributes. Ethically, each enters the scene with completely distinct positions vis-à-vis liberty: one (Owner) has it, the other (Slave) does not; juridically, as well, vis-à-vis property: one (Slave) is and the other (Owner) is not. When positioned against each other, as persons (humans) we find that the Slave's predicate is non-liberty and the Owner's is liberty—the latter does not occupy the same position as the Slave. In that juridico-economic formation, the Slave is the only category of persons for whom being property is a predicate. Furthermore, liberty, as an ethical principle, does not even figure into the scene mediated by title (a juridical principle); it only operates in the relationship between the Owner and the State (by which he is protected because a Citizen), not in the one between the slave owner and the enslaved person or between the state and the enslaved person. Met with juridical force (as title/state) and physical force (as property/slave owner), the Slave has no ethical position, no stand before the figure of Humanity. Therefore, she is released to commingle with other existents that are liable to be extracted and expropriated. Thus figured, blackness as the *wounded captive body in the scene of subjugation*, a referent to the juridical authority to deploy total violence, breaks through the categorial and historical separation of the Colonial, the Racial, and Capital, as she exposes how global capital accumulates not only through exploitation but through the violent expropriation of Slave labor.[75]

75 Here is David Lloyd's comment on this passage: "Is a distinct account of the differential place of the indigenous in the regime of raciality on the agenda here? If not, this acknowledgement is a little pro forma. For sure, the indigenous are subject to a no less total violence, but on account of representing an untamed liberty that signifies an absence of property versus those deemed incapable of liberty and requiring coercive labor."

My response is yes; on the other hand, the Indigenous figures differently in the regime of raciality. And I think that Lloyd's framing of the distinction between the two colonial figures, the Native and the Slave, as they are figured by the arsenal of raciality is appropriate. However, my comment here does not so much concern raciality as serve as a reminder of how total violence defined the colonial architecture and its modality of governance, in expropriation of both labor and land. This becomes significant in chapter 3, where I re/compose Marx's equation of value, precisely by retrieving cotton (planted on Native lands) and slave labor. Perhaps here is also a good place to remind the reader that I use the term Native (instead of Indigenous), which is the one that prevails in anti-colonial scholarship. I also want to keep it distinct from the global political category of Indigeneity, which delimits the political position of the enunciation of Indigenous peoples. In sum, like the term Slave, Native refers to a political position of subjugation under the colonial political architecture. Highlighting how both the Native and the Slave were governed through the deployment of total violence is a contribution to the project articulated by many, in particular the collection edited by Tiffany Lethabo King, Jenell Navarro, and Andrea Smith, *Otherwise Worlds*.

CHAPTER 2
“the most perfect hallucination”

> Yes, maybe what? Well, maybe, if I wasn't completely out of my mind, if I wasn't in the middle of the most perfect hallucination I'd ever heard of, if the child before me was real and was telling the truth, maybe he was one of my ancestors.
>
> Maybe he was my several times great grandfather, but still vaguely alive in the memory of my family because his daughter had bought a large Bible in an ornately carved, wooden chest and had begun keeping family records in it. My uncle still had it.
>
> Grandmother Hagar. Hagar Weylin, born in 1831. Hers was the first name listed. And she had given her parents' names as Rufus Weylin and Alice Green-something Weylin.
>
> "Rufus, what's Alice's last name?"
>
> —Octavia E. Butler, *Kindred*

Not knowing how she arrived there might have become a second—or even third—concern as Dana realized that she was deep into her family history. She knew, for sure, that her "several times" great-grandfather was her "several times" great-grandmother's Owner. That much was given away by his name.[1] A last name that recalled—only more immediately than those of other black persons, others descended from enslaved persons—that her family's origin was defined by something that differs from what most understand as familial relations. And yet there she was, talking to, seeing, touching her ancestor-Owner. There she was. His life in her hands. Knowing that she could not take for granted the fact that if he had hers in his hands it would not render that world any less dangerous to her than had she not descended from him. Knowing Alice's last name might verify her experience, establish it as something that was indeed happening. Knowing Alice's last name might confirm or reject it as a *reality* that, though not the hallucination she conjectures, would, as it turned out, be equally improbable.

Would confirming Alice's last name make much of a difference? Would it render meeting her Owner-ancestor less improbable? Probably not. However, it would not make it something beyond the realm of possibility. After all, there was the Bible

---

1 Butler does not give the precise generation but uses the phrase "several times great grandfather" to refer to Rufus.

and the last name. Perhaps other memories and mementos were hidden in someone's closet somewhere. More importantly, in a way she has always been there (in/as Alice), as Alice's possible offspring's possible offspring's possible daughter. Still, she is not there as Alice's "several times" great-granddaughter—that could never be the answer to a question about where she came from or who she was. From the point of view of that world, it was impossible: Alice did not have children; she was barely no longer one. From the point of view of Dana's world, it was improbable but also incomprehensible because, if she were to try to answer the question of who she was, she would have to answer in a way that did not belie the fact that she had never been enslaved. And yet, even if she could try—as she did—she would find that it does not matter, then/there, that she was not or had not been anyone's property. Existing as a black woman in antebellum Maryland was not safe, as she found out more than once. The "truth," that unmistakable aspect of that reality—in which that boy, her "several times" great-grandfather, needed her to remain alive and her "several times" great-grandmother was still childless—made it all the more important and yet useless to know whether she was hallucinating or indeed there/then.

Nothing she had book-learned about how it was back "then" had prepared her for the kind of life-learning she was to get while there/then. The first time, on the river, she was sure Rufus's mother would have killed her (or had her killed) had she not fainted; that Dana was saving her five-year-old son from drowning would not have made any difference. Dana was a black woman and therefore a Slave. She was not one of the Weylins' Slaves, so she must be a runway. Nothing but a runaway and, as such, intrinsically dangerous to (Slavery as an institution) the white folk. A nobody to the farm's black folk. Nothing to them, and also someone they would not know where to place. A black person from a different spacetime moment. From there/where black folk read, write, and do not exist under the threat of the whip, or worse. There was nothing that she could do to control how much others would know about her. And she did try. Every now and then someone caught a contradiction, an untoward gesture, a sign that she did not understand what was expected from her as a Slave. And it was as a Slave that she had to fulfill her charge, to prevent her Owner-ancestor’s death, so she herself would come to life, to exist.

Among many things that Dana, as someone living in 1976 Los Angeles, did and could know about antebellum Maryland was the fact that her skin color rendered her a captive. This was not a matter of personal identification, though she did exist like the other black persons on the Weylin plantation, both enslaved and free. Back then/there, what mattered was not her first-person approach to that world but that, in that world (the colonial political architecture where Slavery was the main economic modality), she occupied a third-person position—but one referred to as a she or a her that has the juridical status of an “it,” that is, of property. The association of skin color and property status was such that even if she had papers proving her to be a free black person, it did not guarantee that she would not have to exist as a Slave.

How could it possibly make sense? Why would a young black woman be sent there/then to save the life of a white male child? An impossible task: someone who then/there was always in fear for life and limb did not, could not have the power to protect the white child of a Slave Owner. Whether or not she belonged there, regardless of whether she was indeed there/then, Dana was certain—and would be reminded over and over again—that her position in that world, Rufus and Alice’s world, was not so much precarious as it was fully and well defined. Whether or not she had papers or Rufus’s father had papers showing his ownership of her—his claim of title over her—she was a Weylin Slave. That she was also a member of the family is one of those possible and probable things that do not receive much attention these days. Nowadays, neither the biological (blood) nor the juridical (title) ties Owners and Slaves had back then/there are given much import—though she and her husband, Kevin, knew that such relationships, filial (blood) and juridical (marriage), in their day, nowadays, were not accepted by all. They also knew that this is not because white persons were once Owners and black persons their Slaves. The explanation is that white and black persons do not match, there are too many differences, too much history. Interracial filial and romantic relationships—especially in the mid-1970s, Dana's here/now—were met with suspicion at best. Who is to say, Dana could concede, that, just as the Weylins' Bible had remained in the black family, the white Weylins did not inherit a share of the black bodies that were expended in the cultivation of their ancestors' farmlands.

For that is just as possible as Dana being back there/then, wondering if she is saving the life of her Owner-ancestor. Before she learns Alice's last name, the question of what was happening—of her experience, what was happening to her—would remain undetermined at the level of *reality* but not at the level of *truth*. Because Dana's "several times" great-grandfather could have been a Slave Owner, it was *probable*—and knowing Alice's last name would ascertain if it was true—that Rufus was indeed him. Because when Dana was born Rufus (and Alice) had been dead for decades, it is not *possible* that that person in front of her, Rufus, was indeed him. Nonetheless, since Rufus is her Owner-ancestor, and she was saving *his* life, irrespective of whether the experience was *possible* or *real*—whether it was possible for her to be *real*ly (spatiotemporally present) in 1830s Maryland (and not having a dream or hallucination)—Dana's charge, although incomprehensible, is thinkable.

"an unasked question"

> Natural cognition begins with experience and remains within experience. In the theoretical attitude which we call the "natural" [...] the collective horizon of possible investigation is therefore designated with one word: It is the world.
>
> —Edmund Husserl, *General Introduction to a Pure Phenomenology*

> Between me and the other world there is ever an unasked question.
>
> —W. E. B. Du Bois, *The Souls of Black Folk*

Whether the *world* Husserl and Du Bois recall is one and the same may never be established. Each statement, no doubt, addresses it in distinct ways: Husserl’s *world*, in this commentary on the “natural attitude,” encompasses the objects of scientific knowledge; Du Bois’s “other world” presumes humans existing in a racially configured landscape. More importantly, each statement records a moment in post-Enlightenment thinking in which one can identify at least two orientations that mark the dis/continuities between nineteenth- and twentieth-century thought. This shift established the basis for comprehending racial subjugation because it marked a redeployment of the *transparent I* that explicitly rejected but did not dismantle the nineteenth-century scientific constructions of the Human. Du Bois’s meditation on experience signals a critical venue with both an ontological and a sociological line of interrogation, while Husserl’s meditation opens up an ontological and anthropological route. At that crossroads I find social-scientific elaborations (sociological and anthropological) that signal later operations of raciality, that is, that which becomes evident when one focuses on the four-way intersection composed by the juxtaposition of their meditations. There it is almost impossible to miss the onto-epistemological blind spot that sustains each of the four directions. That spot is the point at which the *human body* troubles any settled sense of *world*—in particular, of existence under the epistemological conditions governed by historicity. This blind spot figures what blackness rendered as the wounded captive body in the scene of subjugation cannot but expose, which is how the tools of raciality, such as ethnicity, operate in such a way as to transform (explain) effects of total violence into evidence of (the effects of) racial (moral) difference. Here I find what is perhaps the greatest impediment to advancing a critical program that addresses the joint workings of the Colonial, the Racial, the Juridical, and Capital in the global present. More directly, the blind spot assembled by this epistemological rearrangement preempts questions such as whether, and if so, how, raciality refigures coloniality, given that throughout the twentieth century it has consistently authorized deployments of total violence otherwise unacceptable in the liberal polity. Such a question, I think, leads to a consideration of the interplay both of the symbolic (scientific and historical) and the juridical (the structures of the state and cisheteropatriarchy) and of the ethical and the economic moments, given the significance of transparency in the current global political architecture.

Regarding the kind of exploratory work required by the examination of this blind spot, let it be noted that the task is not the peeling off of layers. The blind spot is not so much a meeting point as it is the mark of a departure. A cut. A mark of a double severance signaled by Phenomenology's retrieval of the Human from the grips of an apparently unrestrained scientificism (here I am thinking of Herbert Spencer's determinism and Auguste Comte's positivism),[2] which coincides with Anthropology's (here I am thinking of Franz Boas's discipline-founding studies) disavowal of the body (organic forms and functions) as the causes of human mental (moral and intellectual) attributes.[3] The double disavowal of the nineteenth-century project of uncovering the laws and forms of nature responsible for Human uniqueness and variability intended to rescue the human (mind-body) from the determinations of scientific reason. The cut is signaled by a turn, as considerations of self-consciousness—now renamed Subjectivity—move to retrieve it as an interior/temporal thing along with statements that elaborate on the separation—between the self-positing mind and world—that sustains Human uniqueness.

This effort ushered in the shift from a determinative (scientific) to an interpretive (historical) regime of the post-Enlightenment episteme. It had several consequences, all of which account for the current inability to engage the racial as a *proper* modern political concept. Three of them are significant here: first, the

---

2 For a contemporary critique of Spencer's, Comte's, and other nineteenth-century determinative proposals for sociology, see generally Georges Canguilhem, *A Vital Rationalist: Selected Writings from Georges Canguilhem*, ed. François Delaporte, trans. Arthur Goldhammer (New York: Zone Books, 2000).

3 See Franz Boas, *The Mind of Primitive Man* (New York: Free Press, 1963).

Human was united with the world, which was no longer solely the effect of laws of nature but was approached (in sociology and anthropology) as expressions of human history and culture; second, racial difference, which in the nineteenth century was reconfigured as a scientific tool for the investigation of Human existence (and which then shared with the notion of the nation the utmost position as a political descriptor), would, throughout the twentieth century, be transformed into a datum (physical trait) deemed relevant only insofar as it effects mental representations ("meanings"); third and most important, because racial difference would become relevant at the level of the symbolic (cultural or ideological) in the interpretive episteme, the "color line" was approached as a *moral* (social) problem, a residuum (owing to the lack of education in modern principles, a mental failure) that could be resolved (with the disappearance of the racially different, that is, the non-white) or with the further education of white minds in liberal mores.

What I am highlighting here is how this retrieving of the world (as directly accessible to self-consciousness) and re-signifying of racial difference as a residuum (a datum, a mental leftover of the unenlightened past to be studied and eliminated) institutes a gulf between a refiguring of self-consciousness that prefigures existence before the immediately accessible world Husserl describes *and* a self-consciousness for which existence (because defined by/as datum) always already prefigures how the (social) world perceives his/her (racially determined) body.[4] Lurking over this blind spot, however, the racial body—the human body produced by the tools of the

4 Eventually, one does grasp some of what Du Bois had in mind when he says, "And yet, being a problem is a strange experience,—peculiar even for one who has never been anything else, save perhaps in babyhood and in Europe"—in the second paragraph of "Of Our Spiritual Strivings," the first chapter of *The Souls of Black Folk* (New York: Bantam Books, 1989), 2. In his 1961 autobiography, he expands: "I found myself on the outside of the American world, looking in. With me were white folk—students, acquaintances, teachers—who viewed the scene with me. They did not always pause to regard me as a curiosity, or

Science of Man—recalls how whiteness was reconfigured to signify that to which Husserl returned (*transparency*) in order to rescue the Human from scientificism. On the one hand, precisely because the racial body becomes a datum in the reconstitution of anthropology, with its refiguring of its object and method through historicity, it was not surprising that Husserl's project apparently reconciled his claims concerning the universality of the European lifeworld with other contemporaneous/contiguous modes of human existence or experience and their corresponding lifeworlds and historicities.[5] On the other hand, for Du Bois, who would mobilize sociological methods in investigations of "Negro conditions" in the early twentieth-century United States, the quest(ion) for self-consciousness directed attention to the economic (discrimination and exclusion) and juridical (Jim Crow laws and lynchings) dimensions of existence. Not surprisingly, in the two decades after the publication of *The Souls of Black Folk*—as Du Bois embraced historical materialism—Robert E. Park, a framer of the sociology of race relations, takes Du Bois's statement on double consciousness as a descriptor for and evidence of the harmful (unbecoming) mental (moral and intellectual) effects of the improper attitudes and prejudices

something sub-human." That was in 1892. W. E. B. Du Bois, *The Autobiography of W. E. B. Du Bois* (Oxford: Oxford University Press, 2007), 99.

5 Husserl's considerations of lifeworld as it builds on Kant's effort start from the double function of the understanding—self-reflection and its "concealment [...] ruling as constitutive of the always already developed and always further developing meaning-configuration 'intuitively given surrounding world.'" Here he postulates the pregivenness of the world as presupposed by scientific approaches to it, and that "this surrounding world has only the ontic meaning given to it by our experiences, our thoughts, our valuations, etc.; and it has the modes of validity (certainty of being, possibility, perhaps illusion, etc.)." At the same time, "it is pregiven to us all quite naturally, as persons within the horizon of our fellow men, i.e., in every actual connection with others, as 'the' world common to us all." Edmund Husserl, *The Crisis of European Sciences and Transcendental Phenomenology*, trans. David Carr (Evanston, IL: Northwestern University Press, 1970), 104, 105, 122.

entertained by white US Americans toward their racially different countrypersons.[6] Yet another indication of the departures I mentioned earlier, this convinces me that Du Bois's comment on the "other world" (and the "problem" it takes him to *embody*) suggests that only a move to the figurative (away from this still interpretive moment) will allow the radical gesture (a complete break with the post-Enlightenment onto-epistemological program) hosted in the blind spot from where Phenomenology, Anthropology, and Sociology depart.

Returning to the argument regarding the onto-epistemological significance of raciality, how it populated the global space with a spatially constituted (exterior) version of the Subject, is not an attempt at correcting the rendering of self-consciousness (in Phenomenology as well as Sociology and Anthropology) that marks this interpretive moment. It is a contribution to the dissolution of Subjectivity (self-consciousness) and *its* world. For what renders Dana's charge incomprehensible is not her blackness but the unpayable debt, the fact that her existence required the existence of another who held the authority to decide on her life and death. Her obligation is to keep alive someone who could kill and rape her at any given time. Knowing that obligation does alter Dana's "self-consciousness," her "natural attitude" as a "first person" who posits the (pregiven) world as real. Her response, however, is not a bracketing, a suspension of reality and a contemplation of what resists the gesture, that is, her "pure I."[7] That option is not available to her because early on, during her first trip, Dana realizes that existing as a black person in antebellum Maryland means having one's physical integrity always at risk. Responding to her obligation to keep Rufus alive means to *return* physically to a moment where/when the black person's body, the captive body, has no

6 For an examination of Park's appropriation of Du Bois's double consciousness, see Ferreira da Silva, *Toward a Global Idea of Race*, 158–62.

7 These are references to Husserl's refiguring of self-consciousness (as pure I/subjectivity), which has been crucial to the forming and unfolding of the interpretive moment.

claim to protection. Juridically determined as property (chattel), the Slave is always available for the Owner's enjoyment, as an object of entertainment and punishment. That world—actually, both of Dana's worlds, her present and her family's past—is not posited, it is bequeathed, as signaled by Alice's last name, Greenwood Weylin, the family heirlooms (her Bible), and her black body. That *world* has a place for her before she comes into it. Indeed, the post-Enlightenment colonial context was not one but two worlds, as Fanon describes,[8] and the inhabitants of each were separated by skin color, which functioned as a mark for their juridical status: Slave and Owner (property and proprietor), and Native and Settler (Indigenous inhabitants and conqueror-settlers). Precisely this context refigured in blackness is disappeared in the blind spot, that covering of the cut from which current ways of comprehending the political architecture of the global present are derived, but also which indicates how in this still interpretive moment the comprehension of racial subjugation has been reduced to the simplistic inference that it functions like a stereotype.

The most perverse and lasting aspect of raciality and its operators—that is, its tools of comprehensibility as strategies of engulfment and particularization[9]—may be how, as Spillers notes about ethnicity, they manage to render the consequences of accumulated (past and present) total violence into effects of

8 Fanon, *Wretched of the Earth*, 35–94. By qualifying it as a post-Enlightenment colonial context, I am highlighting how the Racial—as produced in nineteenth-century anthropology—operated in that version of the colonial political architecture, which is the one Fanon describes, in which the concept of the nation would be part of the anti-colonial lexicon.

9 Elsewhere I have introduced the phrases "strategies of engulfment" ("scientific concepts that explain other human conditions as variations of those found in post-Enlightenment Europe," such as the concepts of the racial and the cultural) and "strategies of particularization" ("categories of human beings deployed by the sciences of man and society") for describing the tools of knowledge produced by racial knowledge in the nineteenth and twentieth centuries. Ferreira da Silva, *Toward a Global Idea of Race*, xvi.

racial (atemporal) difference. How does this work? An effect of blackness as a social-scientific category (a tool whose force or explanatory value rests on necessity) is that it closes the circuit of signification, as I discuss later in this chapter. It explains the workings of total and symbolic violence with regard to a black person as an effect of her body's organic (internal and external) forms and functions. This results from how racial knowledge deploys formality and efficacy in the manufacturing of its strategies of engulfment and particularization. Ethnicity, as discussed in the previous chapter as a strategy of engulfment, performs that role in statements that attribute pathology to female-headed families and "black families" because there is a correlation between this kind of family formation and black persons' household composition, and from this correlation the concept of ethnicity produces the notion of the "Negro family." If the question is asked why most black persons live in female-headed households, the answer will refer to the absence of the father and statements on their pathological masculinity, and will include *causes* such as discrimination, exclusion, and criminalization. For when the question is asked why black men are discriminated against, excluded, and criminalized, the answer will be because they are black—because in regard to employment, salary, and the legal system, white decision-makers entertain unbecoming beliefs and attitudes about blackness and black persons. Skin color (blackness) is the first and final descriptor in this explanatory train. Existing in social conditions created by the institutionalization and proliferation of negative meanings attributed to blackness, sociologists explain, black persons respond with unbecoming ideas and behavior that results in pathological situations such as the larger number of black families headed by women. This is as far as interpretive thinking—which presumes that unbecoming beliefs beget unbecoming practices that beget more unbecoming ideas and practices—can go. Not too far at all because the circuit closes quickly, as blackness is the trigger of both the question and the explanation given in the answer.

How to break this logic? An option here is to attend to this closed circuitry (the mythical effect, to recall Spillers's descriptor) of ethnicity and other tools of raciality when deployed to account for racial subjugation. Instead of taking the beaten interpretive path and focusing on signification, I follow the figurative trail signaled by the wounded captive body in the scene of subjugation and attend to the composition (both shape and content). Looking closely at the *what* (elements) and *how* (arranging) of its configuration—and without asking the *why* (purpose) of, and by which means (the efficient cause), it is deployed—I move to locate *what* (the movement itself that) renders possible the postulation of an identity between *cause* and *effect* and to show how it results from substituting the moral for the juridico-economic. Read in such a way, it is almost impossible to miss the operations of juridical arbitration in racial subjugation that both precedes or follows as authorization for total violence. Exposing this internal and yet occluded juridical element, I propose, renders it possible to denaturalize the scene of racial subjugation—that is, to retrieve racial difference from its condition as a residuum or datum and to place it in its proper political/symbolic (scientific) stage. A most important step in this groundwork, which the wounded captive body in the scene of subjugation performs in this chapter, is to release blackness (and other signifiers of racial difference) from the constraints of understanding and to make it available to the imagination and the capacity to contemplate existence without the movement of determinacy, which is institutive of both juridical and scientific assemblies.

My second guide here is Saidiya Hartman's *Scenes of Subjection*, where I find, both in the content and mode of presentation of her analysis, the wounded captive body in the scene of subjugation exposing the Juridical contours of the cut that inaugurates the interpretive moment of the post-Enlightenment episteme.[10] Tracing repetitions of terror in scenes of enjoyment and punishment (noting how indistinguishable these

10 To recall: Juridical here refers to authority as linked to the figures of the State, the Patriarch (which attaches to cishetero manhood), and the Slave Owner.

were), she suggests a generative setting for reflection—the scene of subjugation where one can appreciate the im/possibility of empathy before "suffering materialized by the display of the tortured body or endless recitations of the ghastly and the terrible."[11] That moment, I find, indicates the ethical contours of the onto-epistemological blind spot at the intersection of Husserl's ontological and anthropological routes (for rescuing the human from science) and Du Bois's ontological and sociological lines of interrogation (of the racial world). Further, her analysis of scenes of subjection unfolding under the expositive moral philosophy that prevailed until the end of the nineteenth century shows that attempts at capturing a black *interiority* in (reenactments of) the scene of total violence fail precisely because the very aspects of the scene that attain Humanity and Subjectivity—that is, leisure, desire, and sentiment—are thoroughly juridically preformed.

An otherwise (under the interpretive regime) impossible site for reflection becomes available through questions that register how intersubjectivity—phenomenology's ethical substratum—does not belong in the scene of total violence. Hartman writes:

> Can the white witness of the spectacle of suffering affirm the materiality of black sentience only by feeling for himself? Does this not only exacerbate the idea that black sentience is inconceivable and unimaginable but, in the very ease of possessing the abased and enslaved body, ultimately elide an understanding and acknowledgment of the slave's pain? Beyond evidence of slavery's crime, what does this exposure of the suffering body of the bondsman yield? Does this not reinforce the "thingly" quality of the captive by reducing the body to evidence in the very effort to establish the humanity of the enslaved?

Each of these questions accepts the answer that the recognition of the Slave's Humanity requires a bodily substitution, that is, that "the white body be positioned in the place of the black

---

11 Hartman, *Scenes of Subjection*, 4.

body in order to make this suffering visible and intelligible."[12] However, such occupation is both possible and required because the wounded captive body in the scene of subjugation—which, as Dana's predicament remembers and the Dred Scott decision establishes, the black body always signifies—figures a juridical form that exists at once as person and property: as person, she harbors feelings, will, desire, while as property, she hosts the Owner's authority (liberty expressed as/in the right to deploy total violence).

What I read in Hartman's analysis is the conundrum blackness hosts, which enters into the very constitution of the post-Enlightenment political architecture. For what is rehearsed in the scene of subjugation is a juridical relation involving two human existents in which one has a life-and-death authority over another, which does not derive from their previous interactions as persons but from a market exchange in which one bought a title over the other. This situation creates two distinct descriptors, each linking the juridical relation to a different moment of the political—for the Slave, fungibility (economic), and for the Owner, dignity (ethical). As I elaborate later in this chapter, this poses a challenge that neither phenomenology nor the interpretive (historical) versions of the social-scientific (sociological and anthropological) project (assembled at the same time) can contemplate without breaking into unrecognizable pieces. For if one sets aside the basic utilitarian moral framework (and its romantic tinge) that governed antislavery discourse, there remains the presentation of Subjectivity and Humanity as *interiority* that is also common to the interpretive (scientific, historical, and structuralist) philosophical orientation that phenomenology gifted the twentieth century. Consistently, the sociological projects it inspired re-present this im/possibility of a black interiority when they rewrite blackness as a signifier of pathological social institutions (Moynihan's "Negro family") or social subjects (economist Gunnar Myrdal's asocial black youth) whose existence expresses an affectable

12 Hartman, 19.

self-consciousness, which in turn expresses social conditions created by racist ideas entertained by white persons.[13] Here skin color (blackness) refers to an interiority that is through and through a vessel that holds and conveys the affectability—the social pathologies, like Moynihan's black family—sociologists of race relations argued is inherent to social configurations informed by racial (and cultural) difference.

Neither through Husserl's natural consciousness (the first person) nor through his pure consciousness (in phenomenological reduction) does Subjectivity immediately recall the juridical figure of the Slave and the scientific figure of the black (skinned) social subject. Instead, it registers how the white subject governs (through the legal form of title) the juridical condition of the former and (through a philosophically postulated and scientifically re-signified *transparency*) the symbolic (scientific) construction of the latter. Precisely for this reason, both Du Bois's sociological studies and Husserl's phenomenological philosophy would also take racial difference as a datum:[14] the former by taking a historical orientation in his sociological studies of how racial

---

13 Gunnar Myrdal, *An American Dilemma: The Negro Problem and Modern Democracy* (New York: Harper & Row, 1962).

14 In the case of Du Bois, racial difference is a given, in terms of how his point of departure is a "Negro American" condition fundamentally different from white Americans. I am not suggesting that he conceives of this in terms of an essence. Like Chandler in *X—The Problem of the Negro as a Problem for Thought*, I read Du Bois's approach as an articulation of a sociohistorical perspective. Husserl's take on racial difference is indirectly presented, and it (expectedly) presents it in terms of cultural difference (already delineated by racial difference) along the lines of Boas's cultural anthropology. As, for instance, in his elaboration of lifeworld: "We have a world-horizon as a horizon of possible thing-experience [*Dingerfahrung*]. Things: that is, stones, animals, plants, even human beings and human products; but everything here is subjective and relative, even though normally, in our experience and in the social group united with us in the community of life, we arrive at 'secure' facts [...]. But when we are thrown into an alien social sphere, that of the Negroes in the Congo, Chinese peasants, etc., we discover that their truths, the facts that for them are fixed, generally verified or verifiable, are by no means the same as ours." Husserl, *Crisis of European Sciences*, 138–39.

difference configured the post-Emancipation United States, and the latter by taking as a matter of fact the anthropological premise of the correspondence between physical traits, places of origin, and forms of consciousness (and the peculiar historicity of each lifeworld). In short, historicity, the ontological horizon of Subjectivity (the twentieth-century refashioning of the *transparent I*), which rules the interpretive episteme, does not, as I have argued elsewhere,[15] carry raciality, for reasons that I will further elaborate later in this chapter.

"Things which are equal"

> First Axiom: Things which are equal to the same thing are also equal to one another.
>
> Second Axiom: If equals are added to equals, the whole are equal.
>
> Third Axiom: If equals be subtracted from equals, the remainders are equal.
>
> Fourth Axiom: Things which coincide with one another are equal to one another.
>
> Fifth Axiom: The whole is greater than the part.
>
> —Euclid's axioms

"I am a marked woman. [...] If I were not here, I would have to be invented," Hortense Spillers writes at the opening of "Mama's Baby, Papa's Maybe."[16] Whatever move renders Dana's charge comprehensible must include a kind of total demolition of this statement—following a list of stereotypes for black women and preceding the discussion of Moynihan's deployment of ethnicity—demands. That work then has to go beyond denouncing or opposing objectification. An argument that exposes dehumanization or a critique of objectification—at least not one that would consist in spelling out why it is a bad thing—though

15 This argument has been developed in Ferreira da Silva, *Toward a Global Idea of Race*, 17–90.

16 Spillers, "Mama's Baby, Papa's Maybe," 65.

important, is not sufficient. Why? For one thing, the very same interpretive episteme that abhors stereotyping for its robbing of interiority and temporality left untouched the effects, tools, and operations of scientific reason that assembled the tools of categories of raciality in the determinative moment. More importantly, the demand for inclusion—to be seen as Human and/or treated as Subjectivity—does not trouble the grammar that Spillers recalls needs her, needs the black woman and all the common names—the stereotypes (Sapphire) and the racial category (black matriarch)—that hold her hostage as symbol with the same intensity as the lash held the Slave as laborer. And these common names that cover up the "high crimes against the flesh," like the lash, do not annul/annihilate whatever she might signify or will in that very moment when they halt her.

What exactly is the political/symbolic work of the stereotype and the racial category? How do they participate in subjugation in the post-Enlightenment period? Both metaphorically and metonymically, stereotypes function like any other modern abstractions (categories and concepts), that is, they rehearse a mode of signification (of creation and mobilization of sense and meanings) whose terms and movements substitute for and preempt whatever else might be constitutive of or related to the person or thing to which they are applied. To be sure, the *fixing* (determining) effect of stereotypes and modern scientific tools (categories), in general, derives from how necessity and the onto-epistemological descriptors and pillars through which it operates establish these composites, whose parts play (signify) regardless of what its target does or says. Or, more directly, their *objectifying* (separating, subsuming, and relating) capacity derives from how they establish a relationship between that which they capture and their intrinsic valuative effect.[17] Nevertheless, they differ in that, for instance, the valuation

17 This is in the case of stereotypes that result from the effect of fixing, which render the persons to whom they are addressed not fully human since they lack the liberty to be seen for who they are (interiorly) and are robbed of the presumption that can change or self-actualize (temporally) by the force of their will and desire.

targets interiority (stereotyping fixes mental traits to exterior ones) and exteriority (categorizing fixes exterior traits [appearances] to interior ones [essence]), and also in terms of how their relation to truth is regarded: stereotyping is dismissed as a misapprehension, and modern scientific tools host the weight of logical (categorical or hypothetical) reasoning that guarantees determinative signification.

While generalizations do take the form of *objectification*—which is the form of third-person (she is) and even some second-person (you are) predications of quality (statements on being)—as in stereotyping, scientific predication is considered the hallmark of *dehumanization*. Not in the sense that it refers to human existents as comparable to every other thing in the world—though this is the case. Under the post-Enlightenment epistemic regime, the human mind (not the person, that is, the mind-body composite) connotes and denotes *uniqueness*: it matters as *homo historicus*, the interior-temporal thing, the thing with individuality, or the singular exemplar of utmost generality, the sole existent with *dignity*. Treating a person on the basis of a presumed membership of a "group" (stereotyping) or as an object of knowledge (ethics paperwork for social-scientific studies remind us of it every time) is an assault on their *uniqueness* because it expresses a disregard for interiority. More importantly, under the interpretive moment, because the gesture obviates Subjectivity, it robs the person of the qualities that tell that the Human is singular among other existing things, that is, the qualities of *liberty* and *dignity* it acquires in its ethical figuring as the *transparent* (self-determined because self-knowing) *I*. If, however, the Category of Blackness has been constructed by the Science of Man and reconstructed by the Sociology of Race Relations to signify what does not fall within the range of the ethical concepts of liberty and dignity, then prior to any attempt at re-signification, a first step must be to examine the very composition of this symbolic construct, which carries undeniable ethical efficacy.

Toward doing so, I activate the wounded captive body in the scene of subjugation from where she re/de/composes that which renders Dana's predicament incomprehensible, namely the racial dialectic, that is, the logical circle that resolves the cause and effect of racial subjugation as racial difference. This section covers the first of the three moments of this re/de/compositional presentation. Beginning from the end, in a way, I first dissemble the “blind spot” that internally organizes the interpretive moment of the post-Enlightenment epistemic regime in order to expose how *necessity* supports both the figure at its center, Subjectivity, and those whose first names are incessantly overwritten by *objectification* (racial stereotyping or coding). Further re/de/compositional moves in the next two sections describe *determinacy*, which is the movement of signification *necessity* sustains, and prepare the terrain for its traversing through a consideration of how it establishes the (de)limitations that maintain post-Enlightenment thinking.

“a thousand reasons”

> The slave master had a direct interest in discrediting the personality of those he held as property. Every man who had a thousand dollars so invested had a thousand reasons for painting the black man as fit only for slavery. [...] The holders of twenty hundred million dollars’ worth of property in human chattels procured the means of influencing press, pulpit, and politician, and through these instrumentalities they belittled our virtues and magnified our vices, and have made us odious in the eyes of the world.
>
> —Frederick Douglass, “The Color Line”

Why has so much and yet nothing changed in regard to deployments of total violence against black persons since 1881? Though following different procedures, what drives Frederick Douglass’s argument in “The Color Line” is not that different from what moves my own interest in the unraveling of the racial dialectic—that is, an elucidation of blackness’s capacity to orchestrate the juridical moment of the post-Enlightenment political architecture. Not surprisingly, like Douglass, I too choose to confront the symbolic moment when considering blackness as the defining aspect in subjugation.

Unwilling to accept the argument that "race prejudice" is universal, a *natural* (instinctive) human reaction to racial difference, Douglass advances a logical argument against it. He begins by analytically dismounting this thesis through a consideration of seven points, with which "all would agree."[18] And he reaches the one possible conclusion: "Out of the depths of slavery has come this prejudice and this color line."[19] The color line is not the effect of a *natural* (white) mental (moral and intellectual) attribute, and racial difference is not *expressive* of (black persons') mental (moral and intellectual) attributes, he argues. Why? Because, once the "undesirable conditions" that are "coupled" with the color (black) disappear "there will be no color line drawn."[20] What he offers then is a description of how the color line renders blackness a condensation of the juridical and economic components of the colonial political architecture.[21]

When the color line was articulated to figure segregation and Jim Crow in the later nineteenth and the twentieth century, it was commonly constructed as a badge of inferiority (of slavery or servitude) or the cause of a "feeling of inferiority."[22] To be

---

18 Frederick Douglass, "The Color Line," *North American Review* 132, no. 295 (June 1881): 575.

19 In doing so, he advances as probable "causes" for prejudice white Americans' desire for power and domination and the "undesirable" (poverty, dependence, servility) social conditions under which black persons lived. Douglass, 573.

20 Douglass, 575. Unlike the first version of the sociology of race relations, Douglass's text does find a solution in the disappearance of the physical markers of racial (cultural) difference.

21 I am borrowing Freud's term and meaning to refer not to a psychoanalytical process but to an elemental one: condensation is the phase transition from gas to liquid with which I capture how a term transits from the modern domain of ideas to that of emotions (feelings).

22 Two landmark and competing (but not necessarily) antagonistic US Supreme Court decisions, *Plessy v. Ferguson* (1896) and *Brown v. Board of Education* (1954), deploy these descriptors, which would become dominant but do not capture Douglass's argument regarding the color line. In *Plessy v. Ferguson*, the decision that authorized Jim Crow, the majority opinion of the court rejected Plessy's argument that "enforced separation stamps the colored race with a badge of inferiority," and argued that "if this be so, it

sure, both of these meanings became central to the arguments for racial equality and the works that belonged to the interpretive (historical) version of race relations. Evidently, when the

---

is not by reason of anything found in the act, but solely because the colored race chooses to put that construction upon it." In his dissenting opinion, Justice John Marshall Harlan states that, to the contrary, "the arbitrary separation of citizens, on the basis of race, while they are on a public highway, is a badge of servitude wholly inconsistent with the civil freedom and the equality before the law established by the constitution. It cannot be justified upon any legal grounds." Plessy v. Ferguson, 163 U.S. 537 (1896), 551, 562. Of note here is how the majority opinion dismissed the claim with an interpretive (subjective) argument, while Justice Harlan chose to highlight the "objective" aspect, in particular the fact that the highway (the railroads) is a public space, indicating that legally authorizing segregation would make it—as it did—a public (state) decision and practice.

Harlan's opinion is similar to Douglass's reading of how blackness comes to signify slavery, which, as noted above, is an attribution made not by black persons but by white Americans, including the state. As it turned out, the basis of the argument presented by the majority opinion of the Supreme Court for the Plessy case—inferiority—would be the one deployed by the majority opinion of *Brown v. Board of Education*, the landmark decision against racial segregation in the United States: "To separate them [children in grade and high schools] from others of similar age and qualification solely because of their race generates *a feeling of inferiority* as to their status in the community that may affect their hearts and minds in a way unlikely ever to be undone" (my italics). That interpretation was, as expected, supported in a footnote by scientific evidence (a liberal version of the sociology of race relations) provided by sociological and social-psychological works: "K.B. Clark, Effect of Prejudice and Discrimination on Personality Development (Mid-century White House Conference on Children and Youth, 1950); Witmer and Kotinsky, Personality in the Making (1952), c. VI; Deutscher and Chein, The Psychological Effects of Enforced Segregation: A Survey of Social Science Opinion, 26 J.Psychol. 259 (1948); Chein, What are the Psychological Effects of Segregation Under Conditions of Equal Facilities?, 3 Int.J.Opinion and Attitude Res. 229 (1949); Brameld, Educational Costs, in Discrimination and National Welfare (MacIver, ed., 1949), 44-48; Frazier, The Negro in the United States (1949), 674-681. *And see generally* Myrdal, An American Dilemma (1944)." Brown v. Board of Education, 347 U.S. 483 (1954), 494 (italics in original).

color line is presented as a badge or cause of a feeling, it fits perfectly in the interpretive episteme—and can be reconstructed in psychological, anthropological, or literary terms. Neither set of disciplinary tools and formulations can capture Douglass's description, however, for it indicates the process of *transformation* of the same components, one in which blackness seems to afford anyone or any institution in the post-Emancipation era (that is not named/identified/constructed as black) the *juridical authority* (on which rested the Owner and other whites' liberty and dignity) to deploy total violence. In doing so, Douglass's rendering of the color line is perhaps the earliest announcement of the racial event, that is, the form of the scene of black subjugation, the one that the racial dialectic obviates by rendering blackness (as racial difference) the cause and effect of racial subjugation.

The activation of the *wounded captive body in the scene of subjugation* permits the tracking of what is operative in every repetition of the racial event, that is, the very political form that ignores history. That which happens without time and regardless of place is also without historicity (interiority/temporality) and does not call for speculations about Subjectivity, that is, the preferred grounds of the interpretive episteme, mental attributes, capacities, feelings, beliefs, meanings, and so on. Under the guidance of the figure that hosts blackness as the *ongoing present* of a *common refusal*—for which I assembled borrowings from Spillers, Hartman, and Moten—I perform three movements of re/de/composition. First, as I have already started doing, I read the wounded captive body in the scene of subjugation in Douglass's rendering as playing out in the drawing of the color line, namely focusing on *economic* expropriation ("a thousand reasons") and the *juridical* relation ("property"),[23] and the Owner's self-interest from which the arguments about black persons' mental (moral and intellectual) deficiencies derive. Second, in this chapter I read in Hartman's analysis of the scenes of physical violence how the person whose captive body is under

23 Douglass, "The Color Line," 573.

torture is both presumed to be and yet not made present as an *interior* thing. For, as proposed in the previous section, that body, her body, in the scene of subjugation, recalls both the Owner’s (juridical) right to elicit obedience through violation or humiliation and the white abolitionist’s—the spectator who abhors the scene—ethical ability to claim her interiority (feelings, fears, desires as available) for himself. Hidden between this juridical *authority* and ethical *prerogative* is something that could be called (but which I refuse to call) a black Subjectivity, which, precisely because inaccessible, figures at once excess (the Owner’s extended authority to force enjoyment) and opaqueness (no one could know, that is, grasp, what went through the captive’s mind when her body was shackled or beaten or raped or just confined to the Owner’s estate).

What becomes possible when the wounded captive body in the scene of subjugation, a ray of blacklight, illuminates the blind spot that supports the racial dialectic?[24] Many more venues open for this question than are possible to track in this text, or in any textual elaboration of this question, for that matter. I track three in this chapter. A first venue takes me to a consideration of how a juridical figuring of blackness, which refuses the demand to become an interior/temporal thing, confronts the *transparent I* and its rule over the interpretive episteme. A second venue goes a bit deeper and reconsiders *world* and its *transparent I* in view of how necessity sustains raciality’s symbolic work and its own version of the *transparent I*—and, as other scientific renderings, it preserves *him* in *liberty*. Finally, the third venue de/composes the *transparent I* and *world* toward the image of existence that emerges when her flesh, exposed through lacerated black skin, troubles the symbolic (onto-epistemological) arrangement that governs what Hartman calls the afterlife of slavery.

24 When considering the scene of subjugation, it is crucial to attend to Hartman’s presentation of it, in particular her indication of an in/distinction between enjoyment and punishment. Hartman, *Scenes of Subjection*, 17–114.

"the evidence"

> The colored people of this country [...] carry in front the evidence which marks them for persecution.
>
> —Frederick Douglass, "The Color Line"

W. E. B. Du Bois's phrase "between me and the other" signals a "first person," a position of enunciation that, as Nahum Chandler proposes in *X—The Problem of the Negro as a Problem for Thought*, announces a discourse that troubles the very basis of oppositional (hierarchical) logic and the claims to identity or purity it supports, that is, the very "logic of being." Following the trajectory of Du Bois's discourse, attending to its implications for its own political context (post-Reconstruction United States) and what preceded it (Slavery), Chandler delineates what he calls an African American (Africanist or diasporic) position of enunciation that renders explicit the "question about the forms of historical existence and grounds of reflexive identification" for both African Americans and European Americans.[25] That position, its question(ing) of an enunciator (on one side of the relation figured by "between"), which he aptly names "an exorbitance," also requests a reconsideration of the *world* that, I find, must accompany any re/de/composition of the context of signification (the political/symbolic moment) in which the modern theme of being makes sense.[26]

How? How to ask the question of the *world* without presuming a position of enunciation that is in the *world* but not the same as it, not of it? More directly, is it not that every time the word is said—in this sense, as the referent, that which is to be predicated—the position of enunciation is immediately

25 Chandler, *X—The Problem of the Negro as a Problem for Thought*, 12.

26 For an argument that deals directly with Du Bois's thinking as a challenge to phenomenology and other ontological accounts, see R. A. Judy, *Sentient Flesh: Thinking in Disorder, Poiesis in Black* (Durham, NC: Duke University Press, 2020).

occupied by something like a Subject? From Descartes to Kant and Hegel to Husserl and Heidegger, that which exists or happens (res extensa, Nature, or *world*) is implicated in the delineation of the Subject of (universal, transcendental) reason. However, something else happens, as Chandler forcefully describes, when Du Bois qualifies *world* with the adjective *other*—"between me and the other world" signals a pre-position, that is, that there is no such thing as *world* but *a world* that is predicated on the presence of "other" and a presumed *transparent I*, as given by the position of enunciation (pre-posed, that is, "me"). Hence if one grants the existence of two worlds—of "me" and of the "other"—there becomes possible, even if not probable and never actual, something similar to but no longer *a world* without and beyond either. Certainly, as Chandler pursues, the pre-posed/pre-positioned enunciation ("me") questions any simple oppositional pairing that does not immediately also question the self-sufficiency of both terms/positions.[27] However, I find it does more. If the pairing of "me" and "the other" challenges the whole basis of Western metaphysics, as Chandler correctly argues, it does so because it renders both worlds (of "me" and of "the other") a world that Du Bois's phrase says is divided—there is "me," a space (between) occupied by the question (about being a problem), and "the other world." As such, when confronted with a *first black person singular*, the world is mapped, troubled, and complexified by what "the other" (and their world) takes blackness to be/signify. Nonetheless, the division also indicates that there is something like *a world* that exceeds "me" and "the other," which cannot be brought into discourse because the ("me" and "other") worlds only exist because pre-posed, that is, with and out of (without) it.

That world is a future world and a past world; it is even another world, a virtual world, or not a world at all; it is a possible world, perhaps one among many possible and not probable

27 Recall my earlier comments, in chapter 1, on Hegel's scene of the life-and-death struggle into which both self-consciousnesses enter as self-sufficient entities. Hegel, *Phenomenology of Spirit*, 108–16.

worlds—and as such it is nothing like *a world* because it neither presumes nor posits nor produces something like a Subject (whether transparent or affectable). However, because of the needs of the moment of this chapter, because it requires a (confining, structuring) context, for now I will call it *a world*, one in which the question about a (human) being that is a problem, which, as we know, is another way to refer to "the color line," makes sense. A phrase that, we learn from Douglass, recalls the wounded or dead captive body in the scene of subjugation and, along with her, the juridical and economic conditions under which she figures domination and self-interest. For this reason, the question (about the being of a being that is a problem) and the answer do not make sense in the interpretive episteme. It is not that the question cannot be answered (hence its signaling of an exorbitance that, Chandler argues, "Du Bois's discourse" exemplifies); it is that it cannot be formulated if both the questioner and the questioned exist in the world of Husserl's natural consciousness or pure consciousness, or Heidegger's Dasein.

Let me elaborate on this impossibility of asking the question by recalling two statements that mark the early twentieth-century shift from the determinative to the interpretive moment of the post-Enlightenment episteme, namely, the disavowal of the project of the Science of Man to assemble Cultural Anthropology and the framing of Phenomenology. Each, as we know, took a different route: one (Franz Boas) would build a scientific approach to culture, and the other (Edmund Husserl) claimed the task of properly framing a scientific philosophy. The first combines two works by Boas: the 1912 study that challenged the scientists of Man's claims regarding racial types by showing physical changes in second-generation immigrant children in the United States, and the 1911 book *The Mind of Primitive Man*, which presents a scientific method for the study of mental (moral and intellectual) phenomena that focuses on mental content and not bodily forms. What was to become known as Cultural Anthropology, as I have argued in *Toward a Global Idea of Race*, retained the categories of racial difference, which lost their status as scientific indicators of mental conditions but not the role as *natural* (datum) markers of human difference, born out of interbreeding in isolation in their places of origin. Not surprisingly, the second statement, Husserl's *General Introduction to a Pure Phenomenology*, which was published a year after Boas's 1912 study, repeats the same gesture of disavowal—targeting psychology—of nineteenth-century determinative episteme's projects by uncovering the laws or forms that account for the human condition. While both attended to the presuppositions and methods applied in the previous century's attempts at determining the human mind (through bodily forms or thought processes), treating it as any other thing of the world, neither Cultural Anthropology nor Phenomenology considered how these attempts—their concepts, categories, and formulations—would become part of how the world itself (in particular the human existents in it) would be described.

Neither project takes on the critical path Douglass rehearses, the one that refuses the *naturalization* of racial difference (as datum) by challenging the scientific *determination* of race prejudice (a mental content)—as a natural trait of white populations (physical forms). Had Husserl followed Douglass's path, his figuring of the *transparent I* (natural attitude, pure consciousness, or even historical consciousness [lifeworld]) would be untenable. Had he taken into account how raciality populates the world with different types of human beings, Husserl would not have posited a natural attitude, "the first person singular," the one who, when "seeing, touching, hearing, and so forth, and in the different modes of sensuous perception, [has] corporeal physical things with some spatial distribution or other [that] are *simply there for me, 'on hand,'* in the literal or the figurative sense."[28] To be sure, attending to how the world—in particular as shared with other humans—had been mapped by determinative knowledge would not make impossible the rescue of the *transparent I* (refigured as pure consciousness) by repositioning it in a Kantian

---

28 Edmund Husserl, *General Introduction to a Pure Phenomenology*, trans. F. Kersten, bk. 1 of *Ideas Pertaining to a Pure Phenomenology and to a Phenomenological Philosophy* (The Hague: Martinus Nijhoff, 1983), 52 (italics in original).

a priori.[29] Perhaps this was the most important and needed move as *homo historicus* began to assert its rule under the interpretive episteme. For Husserl's gesture, which rescues the *transparent I* from the position of being like any other thing in the world described by the tools of scientific reason, did not abandon the world under the microscope of determinative knowledge. For him, reality—"the reality of the physical thing taken singly and the reality of the whole world"—is "only intentional, only an object of consciousness."[30] Recomposed with the essence (the in-itself Kant said was of no concern to scientific knowledge) in Phenomenology, the world is fully in the grasp of the *transparent I*, it becomes the *surrounding world*, the elimination of which would not bring about the destruction of "the being of consciousness."[31] This restating of separability—between the Human and the world and between other existents and events—delimits what in the post-Enlightenment episteme becomes the basis of humans' uniqueness. With the difference being that here, besides exteriority (spatiality), non-Human existents and events also acquire an essence (a formal interiority) by virtue of which they are immediately available to the phenomenological (pure) consciousness.

This definitely does not capture Du Bois's and Douglass's descriptions of existence, in which "the color line" figures the political (juridico-economic) position the category of blackness comprehends, that is, one in which everything exists "between"—where the "natural attitude" before or in the *world* is not self-determination (now renamed intentionality) but affectability, for in it every (black and white) "I" emerges pre-positioned. From there, whatever is (of) the world can never be excluded because the *first black person singular* is already anticipated

29 It is relevant to recall that the phenomenological project in this articulation is "to acquire a new region of being never before delimited in its own peculiarity," which is the region of "'pure mental processes,' 'pure consciousness' with its pure correlates of consciousness and, on the other hand, its 'pure Ego.'" Husserl, 64.

30 Husserl, 113.

31 Husserl, 110.

(not by stereotypes, those come about eventually) as a referent of a *juridical* relation (title/property) and comprehended by a *scientific* category that renders that particular consciousness an effect of bodily forms that position an enunciation that exposes the world as inhabited by *modern* beings always in a given political (juridic, symbolic, ethic, and economic) architecture.[32]

Under the interpretive moment of the post-Enlightenment epistemic regime, sociological and anthropological projects populated the *world* described from the position of the *first black person singular*. Keeping with the nineteenth-century determinative orientation they replaced but did not displace, these projects of knowledge address that person as a (social) *being* doubly determined (affected)—as a (physical) object of discriminatory ideas and practices and a (mental) object, the study of which would uncover how white minds (mental content) constitute (through intentionality) the social (moral) *world*. Though the juridical and economic dimensions of racial subjugation were described and investigated, as noted in the previous chapter, they are secondary to that which is placed as the origin of racial subjugation, which is white persons' negative mental (moral and intellectual) responses (prejudice, beliefs, ideology, stereotyping) to black (and other non-white persons') physical traits. Racial difference, however, is considered either a *datum* (indicator of cultural [mental and moral] differences) or a *residuum*, a leftover from Europe's premodern (moral) past. Either way, in the case of the *first black person singular*, skin color, as Douglass registered, is at the beginning and the end of the explanation or justification for decisions and actions that harm or benefit black persons. For this reason, I have chosen not to remain within this interpretive closure and from here to try to provide an account of "black being" without objectification, or to rehumanize and/or delimit a black Subjectivity. Instead, I activate the wounded captive body in the scene of subjugation, which recomposes the interpretive episteme in confronting how

32 For this whole argument, see generally Ferreira da Silva, *Toward a Global Idea of Race*.

skin color performs the work it does—a move that takes me back to the Kantian program, that is, to the philosophical intervention that has sustained both the determinative and the interpretive moment of the post-Enlightenment episteme, which set up the conditions for assembling the Science of Man and the framing of phenomenology.

"objects of possible experience"

> Now we call the synthesis of the manifold in imagination transcendental if, without distinction of the intuitions, it concerns nothing but the connection of the manifold *a priori*, and the unity of this synthesis is called transcendental if it is represented as necessary *a priori* in relation to the original unity of apperception. Now since this latter is the ground of the possibility of all cognitions, the transcendental unity of the synthesis of the imagination is the pure form of all possible cognition, through which, therefore, all objects of possible experience must be represented *a priori*.
>
> —Immanuel Kant, *Critique of Pure Reason*

If the *probable* and the *possible* belong to different registers—that is, using Kant's language, the Understanding and the Imagination, respectively—what is *real* (as opposed to imagined) and what is *true* (as opposed to what is an error) do not need to coincide. Hallucinations, daydreams, dreams in general may include content that is true—in terms of whether or not there is evidence for it to be so—but not real—if one defines *reality* in terms of the "actual [spacetime] existence" of a thing. Though in both cases it is a matter of judgment—three different statements to be precise—they are not necessarily of the same kind or, better, in the post-Enlightenment episteme, they do not operate at the same level. For if what is or is not *probable*, or the attribution of truth, refers to the *validity* of the statement, the statement of whether something is possible (as opposed to impossible) refers to the *form* of the statement, and the statement regarding *reality* refers to the *thing* being judged.

What makes Dana's charge thinkable is precisely what makes it *probable*: the fact, confirmed by finding out Alice's last name, that one of her ancestors was an Owner. Now this is given by the last name as index of a juridical relation—Dana as a descendant of Slaves indicates two possible relations in the antebellum United States, of title (property relation) and of marriage (family relation). Similarly, Dana's blackness enjoys the same validity—if we recall that with or without papers proving her status as a free black woman, like Dred Scott, she would still be submitted to the authority of any white person if caught without Rufus's protection—evidence of her juridical status as property. Moreover, this status extends beyond Slavery, as the racial event materializes in the many cases of police shootings of black persons and prosecutors' failure to charge; the racial dialectic supports the courts' consistent failure to deliver guilty verdicts in such cases. The Category of Blackness has come to acquire the same validity that last names and title papers have in establishing a juridical relation because of its construction as a scientific category. What needs further consideration is its relation, for centuries now, to how black skin color indexes the juridical position of the Slave.

Almost two decades after the abolition of slavery, Frederick Douglass presents a case for how the juridical and economic conditions of black persons show that slavery extended into the 1880s. Employing a logical procedure to present his argument against the Science of Man's explanation of race prejudice as an effect of physical differences,[33] Douglass challenges how racial difference had been deployed as the *cause* for the conditions in post-Emancipation United States that maintained the black population in de facto *economic* dispossession, a situation that differed little from how they lived under the regime of slavery.

---

33 Though he mentions their arguments, Douglass does not spend much time discussing the scientific projects that described "the prejudice of race" or "the prejudice against color"—the "so-called natural, instinctive prejudice"—as an "ineradicable part of human nature," that is, as the effect of "any fixed and universal law of nature." Douglass, "The Color Line," 567, 570, 572.

Nevertheless, the same modern symbolic (scientific) construction of racial difference Douglass challenges—"a natural, instinctive, and invisible attribute of the white race, one that cannot be eradicated; that even evolution itself cannot carry us beyond and above,"[34] that is, that which explains "race prejudice" among whites—is redeployed by the sociology of race relations, and is a component of the racial dialectic, without addressing how this determinative statement was inherited from the very Science of Man it deplored. This is so because necessity is the ground shared by Douglass's argument, the findings of the Science of Man, and both versions of the Sociology of Race Relations.[35] I will

34 Douglass, 569.

35 Logical necessity: under the principles or laws of noncontradiction, the excluded middle, and identity, syllogism would govern medieval scholastic philosophers' disputationes. The basic statement is that the proof that something is true resides in how it could not be otherwise. Syllogism renders such an analytical move immediately: proposition 1 (if *a* and *b* are the same) and proposition 2 (if *b* and *c* are the same) lead necessarily to conclusion A (then *a* and *c* are the same). Verification, observation of *c*, or comparing *c* to *a* are not needed. Euclid's axioms constitute the same procedure mathematically. Instead of identity, axioms 1 to 4 establish equality. Through its workings in mathematical proofs, necessity would remain crucial in modern thought, particularly in Natural Philosophy/Newtonian physics. Key to the claim that the human mind could know the things of the world with certainty when relying on its unique capacity, logical reasoning through the assignation of identity, whether through quantitative (mathematical inference) or qualitative (determination of presence and absence) reasoning, sustained, respectively, Natural Philosophy and Natural History. Necessity, it is crucial to emphasize, does not refer to the *how* of the statement (the form of the judgment, that is, whether or not it is about the existence of something) or to the *what* (the quality of the thing, that is, whether or not a thing is real). Using Kant's language, it is a condition of possibility for knowledge with certainty—the other one for him is strict universality. It is, like Descartes's account of how he determines the first principle of his philosophy, a procedure for knowing, that is, logical reasoning, which he finds as the only unquestionable reality. From this, he concludes that the mind, or the *I Think*, which performs the steps of logical reasoning, is nothing else but logical, that is, formal. His procedure is logical by exclusion, that is, every step includes the assertion of a possibility,

return to this argument later. Taking a step backward—since I have already provided an outline of the philosophical shifts that ushered in the interpretive episteme—I will first outline the Kantian program, which supports the determinative episteme and provided the departure point for Hegel's version of the scene of history and Husserl's outline of Phenomenology.

Perhaps the hold the Kantian program has had over post-Enlightenment thinking results from how its interiorizing of knowledge is a concession (an acknowledgment of the limits of rational knowledge) that performs like an unquestionable victory. The program itself relies on the determining power of the Understanding, that is, on the formal conditions of possibility for knowing with certainty, and its force (which accounts for its victory) resides in the postulate that links this possibility to something of the order of the speculative, which is a final or purposive principle of Reason. Here I am referring to what Kant in *Critique of the Power of Judgment* calls the "law of the specification of nature," which is the "*a priori* principle" guiding the power of judgment (both determinative and reflective). This principle, Kant postulates, "assumes in behalf of an *order of nature* cognizable for our understanding in the division that it makes of its universal laws when it would subordinate a manifold of particular laws to these."[36] Linearity, as obtained in this principle, can be presented in terms of *mathesis* and *taxonomia*: on the one hand, the species can be displayed along a line, which would stand for the genera, and presented as gradations, with or without a hierarchy; on the other hand, they can be arranged in a grid, with the genera designating the table and the species

inferences from this possibility, and rejection of this possibility through the fact that the inferences fail to hold. All that he is left with at the end is the certainty that the only thing that resists his doubting exercise is the very process of doubting, which is also, in turn, the application of logic seeking not to prove but to disprove everything.

36 Immanuel Kant, *Critique of the Power of Judgment*, ed. Paul Guyer, trans. Paul Guyer and Eric Matthews (Cambridge: Cambridge University Press, 2000), 72 (my italics in last quote).

distributed in the slots that compose it.[37] Because it is a subjective element, Kant's principle could be called a precondition for scientific knowledge. I call it the *image of existence*, which is presupposed in both the determinative and the interpretive moments of the post-Enlightenment episteme.

On this principle rests the Kantian conceptual edifice, for without the principle, neither the formal rendering of the knowing subject and its object—the very notion of the *object* which grasps it under/in *relation* with others—as Nature nor the construction of existents and events as always already determinable, that is, as phenomena, would hold. The consequences of Kant's articulation of the transcendental are numerous. For now, however, I am primarily interested in pointing out how this image of existence (the *order of nature*) facilitates the retaining of necessity under the reinscription of the Cartesian inaugural statement, which obtains the fundamental separability (between res extensa and res cogitans), now in terms of the separation between a natural (of *objects*) and a moral (of the *I Think*) world. Having already been released from syllogism—for instance, in Galileo's recuperation of Euclid's mathematization of the principle of identity in terms of the principle of equality—in the Kantian program, necessity is ushered to the core of knowledge, that is, beyond its application in mechanics. The first and most important move, in *Critique of Pure Reason*, is precisely the concession, that is, the abandoning of any pretension to know the essence of (and with it, the final cause for) existents and events—both of which Kant captures with the term the Thing (*das Ding*)—expressed in the postulate that scientific knowledge is concerned with their appearances, with how they affect the mind, in a way mediated by the formal (pure) intuitions of Space and Time. That concession makes everything in the world accessible to the rational mind because it already modifies things in

37 For a description of these terms in the epistemic regime ("classical" order) in which they allegedly prevailed, see Michel Foucault, *The Order of Things: An Archaeology of the Human Sciences* (New York: Vintage, 1994), 71–77.

their very presentation—that is, insofar as they are of interest to knowledge, they are objects. When considered in connection with the law of the specification of nature, which in turn rests on the principle of the purposiveness of nature, both of which are subjectively held, the formalization of sensation (the moment in which things affect the knowing subject) completes what can be called the occupation of existence with the *I Think*. In short, the interiorization of the conditions for the possibility for knowing facilitates the expansion of necessity between abstract mathematical descriptions of earthly and heavenly events (movements) also (and perhaps only) because it mobilizes the very linearity that supported Galileo's recuperation of mathematics against the Aristotelian orthodoxy, which it puts into operation in the onto-epistemological descriptors (formality and efficacy) and pillars (separability, determinacy, and sequentiality) that characterize post-Enlightenment thinking.

Three moves that unfold Kant's response to Hume's questioning of the mind's ability to grasp the universal give us a sense of how this was accomplished. First, it is the radical statement that even though scientific knowledge requires experience, knowledge "independent of all experience" is possible—that is, what Kant identifies as that which guarantees the certainty of a judgment, namely necessity and strict (or absolute) universality. The significance of necessity is presented immediately: "If a proposition is thought along with its necessity, it is an *a priori* judgement; if it is, moreover, also not derived from any proposition except one that in turn is valid as a necessary proposition, then it is absolutely *a priori*."[38] Strict universality results from a judgment arrived at by comparing something (through induction) that admits exceptions and something that admits no exception. Both necessity and strict universality are peculiar to *formality* (the manner of presentation of objects and arguments proper to mathematical reasoning) and *efficacy* (as

38 Immanuel Kant, *Critique of Pure Reason*, trans. and ed. Paul Guyer and Allen W. Wood (Cambridge: Cambridge University Press, 1998), 137 (italics in original).

observed phenomena are described in terms of the cause-and-effect relation).[39] Beyond observation, efficacy also operates formally at the level of the Understanding because, for Kant, the task of scientific (synthetic) knowledge is to subsume "the manifold of appearances" already "ordered under certain relations" (by the pure intuitions of time and space), that is, already as form.[40] Efficacy refers to this movement of subsumption, which consists in the "third thing necessary for cognition," that is, as the "pure concepts of the understanding," the categories that correspond to the logical functions of judgement" (quantity, quality, relation, and modality)—through these "certain intuitions are determined in regard to the synthetic unity of their consciousness as contained under these functions."[41] Both onto-epistemological descriptors that obtain *necessity* would rule the post-Enlightenment episteme. On the one hand, formality is articulated here as belonging to the conditions of possibility for knowledge in general in terms of the intuitions (through which an object is given as a phenomenon) and conceptions (the logical functions that are the rules they are subsumed under) through which what exists and what happens, under scientific knowledge, become Nature. On the other hand, and more importantly, efficacy becomes an attribute of cognition from the very moment of apprehension (of the Thing as phenomenon), that is, as it appears in spacetime, through the synthesis produced by imagination, to the unity given by the laws or categories of the Understanding.

---

39 "If one would have one [example] from the commonest use of the understanding, the proposition that every alteration must have a cause will do; indeed in the latter the very concept of a cause so obviously contains the concept of a necessity of connection with an effect, and a strict universality of rule that it would be entirely lost if one sought [...] to derive it from a frequent association of that which happens with that which precedes and a habit (thus a merely subjective necessity) of connecting representations arising from that association." Kant, 138.

40 Kant, 155–56.

41 Kant, 211–12.

Undoubtedly, these are distinguishing aspects of post-Enlightenment thinking; however, they are fully operative under Kant's more general proposition, which obtains linearity in the very description of the productive moment, which is contingent upon both separability as articulated in the Cartesian inaugural statement and Kant's own privileging of the pure intuition of time in his description of the productive (determinative) moment in knowledge. Following *separability*, because it provides an aspect of Kant's image of existence (an order with different levels of abstraction) that comports with the idea that one thing affects another (body and soul as different substances) as well as the idea that what causes something to happen is not the same as what happens (the soul commands the body), *determinacy* is yielded by the view that the business of the Understanding (scientific knowledge), which is synthetic (productive) knowledge, is to subsume impressions (gathered by intuition) linearly (successively)—after these are synthetized by imagination—under logical functions or categories. "It is only because we subject the sequence of the appearances and thus all alteration to the law of causality that experience itself, i.e., empirical cognition of them, is possible; consequently they themselves, as objects of experience, are possible only in accordance with this law."[42] In that lies the possibility of *determinacy*—in other words, the view that productive knowledge operates linearly, as does the cause in relation to the effect. In the Kantian program, then, formality issues from the analysis of the conditions for knowing with "objective validity"—that is, efficacy, whose criteria are necessity and the strict universality of the statements, becomes the general descriptor of the process of production of cognition.[43] This is

42 Kant, 305. For a discussion of Kant's account of time in regard to raciality and the political, see Rei Terada, "The Racial Grammar of Kantian Time," *European Romantic Review* 28, no. 3 (2017): 267–78.

43 The contrasting images here would be: Locke's empty mind encountering and working with impressions given by the things of the world; Leibniz's intelligent soul (the mind) trying to decipher the other entelechies the divine creator had populated the universe with; and Hume's habitual process of recognizing

a moment of knowledge in which the mind deals with its own creations, that is, the "impressions" gathered through sensation, which are already mediated by the formal (*a priori*) "intuitions" of space and time and the conceptions (or categories or rules) of understanding. Those are the *a priori* conditions of possibility for experience in general, insofar as they are phenomena, that is, that which is perceived in space and time.[44] Efficacy integrates the very design of the Kantian tools and procedures, namely the categories or logical functions of understanding. The fact that Kant models them after the different kinds of judgment (quality, quantity, relation, and modality) describes the Understanding's task as a *juridical* task, that is, a determination/decision—or the subsumption of the impressions (gathered by intuition) and synthesis (operated by the imagination) under the rules (categories or conceptions) it gathers into conceptions.

Much unfolds from how necessity operates intrastructurally in modern thinking. Some of it will be discussed in the next section and in the following chapter. Before proceeding, let me map out how the Kantian program weaves necessity into the intrastructure of modern thinking: (a) in the view that knowledge is concerned with (and productive of) nature (as conforming to the law of phenomena in space and time), which is always already an effect of the categories (the rules or laws of thought) that, because *a priori*, have the attributes of strict necessity and absolute universality, hence objective validity; (b) in reducing knowing to determination (judgment, decision, subsumption), that is, as having its own efficacy, in the writing of judgment as the act of subsuming intuitions and conceptions under the rules (categories) of the Understanding, that is, of deciding how necessity operates (with the force of law) in these relations between a subject and a predicate. With this, Kant, the last of the classical philosophers, made available to the following phase of the modern episteme, the post-Enlightenment regime,

---

repetitions without daring to state anything other than that they do happen.

44 Kant, 51.

a program for knowledge that retains necessity (mathematics) as the ground for knowledge, relies on how *formality* becomes a distinguishing attribute of the tools of modern knowledge and the objects these produce, and presumes *efficacy* both as descriptors of what happens and as the effect of knowing itself, that is, as *determinacy*.

Necessitas

> A boy of this color is found in his bed tied, mutilated, and bleeding, when forthwith all ordinary experience is set aside, and he is presumed to have been guilty of the outrage upon himself; [...] and every effort is made to entangle the poor fellow in the confused meshes of expert testimony (the least trustworthy of all evidence). [...] If an unarmed colored man is shot down and dies in his tracks, a jury, under the influence of this spirit, does not hesitate to find the murdered man the real criminal, and the murderer innocent.
>
> —Frederick Douglass, "The Color Line"

Thinking with Dana's predicament, that is, with the probability that a black person could return to a point in the past to save an ancestor's life—time travel becoming possible would also make it real—allows questions about the ways in which tools of raciality, such as the Category of Blackness, operate when employed in the explanation or justification for something that happens or has happened or is to happen. How is it that the jury faithfully expresses the "spirit" Douglass mentions above, the "insidious influence," met everywhere by the "colored man," who "ceased to be the slave of an individual, but has in some sense become the slave of society."[45] In this regard, I am interested particularly in how blackness (as a post-Enlightenment determinative tool) performs this work—the authorization of deployment of total violence—in, for instance, explanations or justifications for police shootings of unarmed black persons. Even when the evidence

45 Douglass, "The Color Line," 568.

shows no actual (spatiotemporally registered) threat, the argument of self-defense, which I have called self-preservation, is consistently found valid, with the force of necessity.[46]

Similar to Douglass's findings in 1881, a logical pattern still operates today that, virtually every time the explanation or justification for deployment of otherwise unacceptable total violence, renders the person killed the *cause* of their own killing, whether they seemed to be holding a gun (which turned out to be a wallet, in the case of Amadou Diallo) or they moved in threatening way (even after being shot, in the case of Michael Brown). From where, one must ask, does blackness derive such a powerful connection to truth, so strong that it alone sustains the validity of an explanation/justification (by the police officer or nonblack person) against any actual (spatiotemporal) evidence to the contrary? My argument here is that this force resides in the particular way through which the racial dialectic transubstantiates what is politically constituted (by the colonial juridico-economic structure of slavery) into expressions of an organically determined moral deficit (in the case of police shootings) produced by the sight of black skin color (an expression of moral and intellectual deficit).[47]

I examine how blackness manages this shift in the next section. Because the movement is enabled by the notion of universality, which is both premised on and presupposed by juridical and scientific forms, as it figures into them, it is crucial to turn, even briefly, to a consideration of *necessitas* itself. Here my task is to describe how necessity operates in thinking, in particular when the tools of raciality are at work, but without returning to the arguments I advanced when describing the conditions of the production of the analytics of raciality.[48] What I do, instead, is to track how necessity operates within the determinative tools that enter into the composition of the racial

46 Ferreira da Silva, "No-Bodies," 214–17.

47 I elaborate this argument in Ferreira da Silva, "Scene of Nature," 277–80.

48 Ferreira da Silva, *Toward a Global Idea of Race*, 91–170.

dialectic, which is productive of the interpretive (historical) moment of the analytics of raciality. Indirectly, I track its workings through the intrastructure that supports (from within) the reformulation of the *transparent I* as Subjectivity. That is, I track the accompanying emergence of *world* as a theme, or the onto-epistemological regime in which considering something like a black Subjectivity evokes both an exorbitance (which disrupts the subject of Thought, as Chandler suggests) and an absence (which releases existence from the grips of *world*, as I claim).

“impersonal necessity”

> When a scientific proposition is judged to be true, it takes on a retroactive validity. It ceases to be part of the endless stream of forgotten dreams, discarded projects, failed procedures and erroneous conclusions—things, in short, for which someone must shoulder the responsibility. The elimination of the false by the true—that is, the verified—appears, once it is accomplished, to be the quasi-mechanical effect of ineluctable, impersonal necessity. Importing such norms of judgment into the historical domain is, therefore, an inevitable source of misunderstanding. The retroactive effect of the truth influences even one’s assessment of the respective contributions of various investigators to a scientific discovery (an assessment that only a specialist is competent to make), because the tendency is to see the history of the subject in the light of today’s truth, which is easily confused with eternal truth.
>
> —Georges Canguilhem, “The Various Models”

Historicizing truth, to render it contingent on (cultural) “contents” that escape its presupposition, would then be the correct move if we follow through with Georges Canguilhem’s argument as well as Foucault’s and other interpretive philosophers’ postulates. That, however, would not be the most generative move if one is interested in how, under the ruling historicity, nothing much happened to the “failed procedures and erroneous conclusions” of (the truths produced by) the Science of Man. Why is it that raciality so effectively fails to meet the destiny of other nineteenth-century concepts? How is it that the attestation of the dismissal of these procedures does not dissipate their "erroneous conclusions"?[49] How is it that what Douglas saw in 1881 still prevails in 1991 (Rodney King's beating) and 1999 (Amadou Diallo's shooting)—as well as in 2014 (Michael Brown's shooting) and 2020 (Breonna Taylor's shooting and George Floyd's lynching)? How is it that when an unarmed black person is shot, a way to blame them for it will be found? How is it that most (nonblack persons) find it acceptable to consider their killing an attestation of them being guilty and life-threatening to the police? In all these cases, the decision to shoot, the decision not to indict, or the decision to acquit is based on the decision of which accounts convey the "objective reality" of the case, that is, an attempt to "separate fact from fiction."[50] At work here is what I call the

---

49 I am thinking here of Herbert Spencer's mistaken appropriation of the second law of thermodynamics—entropy, indicated by the irreversibility of the direction of energy in a closed system, for instance, heat, which flows from what is hotter (high kinetic energy) to colder (low kinetic energy). This process assumes the arrow of time, the perception that time flows and does so in one direction, along with the conclusion that the system tends toward disorganization. Spencer, however, interpreted it as indicating that the general tendency in "Nature" is equilibrium, which is crucial to the "Law of Evolution" underlying his version of the sociological project:

> The general truth thus illustrated under its simplest aspect, we must now look at under those more complex aspects it usually presents throughout Nature. In nearly all cases, the motion of an aggregate is compound; and the equilibration of each of its components, being carried on independently, does not affect the rest. [...] That this process may be duly realized and the state of things towards which it tends fully understood, it will be well here to cite a case in which we may watch this successive equilibration of combined movements more completely than we can do in those above instanced.

While Spencer contributed to the structural-functionalist approach that would dominate twentieth-century social-scientific projects, the philosophical proposition accompanying it would not survive the shift to the interpretive regime. Herbert Spencer, *First Principles*, 2nd ed. (London: Williams and Norgate, 1867), 274.

50 After the decision by both the grand jury and the US Department of Justice that police officer Darren Wilson's shooting of Michael Brown was not an unreasonable use of

racial dialectic, a vicious, circular logic that renders blackness the *cause* and *effect* of subjugation, that is, the black person is solely responsible for the (total or symbolic) violence enacted. In all such instances of the deployment of total violence, I find Blackness, the category, the modern abstraction resolving each of these events as an instantiation of the divine (natural) law for self-preservation, that aspect of the modern juridical moment, which signals *necessity*.[51] How necessity operates through the Category of Blackness can be appreciated if one attends to how necessity and its onto-epistemological descriptors and pillars enter into the composition of the prevailing explanation for racial subjugation, that is, the racial dialectic.

Thoroughly suffused with necessity, racial difference—the tool of raciality devised in the nineteenth and twentieth centuries—operates at the core of the account of racial subjection produced in the twentieth-century interpretive episteme. Why? Because even though it was assembled according to the prevailing rules and procedures for scientific investigation in the determinative moment, it did not receive the kind of negative attention that one would expect after Phenomenology disavowed that moment. Not because it was ignored, but because racial and cultural difference were reconfigured in the interpretive moment as *raw material*—that is, as a *datum* (natural trait that entices unbecoming representations) and/or a *residuum* (historically surpassed social arrangements that entice nonmodern representations and behavior). Unexamined racial difference, for

force, these words from Robert McCulloch, prosecuting attorney, tell us whose account of the events was considered true or to correspond to the objective reality of the scene of total violence that took place on August 9, 2014, on Canfield Drive in Ferguson, Missouri. "Ferguson Documents: How the Grand Jury Reached a Decision," NPR, November 25, 2014, https://www.npr.org/sections/thetwo-way/2014/11/25/366507379/ferguson-docs-how-the-grand-jury-reached-a-decision.

51 Elsewhere I discuss this operation of necessity as presented in John Locke's articulation of the divine right to self-preservation as the ethical basis for the institution of the body politic. See Ferreira da Silva, "No-Bodies," 214–17.

this reason, would continue to play out in Subjectivity's *world*, though—no matter how (or perhaps because of the) many times we shout that they are social constructs. Precisely their repurposing as sociological constructs—such as Moynihan's "Negro family"—produces a chain of efficacy (efficient causality) that, while constitutive of "the other world," only seems to involve black persons' *reality*.

Seeking to halt this circuitry, this re/de/composing exercise tracks efficacy in the arrangement of determining statements to expose the *necessity* working through them. After these components are retrieved and repurposed through the activation of the wounded captive body in the scene of subjugation, it becomes possible to re/compose the political architecture of the global present by registering how blackness as a scientific construct operates at the symbolic level only because it is inseparable from its ethic, juridic, and economic moments. Every rehearsal of the *scene of nature*,[52] every claim that blackness signals a life-threatening situation and response of total violence, registers an occurrence Douglass wrote about all those decades ago, which plays out every time Dana returns to the Weylin farm. Every one of these instantiations of the *racial event*, of that which happens without time, exposes how historicity—the ontological horizon of the interpretive episteme—affords a limited view of the global political architecture in this early twentieth-first century.

"of an ideological nature"

> You know, the existence in France of a strong current against Muslims is the result of many factors. The first one is colonialism. In the not very distant past, we had the Algerian War, a colonial war against the Algerian people. So the first cause of racism against Arabs and Muslims is of an ideological nature.

---

52 The term "scene of nature" captures how social-scientific signifiers justify otherwise unacceptable deployments of total violence as reasonable—because *necessary* for the self-preservation of the perpetrator—responses to a threat signified by black bodies and black territories. See Ferreira da Silva, "Scene of Nature," 280–87.

> It is a racism that can be traced back to colonialism, this feeling of the superiority of the Western world.
>
> —Alain Badiou

When I first read these comments made by Alain Badiou a 2015 interview, I was surprised. Not so much by how the philosopher of the event deployed efficacy so comfortably, but by how the contemporary left philosopher who postulates that "mathematics is ontology" cannot but think interpretively in regard to Colonial and Racial matters.[53] Nothing other than a historical (interpretive) version of race relations, it turns out, guides his attribution of racism to a lingering colonialism[54]—and his

---

53 Alain Badiou, *Being and Event*, trans. Oliver Feltham (London: Continuum, 2007), 4.

54 I am not suggesting that Badiou's project is internally contradictory. For him, historicity refers to that which escapes the hold of what he calls "the state's metastructure" (Badiou, 174). What I am highlighting, but cannot develop here, is how Badiou's project, in a way, returns to the origin of phenomenology. That is, if Husserl's return to and repurposing of Kant's pure consciousness meant, among other things, rescuing the mind from nineteenth-century determinative projects of knowledge of Man—in this case, psychology—Badiou, also in a move to rescue the subject (now from the assault of women, LGBTQ2+, and the "others of Europe" and their sociohistorical claims of cultural [moral and epistemological] difference), refashions the *transparent I* as a formal (mathematically framed) thing but does not dare to take it out of its proper stage, namely historicity. For instance, in this passage Badiou preempts the obvious, which is the reading of necessity into his mathematical ontology:

> The confusion of the existence of the site (for example, the working class, or a given state of artistic tendencies, or a scientific impasse) with the necessity of the event itself is the cross of determinist or globalizing thought. The site is only ever a *condition of being* for the event. Of course, if the situation is natural, compact, or neutral, the event is impossible. But the existence of a multiple on the edge of the void merely opens up the possibility of an event. It is always possible that no event actually occur. Strictly speaking, a site is only 'evental' insofar as it is retroactively qualified as such by the occurrence of an event. However, we do know one

definition of racism as an *ideological* ("feeling of the superiority of the Western world") hierarchical residuum of what should by now be a bygone nonmodern mentality, but one that republicanism will eventually dissipate. Badiou is not the first or the last French philosopher to count racial and cultural difference as *natural* datum or *historical* residuum, or both. Coherently, his reframing of the *transparent I* as the figure of the *event* seems to aim at something similar to what Husserl sought with his general introduction to Phenomenology. And just as Husserl targets scientific psychology in his challenge to the determinative episteme, Badiou has identified two social-scientific constructions, cultural difference and cultural identity, as the products of the interpretive episteme through which to unleash a formalist attack.[55]

How *formality* grounds Badiou's reframing of the *transparent I* without stripping it of its distinguishing historicity

---

> of its ontological characteristics, related to the form of presentation: it is always an abnormal multiple, on the edge of the void. Therefore, there is no event save relative to a historical situation, even if a historical situation does not *necessarily* produce events. (Badiou, 179; italics in original)

55 In his preface to the English translation of *Being and Event*, Badiou frames his book's project in opposition to what he calls the dominant anthropology of the 1980s:

> In fact, at the time of its publication, this book did not lend itself to immediate comprehension. We were at the end of the eighties, in full intellectual regression. What was fashionable was moral philosophy disguised as political philosophy. [...]
>
> Declarations were made to the effect that all cultures were of the same value, that all communities generated values, that every production of the imaginary was art, that all sexual practices were forms of love, etc. In short, the context combined the violent dogmatism of mercantile 'democracy' with a thoroughgoing scepticism which reduced the effects of truth to particular anthropological operations. Consequently, philosophy was reduced to being either a laborious justification of the universal character of democratic values, or a linguistic sophistry legitimating the right to cultural difference against any universalist pretension on the part of truths.
>
> My book, however, by means of a weighty demonstrative apparatus, made four affirmations that went entirely against the flow of this ordinary philosophy. (Badiou, xi–ii)

reminds us, as the reader may already have noticed, that modern philosophy has only a few tricks in its hat and needs to switch things around once and again. After a century of interpretive moves and firm rejections of determinative procedures and tools, it makes sense that a return to the theme of the Subject would once again rewrite its relationship with the *world* in a way that keeps intact *his* self-determination (as liberty and transparency). Unsurprisingly, this has been accompanied by rewritings of the *object* (and of things) that extend to them something that reads like (Hegelian) self-determination.[56] Without assigning causality, it is possible to see how formality has been recalled in other interpretive departures from Phenomenology—primarily in the latter half of the twentieth century—such as, for instance, those of Michel Foucault or Jacques Derrida, which have provided tools for the critical analyses of racial and other modalities of social subjugation. Foucault's notion of discursive formation and Derrida's deconstruction both decenter and refigure interiority/temporality, the ontological descriptors of the interpretive version of the *transparent I* and its relation to (formal) signification (in discourse or text) in such a way that Subjectivity becomes an effect of the latter.

Though this is precisely the move that makes their critical apparatuses relevant to racial critique, because they remain within the confines of the historical (interpretive) account of racial subjugation Foucault and Derrida offer very little to an anti-colonial and radical black feminist approach. As far as I know, Derrida's only comments on racial subjugation appear in the short text "Racism's Last Word," which is about a 1983 anti-apartheid exhibition. Early in the text he states that racism is textual—"there's no racism without a language"[57]—and he spends a few paragraphs describing racism's movement

56 For commentary on these rewritings, see Denise Ferreira da Silva, "Fractal Thinking," *aCCeSsions*, no. 2, April 27, 2016, https://accessions.org/article2/fractal-thinking/.

57 Jacques Derrida, "Racism's Last Word," trans. Peggy Kamuf, *Critical Inquiry* 12, no. 1 (1985): 292.

of signification. Most of the text (and its argument), however, departs from the task Derrida has assigned to deconstruction. Instead, similar to Badiou, Derrida moves to expose how racism performs the task of a proper ideological tool—he notes how "'discourse' on the concept of race" coexists and inflects liberal structures by injecting segregation and discrimination where they should have no place.[58] Similarly, Foucault engages the Racial from without his own interpretive framework. He does not approach the sociological or political concept of race in terms of subjugation or subjection—which is how he describes the productive effects of power/knowledge. Instead, he traces the emergence and trajectory of what he calls "the discourse of race" (or "race war" or "race struggle") of the Middle Ages. Naming it a "historico-political discourse," a counter-history that depicts society in a "binary structure" but not a hierarchical one, he argues that this discourse constitutes a counter-history of empire (Roman and Catholic) and, as such, goes against the grain of modern European philosophy and the theory of sovereignty, or the "philosophico-juridical theory" of power.[59]

---

58 This is the gist of his commenting on the contradictions state racism (apartheid) harbors as well as "Western" juridico-economic needs—in particular, South Africa's geo-economic strategic positioning during the Cold War:

> No doubt apartheid was instituted and maintained against the British Commonwealth, following a long adventure that began with England's abolition of slavery in 1834, at which time the impoverished Boers undertook the Long Trek toward the Orange Free State and the Transvaal. But this contradiction only confirms the occidental essence of the historical process—in its incoherences, its compromises, and its stabilization. Since the Second World War, at least if one accepts the givens of a certain kind of calculation, the stability of the Pretoria regime has been prerequisite to the political, economic, and strategic equilibrium of Europe. The survival of Western Europe depends on it. Whether one is talking about gold or what are called strategic ores, it is known to be the case that at least three-fourths of the world's share of them is divided between the USSR and South Africa. (Derrida, 294–95)

59 "At a very early stage, we find the basic elements that make the war possible, and then ensure its continuation, pursuit, and development: ethnic differences, differences between languages,

Let me stay longer with Foucault because his rewriting of the concept of race ("back" into the pre-Enlightenment "discourse of races") has broader and deeper implications than Derrida's liberal apology and Badiou's republican dismissal. What I find in Foucault's approach is a diversion resulting from the double movement of his engagement with "the discourse of race." On the one hand, he refuses to consider racial knowledge in his analysis of the modern episteme. Instead, here he locates what he terms the biological transcription, the "theory of races in the historico-biological sense of the term"—"which borrowed its discourse, together with all its elements, concepts, and vocabulary, from a materialist anatomo-physiology."[60] In this transcription, which accounts for the emergence of "state racism," I find something close to a notion of ideology: he describes a "biologico-social racism" as "the idea—which is absolutely new and which will make the discourse function very differently—that the other race is basically not the race that came from elsewhere or that was, for a time, triumphant and dominant, but that it is a race that is permanently, ceaselessly infiltrating the social body, or which is, rather, constantly being re-created in and by the social fabric."[61] On the other hand, he identifies a dissociation, as the theme of struggle in the early

---

different degrees of force, vigor, energy, and violence; the differences between savagery and barbarism; the conquest and subjugation of one race by another. The social body is basically articulated around two races. It is this idea that this clash between two races runs through society from top to bottom which we see being formulated as early as the seventeenth century. And it forms the matrix for all the forms beneath which we can find the face and mechanisms of social warfare." Foucault, *"Society Must Be Defended,"* 60.

60 Foucault, 60.

61 The mobilization of race to the workings of "a centered, centralized, and centralizing power" shifts the discourse from one of two races to one of a "race that holds power and is entitled to define the norm, and against those who deviate from that norm, against those who pose a threat to the biological heritage. At this point, we have all those biological-racist discourses of degeneracy, but also all those institutions within the social body which make the discourse of race struggle function as a principle of exclusion

nineteenth century "tends to erase every trace of racial conflict in order to define itself as class struggle," adding that "it corresponds to a recasting of the theme of the analysis of these struggles in the form of the dialectic, and to a recasting of the theme of racial confrontations in terms of the theory of evolutionism and the struggle for existence."[62] An important shift here, he argues, is that of the role of the State, which, instead of being activated in the war of one race against the other, becomes "the protector of the integrity, the superiority, and the purity of the race. The idea of racial purity, with all its monistic, Statist, and biological implications: that is what replaces the idea of race struggle." An inversion also takes place in his analysis that results from the split between race and struggle, in which struggle is attached to the category of class and race—as the "discourse of race" and not "races"—is appropriated by sovereignty in the form of State racism.[63] Certainly, both make perfect sense. However, "the discourse of race," in addition to the biopolitical elements of "state racism"—"the internal racism of permanent purification [that] will become one of the basic dimensions of social normalization"[64]—also maintain an ethico-juridical aspect that recalls disciplinary power.

My point is: racial knowledge has produced social (moral) subjects that stand differentially before the ethical descriptors (liberty, dignity, and equality) of liberal democratic capitalist architecture. Had he attended to racial knowledge, Foucault might have followed how the diversion in the early nineteenth century he identified was, in the twentieth century, retracted by the sociologists of race relations, who based their descriptions of racial subjugation on the model of "class struggle" and, in doing so, produced a version of the dialectic that, unlike Hegel's and Marx's, does not replicate the linear movement of historical time but instead, as Spillers shows, recalls the circularity

and segregation and, ultimately, as a way of normalizing society." Foucault, 61.

62 Foucault, 60.

63 Foucault, 81.

64 Foucault, 62.

attributed to "mythical" time. However, because he is an interpretive thinker, Foucault limits his approach to the "discourse of race" to the tracking of an "ideological-mythical" tool of the State (in its proclaimed role as the protector of racial purity), and misses how, in the political architecture of the twentieth century, raciality works in the ethico-juridical corner, where the main theme is not *purity* but *authority*.

"people distinguished by marks of racial descent"

> Race relations, as that term is defined in use and wont in the United States, are the relations existing between peoples distinguished by marks of racial descent, particularly when these racial differences enter into the consciousness of the individuals and groups so distinguished, and by so doing determine in each case the individual's conception of himself as well as his status in the community. [...] Race consciousness, therefore, is to be regarded as a phenomenon, like class or caste consciousness, that enforces social distances. Race relations, in this sense, are not so much the relations that exist between individuals of different races as between individuals conscious of these differences.
>
> —Robert E. Park, "The Nature of Race Relations"

> By race relations we do not mean all social contact between persons of different "races," but only those contacts the social characteristics of which are determined by a consciousness of "racial" differences.
>
> —Oliver C. Cox, *Caste, Class, and Race*

Perhaps it was Foucault's position as an interpretive thinker that led him to propose that the modern version of the "discourse of race" gains its political significance from reconfiguring the biological (determinative) version of racial knowledge in the guise of state racism, or perhaps it was his lack of interest in how social-scientific knowledge in the twentieth century produced its own interpretive version of the earlier biological one. Whatever the reasons or conditions that led to this choice, his thesis of the "transcriptions" of the medieval "discourse of race" misses the important factor that, in the interpretive moment, racial difference became a descriptor of a particular kind of relation that both privileges the *subjective* and ascribes to it a role that violates the principles said to constitute modern social (moral) configurations.[65] The historical (interpretive) versions differ in many ways—which I will not recall here. Most significant is the focus on the subjective dimensions (as prejudice, beliefs, or ideology) and, as Robert E. Park and Oliver C. Cox indicate in the quotes above, the focus on how a *natural* phenomenon (racial difference) explains the *social* (moral) phenomenon (race consciousness), which in turn explains how persons are situated in a given political (juridical, economic, symbolic, ethical) configuration.[66] Not surprisingly, then, while the concept of ethnicity, an interpretive tool, maps almost squarely onto the notion of race consciousness, a UNESCO document that once and for all stated the postwar world's rejection of what Foucault names state racism mandated that ethnicity replace the notion of race.[67] Why? Ethnicity's ethical advantage derives from how it does not seem to have the *objectifying* (de-*humanizing*) effect the notion of race has when approached as both *datum* (phenomenon) and *conceptum* (scientific signifier). While it does not have such an effect when employed in the studies of descendants of white/European migrants—in which case it does the kind of objectifying attributed to social-scientific knowledge in general—when employed in studies of

65 The consolidation of the interpretive version of raciality—elsewhere I call it the historical (Marxist and Liberal) versions of racial knowledge—would occur in the mid-twentieth century. See Denise Ferreira da Silva, "An Introduction: The Predicament of Brazilian Culture," *Social Identities* 10, no. 6 (2004): 719–34.

66 As in Park's foundational version, which, at least initially, relied on Science of Man's thesis that reactions to it were instinctual, racial difference was reformulated as datum—a *natural* trait and related mental (moral and intellectual) traits. For an elaboration of this argument, see Ferreira da Silva, *Toward a Global Idea of Race*, 116–71.

67 I am referring to the first statement on race, written in July 1950, in *Four Statements on the Race Question* (Paris: UNESCO, 1969), https://unesdoc.unesco.org/ark:/48223/pf0000122962.

black (or other non-European) persons, as Spillers describes, ethnicity institutes a closed circuitry, a logical circle, precisely because even though it is a concept designed to capture the workings of historical (cultural) difference, it does not dissipate the effects of signification of the scientific (anthropological and sociological) concept of the Racial (both because of how much it shares with the concept and because it was not designed to do that kind of critical work).

That, I argue, results from how racial difference, the determinative tool, remains operative in historical (interpretive) versions of the sociology of race relations and, more importantly, is the very basis for the explanation of racial subjugation the historical versions have assembled. As I noted before, the racial dialectic consists in a closed circuitry, which results in the particular way in which the construction of race consciousness as phenomenon combines the *natural* and the *moral* in the investigation of social (*moral*) conditions. More precisely, in the interpretive moment, the Science of Man’s predication of black body (*natural*) = black mind (*moral*)—that is, that certain physical attributes correspond to mental (moral and intellectual) ones—acquires interpretive significance as that which generates unbecoming ideas. What the racial dialectic performs is the account of racial subjugation assembled by the Sociology of Race Relations in the twentieth century, in which racial difference enters as *natural* datum and/or *historical* residuum.

How the racial dialectic operates becomes evident once one attends to how social-scientific signification models the Kantian program, in particular how it deployed onto-epistemological descriptors and pillars. Though this is an interpretive framework, modern epistemological descriptors provide the necessary effects to warrant a claim to (social) scientific signification. Because racial difference enters the sociological project as a referent to a particular kind of social relation, it functions as a *datum* that provides the basis for the formalization of an *efficacy* that is given empirically and analytically. That is, what is implied in the notion of social relation is a correlation between *ideas* (subjective) and *actions* (objective), and between these *actions* and the *social* (juridical, economic, etc.)

structure (objective). Hence, necessity here operates through formality and efficacy in the very definition of the object of study, namely, the cause (efficacy) for certain economic and juridical circumstances (race relations) and the mental phenomenon (*race consciousness*) it expresses and actualizes. What distinguishes this type of social relations is the fact that it is construed as a social problem, which results from how racial difference gives rise to unbecoming *ideas* (prejudice, belief, or ideology) and (individual or collective or institutional) *actions* (discrimination, segregation, hierarchization) that express premodern principles.

Breaking the circle created by this explanation for racial subjugation takes three steps: the first, preparatory step stays in the text of the Sociology of Race Relations and tracks the delimitation of its field; the second, exploratory step tracks the operations of the determinative tools of raciality (the notions of racial and cultural difference and the categories they yield) in the interpretive version of racial knowledge assembled in the twentieth century; finally, the third, speculative step activates the wounded captive body in the scene of subjugation, where she muddles the presumed transparency of the proper social (*moral*) subject by exposing the violent scene that allows it to emerge as such.

Let me begin by mapping the statement that presents race consciousness—consciousness of racial difference—as a problem. Returning to Park's and Cox's definitions of race relations indicated by the quotes at the opening of this section, I will focus on the implied distinction between *unproblematic* social relations and *problematic* ones. What I do first is to decompose the statement that, in the absence of *consciousness* of racial difference, social relations unfold *unproblematically*, that is, universalist ideas (liberty, equality) inform actions (free and egalitarian) that constitute a free and egalitarian society, and that the presence of racially different persons—in the case of the United States this would be black, Asian, Latinx, and Indigenous persons—cause particularist (discriminatory) ideas, actions, societies. When presented separately, these arguments look like this:

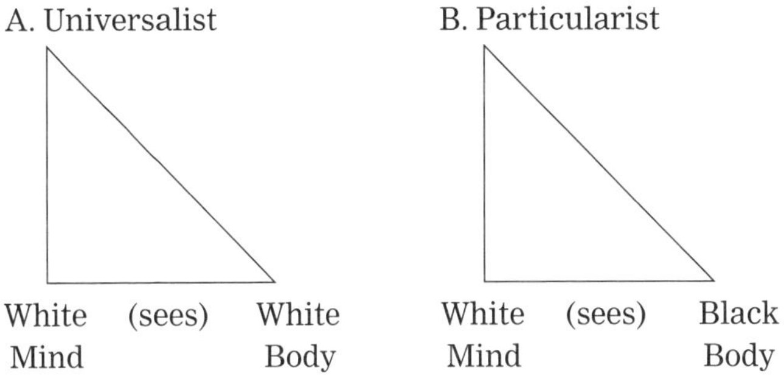

These figures capture the following: (a) a white person (presumably already harboring universal ideas) sees a white person and their ideas remain universalist; and (b) a white person (presumably already harboring universal ideas) sees a black person and their universalist ideas are immediately replaced by particularist ideas (which they may or may not have harbored beforehand; what is important is that these are activated by the sight of a black person). Another way of describing these figures—which is explicit in Park's and Cox's definitions—is that the "natural attitude" of the white person changes by the sight of blackness, giving rise to what the early version of the Sociology of Race Relations termed "racial attitudes." Whatever the relationship is between this sociological concept and Husserl's, there is no question that Phenomenology's description of existence (as *world*)—much like sociology's—does not take into account that determinative knowledge populated *the world* with a variety of Human phenomena determined (classified) according to physical (organic and phenotypical) traits and the mental (moral and intellectual) attributes these supposedly expressed.

My point is that the interpretive version of race relations—which remains the basic one in later approaches to racial subjugation (such as the sociohistorical)—presumes phenomenologically (which can be traced to the versions of Kant, Hegel, and the twentieth century) that the *transparent I* (as Subjectivity) produces (as it represents) the *world* (the immediate world of interaction but NOT the represented world of investigation and speculation!). From this emerges a racial dialectic in which, as Spillers finds in Moynihan's Category of the Negro Family, black persons' social subjugation is explained by blackness, as in the *meanings* attributed to it by white persons. In short, in deployments of the tools of raciality in the study of the social conditions of black persons and populations, a closed circuitry (the racial dialectic) is attained precisely because blackness always already substitutes for the white person.

C. Particularist (white person's racial prejudice, beliefs)

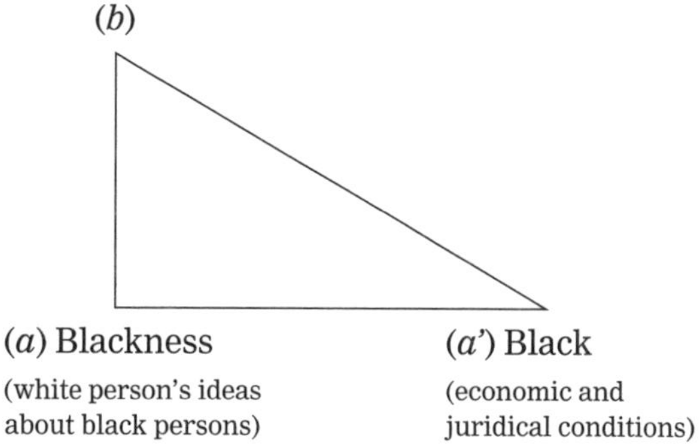

Or, blackness provokes particularist (unbecoming) ideas in the white person's mind (prejudice, belief, ideology), which leads to actions (discrimination and violence) that produce the unbecoming social conditions under which black persons exist.

These figures translate into how, in earlier as well as more recent constructs such as "Negro family" and "black gang member," the social (moral) representations become the explanation for black persons' (juridical and economic) conditions. This deployment of *efficacy* entails that ethnicity functions "mythically," as Spillers charges of Moynihan's report—as it removes the black family from linear time (the form of historicity), it "embodies nothing more than a mode of memorial time."[68] When flattened, that is, when efficacy is imaged linearly ($a \rightarrow b \rightarrow a'$ or a causes b that causes a'), it is easier to appreciate how necessity sustains (social-scientific) racial signification: blackness (whites' particularist ideas that it causes)→unbecoming social conditions

68 Spillers, "Mama's Baby, Papa's Maybe," 66.

(economic dispossession)→Blackness (unbecoming mental contents, Myrdal's pathological, asocial ghetto consciousness, and Moynihan's "tangle of pathology"). However, because the explanation returns blackness as the cause, this is a dialectic ($a \times b$) without linear dislocation (affirmation—negation—negation of the negation), that is, it is a vicious circle: (a) racial difference explains black subjugation (*juridical domination and economic dispossession*) as an effect of (b) white's unbecoming representations of blackness and attendant particularist practices (moral deficit), which result (a') in that maintenance or worsening of black social (subjective) conditions (moral deficit) that leads to further (juridico-economic) deficit.

Not surprisingly, despite the gigantic library of studies about how raciality configures the post-Enlightenment global context, economic dispossession and juridical subjugation of black persons and populations are explained in terms of *subjective* (moral) attributes and not (to proceed with the operating dichotomy) the *objective* (economic and juridical) conditions of existence. Elsewhere I have highlighted how this explanation for racial subjugation, which also functions as justification for racial violence in the courts of law and in the denial of demands for racial justice, doubly renders it exterior (as a residuum) to the post-Enlightenment political architecture, in particular to its symbolic moment, because even when it is described as operating ideologically, it is said to do so by appealing to premodern, irrational, or erroneous representations.[69] For that reason, existing critical tools, which are assemblages of the interpretive episteme, are useless for designing an intervention that describes how raciality operates in modern representation. Let me elaborate this argument with an exploration that tracks how the determinative tools of the Racial operate within the interpretive framework in the production of the logical circle. This move first requires that I take a detour and discuss the frames of the political within which racial subjugation fails to make sense.

69 See generally Ferreira da Silva, "No-Bodies."

"the other no more than itself"

> Thus the relation of the two self-conscious individuals is such that they prove themselves and each other through a life-and-death struggle. [...] And it is only through staking one's life that freedom is won; only thus is it proved that for self-consciousness, its essential being is not [just] being, not the *immediate* form in which it appears, not its submergence in the expanse of life, but rather that there is nothing present in it which could not be regarded as a vanishing moment, that it is only pure *being-for-self.* The individual who has not risked his life may well be recognized as a *person,* but he has not attained to the truth of this recognition as an independent self-consciousness. [...] Its essential being is present to it in the form of an 'other,' it is outside of itself and must rid itself of its self-externality.
>
> —Hegel, *Phenomenology of Spirit*

When Foucault asks, "Can the phenomenon of war be regarded as primary with respect to other relations (relations of inequality, dissymmetries, divisions of labor, relations of exploitation, et cetera)?" he does so in the context of an approach to power that focuses on "relations" and "techniques" of domination and the production of subjects, which are already addressed by a power relation.[70] However, what is at work, he states, is "the manufacture of subjects" and not "the genesis of the sovereign," that is, the figure of juridical power.[71] That being the case, it becomes all the more surprising that Foucault chose to keep racial subjugation as part of his analysis of sovereignty—state racism and its task to preserve racial purity—instead of examining the biological as a site of the production of subjects.[72]

70 Foucault, *"Society Must Be Defended,"* 47.

71 Foucault, 46.

72 Sylvia Wynter does tackle the biological as a site of production of modern subjects. Actually, she embraces it—neurosciences in particular—as providing descriptions of the operation of the human mind that are more adequate than the ones provided by the preferred concepts of the interpretive moment, namely, culture and ideology: "*Both* their [the Pygmy and the French] nongenetically determined and their encoded sociogenic masks are demonstrative of [...] a law-likely functioning, nonphysically

Thus he exposes (the limits of) his critique of sovereignty as the limits of his analysis of the modern episteme. Put differently, what he calls juridical(-political) power plays more of a role in the post-Enlightenment political architecture than Foucault (and Agamben) wishes to concede.[73] Not only because of the role the State (the modern sovereign) has played in securing "society" through management strategies designed to meet the needs of capital at different moments. More importantly, juridical power has remained operative through the transition from the classical order to the modern episteme, a "passage"—in its symbolic (social-scientific) moment—that was facilitated by Kant's transcendental, which grounds authority (in knowledge held by a notion of universality) on necessity.

My point is that the twentieth-century account of racial subjugation (the racial dialectic) figures a closed circuit precisely because the terms inherited from the nineteenth century carry an *authority grounded on necessity*. As described previously, this circle becomes evident when one notices that the explanation begins with blackness (*a*) and ends with blackness (*a'*) because the *cause* of racial subjugation is an *interpretive* construct (white persons' prejudice, belief, ideology, or discourse). Moreover, to the extent that these "causes" are *subjective*, they do not express a Subjectivity that actualizes the *transparent I*. Instead, they are constructed as irrational (*natural*) responses to racial (*natural*) difference. How to disrupt this logic? That, I find, would take the shattering of transparency. For if the form that supports

---

and nonbiologically determined behavior-regulatory principle of causality that is neurochemically implemented." Wynter, in "Unparalleled Catastrophe for Our Species? or, To Give Humanness a Different Future: Conversations," in McKittrick, *Being Human as Praxis*, 57–58.

73 Agamben does not consider how raciality produces moral (social) subjects who can be killed (by the sovereign and his subalterns) without exposing the sovereign's position in regard to the "juridical order"; see Giorgio Agamben, *Homo Sacer: Sovereign Power and Bare Life*, trans. Daniel Heller-Roazen (Stanford, CA: Stanford University Press, 1995). That is, the Owner's and the police officer's *authority* to kill black people is, as the majority opinion in *Dred Scott v. Sanford* states, "morally lawful."

critical and radical versions of the modern political text cannot comprehend racial subjugation because its attribution of causality renders the *transparent I* a mirror that returns blackness as the *cause* of its effects, a figuring of the political is needed that does not rewrite the text as relations in the form of a dialectic, which is but the unfolding of necessity—teleological (Hegel) and eschatological (Marx)—in/as time.[74]

Key to this re/de/composition of the modern political text is how the wounded captive body in the scene of subjugation—at once Human and Thing—fractures the post-Enlightenment ethical scene of value precisely because she indexes blackness and whiteness as *juridical* positions established by title. Juridically delineated, her silhouette exposes the blind spot that historicity (interiority/temporality), in its phenomenological and social-scientific renderings, instituted in twentieth-century critical thought. Through that cut, that is, blackness read as a referent of captivity (and of forced entertainer and forced worker), the total violence characteristic of the Colonial (as a mode of domination) erupts in an interpretive composite. It thus disturbs the apparent tranquility enjoyed by Humanity as an ethical descriptor and by Subjectivity as a sufficient descriptor of the post-Enlightenment social (*moral*) subject.

Let me elaborate how the wounded captive body in the scene of subjugation exposes and sutures this cut, following Hartman's account in *Scenes of Subjection* of how and why *a black Subjectivity* is not retrievable from historical records of enactments of slavery's scenes of total violence—in particular, her comments on how attempts at gathering empathy for the captive (black) person necessarily replace them with the free (white) person, and the captive body is released from any immediate connection with a self-consciousness and its *world*.[75] In other words, the Slave has no commitment to function as a historical

---

74 As indicated above, Foucault's rendering of the "discourse of race" does not help in this work, because his formalist yet fully interpretive approach does not allow for addressing the authority element of sovereignty operating through scientific signification.

75 Hartman, *Scenes of Subjection*, 17–48.

signifier in accounts of the trajectory of the United States as a *society* (nation-state) and of black US American persons as *social* subjects, that is, as constituting a racial group. A poignant expression of this break is how the in/distinction between the scene of enjoyment (of the play of representation) and the scene of punishment (of the acts of violation), especially in accounts offered as a benevolent humanizing gesture (designed to generate empathy), rendered the distinction between fungibility (just as) and dignity (greater than).

Both sets of comments invite consideration of the juridical and ethical elements presupposed and supported by the ontological descriptor Subjectivity, and its ethical correlate Humanity, that would come to rule twentieth-century thought. First, Hartman shows that *humanizing* gestures, the ones that seek to generate empathy by accentuating suffering, rest on a presumed equation of whiteness and Humanity, and she stipulates that the latter alone can successfully mobilize feelings (of sympathy) through the recognition of a common plight. What is also at work there—as Hartman registers when arguing that this articulation of black suffering also performs the work of racial domination—is what makes the Slave (the whole person) available for *appropriation*: the authority the Owner enjoys, as his title over the Slave permits him to decide how to use his property. From this perspective, there is nothing like a Subjectivity (even as white/European/transparent) emerging in this scene, a self-consciousness not mediated by another self-consciousness (which seems to be the point in deployments of Hegel’s lord-and-bondsman passage in accounts of slavery). In fact, it is an effect of its juridical position, where the authority to use the whole captive person (mind-body) rests.[76] What

76 In an interview, Hortense Spillers elaborates on the implications of her argument regarding the centrality of violence in slavery. In particular, she observes how that violence would not be concentrated on black persons who are descendant of slaves but would infuse the whole of the United States’ “ethos.” Excerpts of this recorded interview are featured in a film I made in collaboration with Arjuna Neuman, *Soot Breath / Corpus Infinitum* (2021).

I find here is an interrogation of the figures that would rule the interpretive moment, Subjectivity (ontological) and Humanity (ethical). Such interrogation, then, necessarily confronts the *world* of Husserl's self-consciousness (the first person [the *transparent I*] in both its natural and pure modalities) with the wounded captive body on which its authority is inscribed.

Her wounded flesh, that mark of *authority*, interrupts the movement of substitution (the logical circuitry) precisely because it asks the question: What grounds the authority to violate the mandate—Locke's divine mandate for self-preservation, that demand from the body politic for the protection of life and limb[77]—on which all other modern ethical and juridical forms rest, including liberty and sovereignty? Retracing, as noted in the previous chapter, the movements of Spillers's unraveling of what she calls an "American grammar," my argument follows Hartman's suggestion to delink the captive body from anything that would be named a Subjectivity. (I have in mind, not solely but definitively, sociological and anthropological renderings of the *subjectum*, as these knowledge projects go about explaining/interpreting, respectively, a black *social world* and African *lifeworlds*.) What I find in Hartman's arguments, however, is the exposure of how the transformation of racial difference—from a determinative tool into a (natural) datum and/or (historical/moral) residuum to be studied through an interpretive apparatus—had two reproductive effects. On the one hand, by retaining the prior determinative link between bodily traits, organic forms and functions, and mental (moral and intellectual) attributes, the interpretive methods of twentieth-century anthropology and sociology occluded how determinacy (necessity as it functions in scientific universality) already operated (let's say, as the very perception of racial difference). On the other hand, and through the same move, these interpretive methods occlude how, insofar as blackness is a historical referent (of slavery), it also signals how, in the colonial political architecture, the

77 See generally Locke, *Second Treatise on Civil Government.*

authority of the subject of liberty was held by the force of necessity (as it operates in juridical universality).[78]

Of the many consequences one can surmise, I highlight how the juridical relation that the wounded captive body in the scene of subjugation cannot but recall brings the very notion of Humanity under scrutiny. For this relation reminds not to take for granted that Humanity stands alone. Since its inception in the late nineteenth century, Humanity requested the articulation of a view of racial difference that would prevent it from undermining the extractive and expropriative mechanisms that supported post-Enlightenment Europe's comforts. Two situating moves are unavoidable. First, it is necessary to ask how the juridical notion of *liberty* and its ethical correspondent *dignity* remain primary descriptors, even as the human conditions of existence they describe depended on the captivity and fungibility of the Slave. Second, it is important to attend to how the tools of raciality encompassed and transfigured the colonial juridical mechanism in such a way as to hold back the contradictory nature of the claim to *dignity*. Both moves, I propose, will inevitably expose necessity working in the underground/background, ensuring that the noted contradiction—that is, of liberty (freedom) being enabled by a juridical relation (of the most violent kind)—remains veiled in the relay, that is, through circuitry of substitutions for the juridical by the *moral* (ethical) and the economic by the *natural* (scientific).

What repeats in this circle is the returning of the *cause* and *effect* of violence to the black person, as Douglass commented in 1881, as it places the *cause* for its occurrence in her body. Because its juridical conditions of possibility are displaced by the capacity of the (logical) principle of identity to occlude mediation, the relay between scientific and ethical (which gives the joint operation of the symbolic and the ethical moments) is

78 It may be necessary to recall here that the position of the subject of liberty is occupied by any white person and not only the Slave Owner, as discussed in the previous chapter, because of the correspondence between whiteness and ownership and blackness and captivity.

propitiated by the rendering of the double meaning of evidence. This occurs through a substitution facilitated by the rendering of *equality* in the format of *identity*, where the sign = (equal or equivalent) manages the return by turning *equal* into *the same* or *equality* (equivalency) into *identity*. In both cases, it is important to recall that the "truth" (validity) of the statement of both identity and difference rests on the force (of necessity) that supports analytical moves, that is, the fact that they stand in themselves, supported by their internal elements, without the need for external proof or evidence.

This is precisely because the specific ethical attributes of Man and Humanity, *liberty* and *dignity*, respectively, have been articulated to signal their difference from the Negro (the person as also Commodity)—and not, as one would assume, in its departure from feudal ethical forms; the buying and selling of persons was not a distinguishing aspect of Feudalism. Even a cursory review of philosophical statements that dismiss the Negro will show that all they state is an absence, a lack of the intellectual capacities to entertain the ethical (universal) principles that figure Humanity. In that context, the Negro (the commodity) is not presented as the *negation* (having attributes that compete with and threaten white persons) but as the *negative*, that is, a Human existent, a person who lacks what is specific (*unique*) to the white person (the Owner, trader, or overseer). Thus the Negro is described as Human without any of the traits specific to those who embody the modern ethical constructs, that is, Man/Humanity. It took less than a hundred years for the scientists of Man to try to find ways to fix this (to determine this difference with the tools of the Science of Life) by means of assembling a scientific object, namely the (organic) human body, whose forms and functions accounted for the mental (moral and intellectual) attributes that distinguish the human. Only after the Human body, as an organic existent, comes under the scrutiny of transcendental reason would blackness (of the Negro), as an *object* (that is, a product of the tools of scientific reason) be apparently released from the signifying hold it shared with whiteness.[79] Even this construction, however, has not tamed blackness, as the movement of substitution it has allowed can at any point be stopped, and the *negative* can be released to shine as *blacklight* on the limits of the ethical accounts it supports, which it both signifies and maintains.

That capacity manifests when the *juridical* figure of the wounded captive body in the scene of subjugation recalls the distinction between the economic and the ethical scenes of value through the notions of fungibility and dignity—qualities assigned to the Thing (as Commodity) and the Human, respectively. For what she does, as the Negro, as an existent that is neither/both Thing nor/and Human, is to allow for the simultaneous appreciation of both senses of value: on the one hand, because she refers to equivalence, her fungibility (being commodity) recalls the economic scene of value; and, on the other hand, because she (negatively) refers to excellence (Human incommensurability), her lack of dignity recalls the ethical scene of value.[80] Exploring the gap between these four terms (fungibility/equivalence and dignity/excellence) returns the

---

79 The concept of the racial produces both the white body and the black body as surfaces of signification of mental (moral and intellectual) attributes. For the whole argument, see generally Ferreira da Silva, *Toward a Global Idea of Race*.

80 My rendering of the term fungibility differs from Hartman's primarily because I am retaining it in the economic scene. In her rendering, Hartman takes this economic signified into the ethical scene, where it supports her powerful critique of abolitionist discourses:

> Yet empathy in important respects confounds [John] Rankin's efforts to identify with the enslaved because in making the slave's suffering his own, Rankin begins to feel for himself rather than for those whom this exercise in imagination presumably is designed to reach. Moreover, by exploiting the vulnerability of the captive body as a vessel for the uses, thoughts, and feelings of others, the humanity extended to the slave inadvertently confirms the expectations and desires definitive of the relations of chattel slavery. In other words, the ease of Rankin's empathic identification is as much due to his good intentions and heartfelt opposition to slavery as to the fungibility of the captive body. (Hartman, *Scenes of Subjection*, 19)

attention to raciality's work as a political/symbolic tool, to its primary function, that is, to produce irreducible, unsublatable difference among human collectives.[81] There is no question that Blackness as a category figures the person as an object, that as a category of knowledge it cannot but produce objects or index existents and events as particular expressions of the workings of the "laws of nature," that is, of exterior determinants. My interest here, however, is not in whether this effect of objectification (Commodity or Object) can be overcome or, put differently, whether what is fungible can become noble, or what is articulated as equivalent can be reconstructed as excellent. What this pairing allows me to highlight here is how fungibility, a gift from the wounded captive body in the scene of subjugation, renders blackness as a referent of other sets of laws, the juridical laws of the polity, whose import remains in that correspondence between fungibility and property, of which Hartman reminds us.

Fungibility (the economic signified), an attribute of the Slave, hosts a disruptive potential that dignity (the ethical signified) cannot undermine, which is collapsing the separation of their respective scenes of value—the economic and the ethical. An unsettling possibility in the post-Enlightenment political architecture, it risks becoming actual when one examines how raciality only performs the task it does for interpretive knowledge because its tools, like the concept of ethnicity, retain necessity as it operates in scientific signification. Exploring this requires mapping the underground of the field of knowledge that produced the tools involved in preparing names such as ethnicity and stereotype, to name the two that Spillers deploys in her analysis of social-scientific signification. That move, however, must be more than a description. It must turn each and every piece of it inside out and upside down, beginning with that which has supported Humanity's claim to specificity (transparency, dignity, etc.) vis-à-vis everything else in the

81 For this argument, see Ferreira da Silva, *Toward a Global Idea of Race*, 115–52.

world or in Nature, namely linear temporality or sequentiality as it operates within historicity.

What figuring of racial subjugation avoids the limitations of sociological explanation and of the interpretive moment in general? My choice is a re/de/composition of the racial dialectic, a repurposing of the mirror effect (described previously) that renders blackness the cause (natural) and effect (moral deficit) of conditions of existence that express economic expropriation (slavery, segregation, incarceration) and juridical domination (whipping, lynching, police brutality). Here is the same figure from the previous section, but now I have replaced skin color (black) with the captive body.

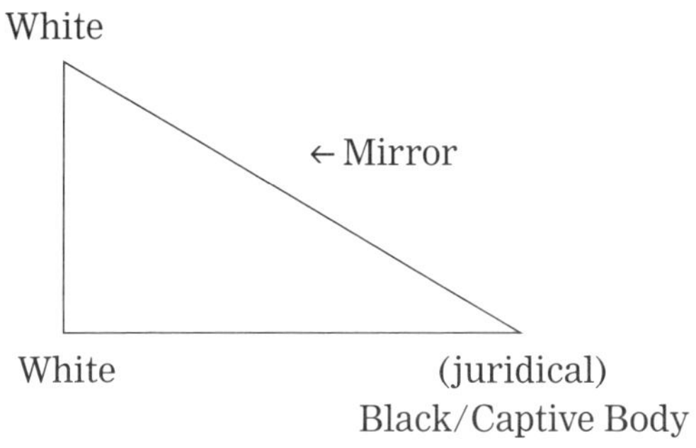

Recall how, when I re/compose the racial-dialectic triangulation by adding the key to sociological explanations—that is, the subjective white element that is always also presented as out of place, a residuum or an error—it becomes evident that the sociological/phenomenological explanation of this particular “natural attitude” is that the circle is created—that is, blackness becomes the cause of blackness—because somehow blackness functions as a mirror that returns whiteness to itself but distorted. Even those who would otherwise exhibit their universalist beliefs before blackness become “racist” (particularist), as the explanation goes. That distortion, however, is not accidental. I read it as the signal that the wounded captive body in the scene of subjugation is left out of the sociological version of the scene of subjugation (the racial dialectic).

Let me now map the wounded captive body onto the political architecture, by releasing it as an incident of blacklight shining into the ethical corner, which distorts the mirror, fractures transparency, requires a shift of the order of presentation. This takes two moves. The first move is simple but has a significant impact. It requires that one begins with blackness, but instead of reproducing the triangle, the captive body doubles it.

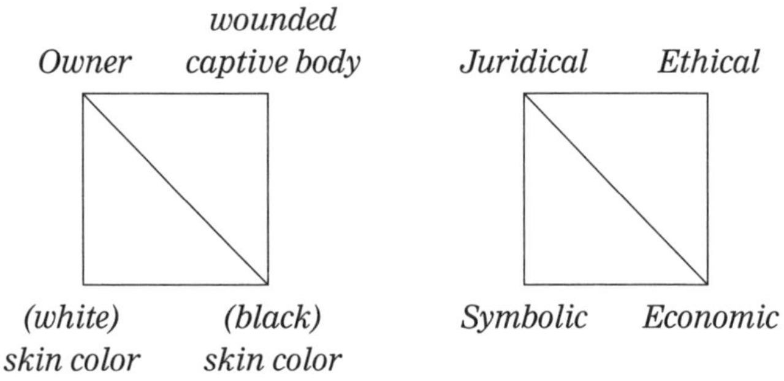

The second is not straightforward: shining as blacklight into the ethical corner, the wounded captive body no longer mirrors the white person's unbecoming ideas and actions; instead she shatters the mirror to expose the juridical and economic moments of the "race relation" as well as how the mirroring is just an effect of the symbolic. What is figured here is the wounded captive body in the scene of juridical subjugation, that is, outside but addressing the interpretive scene of representation—and much in the same way as Hartman describes in the scene of subjection—it signals exorbitance (the excess of violence given by the title form) and absence (the opaqueness of an im/possible interiority/temporality that remains unavailable). That *wounded captive body*—as excess—is not the same as the white body, not because of racial difference and what supports scientific signification, but because they occupy different positions in the juridical scene of subjugation. Blackness also returns whiteness in this register, but returns it as authorized violence. That captive mind—opaque—is not the same as the white mind, not because of racial difference (moral deficit) but because, in the juridical scene of subjection, the interiority (as the play and playground of desire) of the Slave is irrelevant. Total violence is threatened or deployed to contain her will (the moment of expression), to force her to perform her role, to force her to express obedience.[82]

What the wounded captive body immediately does is to recall whiteness as a referent of the Owner and the authority to deploy total violence—as the dead body of the unarmed black person killed by police officers recalls the authority of the State—thereby reinscribing the juridico-economic relation. This re/de/composition is simple and immediate because the wounded captive body in the scene of subjugation recalls History without historicity. As a historical referent of the Commodity, it recalls a juridico-economic feature (Slavery) of the modern political architecture; however, it does not refer to Subjectivity (because her juridico-economic conditions refer to what preceded its ontological ascension). To the extent that hers is a scientifically inscribed body, even in the nineteenth century—and marked with symbolic investments, as Spillers notes—it is so only in the moment of justification for juridical domination (enslavement), and therefore also as a juridical entity.[83]

"elevating disruptions"

> My argument starts with the historical reality of commodities who spoke—of laborers who were commodities before, as it were, the abstraction of labor power from their bodies and who continue to pass on this material heritage across the divide that separates slavery and "freedom." But I am interested, finally, in

---

82 My reading of total violence is inspired by Georges Bataille's analysis of political economy and wealth as "excess energy," which I see as extracted through total violence. In particular, I have appropriated his view of excess energy and repurposed it to consider the material capacity hosted by the wounded captive body as a capacity whose intensity (as figured in high-frequency blacklight) muddles and cuts through the mirror.

83 Studies by Josiah C. Nott and Samuel G. Morton, American apologists of slavery writing in the early and mid-nineteenth century, would have great influence on the development of the project of the Science of Man in the second half of the century.

> the implications of the breaking of such speech, the elevating disruptions of the verbal that take the rich content of the object's/commodity's aurality outside the confines of meaning precisely by way of this material trace.
>
> —Fred Moten, *In the Break*

Legal title afforded the Owner the authority to beat the Slave to death, to destroy her body, but it never assured him the capacity to fully appropriate her mind or the certainty of controlling it. Each and every lash that reaches her skin has the peculiar intensity that comes from knowing there is no limit to the consequences of the beating, but there is a limit to what the beating can achieve. What has happened to it? Where have all these wounds expressed as pain turned into sound, transduced flesh, gone?[84] Nowhere, if considered from a cosmic perspective; that pain turned scream—haptic rendered sonic—continues to reverberate as sound but also as quantic *elementa* (particle wave/matter energy) in the high frequency of blacklight and the high pitch of the trumpet. Transducing also, I propose, describes how the wounded captive body in the scene of subjugation distorts transparency—of the subject's mirror. For how else to describe the process and the operation of what Moten calls blackness, or "the extended movement of a specific upheaval, an ongoing irruption that arranges every line," point, atom, quark, photon, neutron, and so on. Transducing depicts the "resistance of the object"—the scream transduced flesh that transduced into blacklight—in the doubling of the triangle that distorts the interpretive effect of the determinative tools that assembled it. Thus it is the activation of blackness, "the phonic materiality of

84 The conversion of sound into electrical energy has been considered by researchers seeking alternative energy sources. It is made possible by the transducer, a device designed to operate this transformation called transduction—a process that is much simpler than the device. For instance, when a transducer is employed to locate something in water, it captures the pressure waves (sound) that bounce back (echo) when striking something, which the transducer converts into electrical energy.

such propriative exertion" toward the dissolution of the racial dialectic, of its terms, and of the *world* it reproduces.[85]

The wounded captive body in the scene of subjugation returns blacklight, a transduction, that is, an expression of flesh as unrepresentable pain turned radiation, as it recalls the intensive and extensive accumulation of phonons and photons—over five hundred years of extraction of land and expropriation of (the flesh and blood of) bodies that compose global capital. It may be evident by now that the description of the political architecture of the global present I am gathering here does not presuppose or privilege relations. Nor does it return to the theme of sovereignty—as that would basically remain in the terrain of the *transparent I*, that is, the post-Enlightenment figuring of *transparent* self-consciousness as the only self-determining thing. The wounded captive body in the scene of subjugation reflects Dana's predicament in both Rufus's and her present. Her wounded (marked and raped) body, as well as her shrieks—and the love and terror she might and does feel—echo from without the sociological scene but also—as *elementa*—from within every tiny little particle (of signification and exchange) that constitutes the world to which it is applicable, the world in which the racial dialectic makes sense.

By now it may be evident how the racial dialectic renders Dana and the "subprime" borrowers the owners of a debt that is not theirs to pay in the same way it renders the murdered unarmed black person responsible for their killing. For it produces a figuring of *social* relations in which the ethical position of the Other, as in Hegel's passage, emerges in violence. Not, however, in the life-and-death struggle of the lord-and-bondsman presentation of the scene of subjugation. Both positions are four times politically delimited—*scientifically* (racial difference/natural), *ethically* (nonuniversal principles such as prejudice, beliefs, ideology), *juridically* (Owner and Slave Person), and *economically* (Slave Owner and Slave Labor)—since black persons are

85 Fred Moten, *In the Break: The Aesthetics of the Black Radical Tradition* (Minneapolis: University of Minnesota Press, 2003), 1.

descendants of Slaves, as indicated by last names and skin color. Hence they do not express/actualize the *transparent I*: the figure of the other self-consciousness (and in the context of Hegel's text, both self-consciousnesses are others) does not constitute pure being, for both are racially (scientifically) determined. My point is: unlike Hegel's dialectics, where two self-consciousnesses confront each other on purely speculative grounds, here both positions are politically (symbolically, ethically, juridically, and economically) established. This is something that becomes evident at once, after showing the triangulation that both hides and hosts the circle—*a*→*b*→*a'*—surrounding it. It is important to recall here that *b* is hidden precisely because it is not of the order of scientific explanation—but the ethical argument that white people's ideas remain subjective, their own, interiorized, the most that can be expected is to educate them out of these ideas. In any event, the key for this unraveling is to recall how the image of the Other that racial knowledge manufactures is an effect of a double violence, namely the juridical (total) violence that ensures colonial expropriation (of lands and persons) and the scientific productive violence of the tools of modern knowledge that transubstantiate colonial expropriation into a natural/moral deficit (in the Kantian formulation of Nature as conformable to the laws of function of the understanding), that is, a racial deficit.

That Foucault and other European critics in the interpretive regime have not attended to this may be because they intuitively know how racial subjugation threatens their condition of possibility, namely, the very possibility of a pure (and yet historical) self-consciousness able to submit the *world* (as whole, including other humans in it) to phenomenological reduction, whether it is framed substantially or formally. Before the racial event can gather the fragments of interpretive thinking scattered with her activation, the wounded captive body in the scene of subjugation brings the intensity corresponding to the possibility of falling under total violence. She throws blacklight on the excess that instituted her, shattering its most fundamental constituents.

"completely out of my mind"

> "Oh? Then maybe somehow …" I left my voice trail away as my thoughts raced ahead of it fitting things together. The state was right, and the time, the unusual name, the girl, Alice …
>
> "Maybe what?" prompted Rufus.
>
> Yes, maybe what? Well, maybe, if I wasn't completely out of my mind.
>
> —Octavia E. Butler, *Kindred*

Faulty perception, or the seeing, touching, smelling, tasting, or hearing of something that is not real; is it not there or here? Of course Dana thought she was hallucinating. How could her person (mind-body) move instantaneously from mid-1970s Los Angeles to the Weylins' farm in rural antebellum Maryland? But she did. And because she did, it was not a hallucination or a dream. Her ancestors Rufus (Owner-father) and Alice (Free Black mother) were there in the same place, at the same time. She could talk with them, smell them, touch them, hear them. They were real. She was real. And that violates the laws of Thought—or does it? It does, of course. And it also doesn't, obviously. For the presumed contradiction, in the impossibility of a person meeting their ancestors by traversing spacetime, only holds because we think of the body as a solid extended (organic) thing; the *object* of classical physics prevails in our imagination. That renders Dana's travel through spacetime, if it is not a hallucination or a dream, incomprehensible. But if we think of Dana as a person, a cishetero black woman, who, having just moved into her new house in mid-1970s Los Angeles, is yanked out of that moment (time-place) in order to save the life of her Owner-ancestor, we may have a clue for grasping both how the racial dialectic is sustained and how it might be unraveled.

Let me begin with how the wounded captive body in the scene of subjugation figures *existence* without the forms of Space and Time. How she makes it possible to consider what has happened not as something that falls back, behind, in the line of time, but as something operating virtually, both as a possibility before it takes place and as a reality, something that has taken place and is and remains accessible as such (something that is not to come in spacetime). For that to be contemplated, it is necessary to expand our *image of existence* beyond the limits imposed by Galileo's, Newton's, and Kant's Nature as well as Husserl's and Heidegger's *world*—that is, as something that is more than only a matter of the conditions for knowledge that has certainty or objective validity but also beyond the Kantian idea of Nature as conformability with the laws of logic. Such an *image of existence* attends to the cosmic and the quantic, for instance, as one in terms of untemporality (cosmically, that is, all that has happened in the moment of the Big Bang continues to happen on the outer edges of spacetime) and unspatiality (quantically, that is, as the basic components of everything that existed, exists, and will exist are the same particles formed in the initial moment of the Big Bang).

When considered from a cosmic and quantic perspective, Dana's spacetime travels are no longer impossible, for there is no reason to think that the quantic components of her body in 1970s Los Angeles could not be immediately and instantaneously linked with (because they are exactly the same as) the quantic components of the body of the woman who reappeared and repeatedly saved Rufus's life, and vice versa.[86] If the "laws of thought" are thus suspended to make it possible to contemplate Dana's travels as both cosmic and quantic, a whole range of possibilities for thinking become available. When what happens and what exists are approached as matter (raw material), the distinction between *a*, *b*, and *a'* loses its sense, and with it the primacy of the principle of identity/equality (and its correlate, the law of noncontradiction). From a cosmic perspective, antebellum Maryland and 1970s Los Angeles exist in the same cosmic instant, and that indistinction renders it possible for Dana to coexist in

86 This is a reference to quantum entanglement, described earlier. What I am highlighting here is the immediate and instantaneous connection between two particles that have been in contact at some point in spacetime. I am suggesting that Dana's trip may be possible because of the same operations (not yet known by physicists) that render entanglement.

both moments simultaneously and find herself moving from one to another instantaneously.

What this would result in is, among other things, a violation of Kant’s mapping of Quality—as a kind of Judgment (Affirmation, Negation, Infinite) and a Category (Reality, Negation, Limitation)—that is, rendering the distinction between Affirmation and Negation and between Reality and Negation irrelevant, because it (the distinguishing, that is, the determining gesture) would not be able to rely on the presumption of separability and sequentiality. Put differently, affirming that Dana exists simultaneously (as a re/de/composition of quantic *elementa*) in both the past and the present (in 1970s Los Angeles and 1830s Maryland), it cannot be affirmed that she exists only in the past or only in the present, and it also cannot be negated that she exists only in Maryland in the past or only in Los Angeles in the present. All that can be said is that Dana (as a possibility) exists in both moments (past and present). For if sequentiality and separability hold, this is a violation of the principle of non-contradiction, which supports the distinction that A is (reality) and A is not (negation) and the statement that A is something (affirmation) and A is not something (negation). However, even if separability and sequentiality hold, Dana’s existence in both spacetime moments does not violate the distinction that A *is only* something (Limitation) and A *is not* something (Infinite). This is so because, according to Kant, the third elements—such as Infinite and Limitation in regard to Quality—are applications of the combinations of the first and the second, which are not merely derived but request “a particular function of the understanding” because they do not follow in all instances of combination.[87]

To conclude, it is a matter not of determining whether or not Dana exists but of making a statement in regard to the possibility of her existing. Hence, the qualitative form of judgment is relevant—that is, when I say that A is a non-something, or if I say that Dana is nonexistent in 1970s Los Angeles or that she is nonexistent in antebellum Maryland—I make no positive

87 Kant, *Critique of Pure Reason*, 65.

statement on where Dana is an existent. There is no correspondent to where she exists or does not exist; she is just a nonexistent in these two spacetime moments; more importantly, I am not affirming or negating that there are existents in these places and times and that Dana might be an existent in other places and times. Both Dana and whoever does exist remain undetermined; all I will say is that Dana is one that does not exist, the *negative* (NON-antebellum Maryland existent) but not *negation*, that is, I do not say that Dana is NOT the one that exists in antebellum Maryland.

***

What renders Dana's immediate and instantaneous trips to the Past and the East Coast unreal is the fact that they violate sequentiality (the line of time, the sense that it flows and that what has happened precedes what is happening or what will happen) and the separability of space (that two bodies or events cannot occur simultaneously in the same location). To be sure, Dana's travels violate linearity (as sequentiality and separability): from one second to the next she goes from her house in Los Angeles in the 1970s to the Weylins' kitchen in Maryland in the 1830s. Her travels violate the most basic law of logic, which is the principle of identity (both "A is A" and "A is not A" cannot be true at the same time): in regard to time, the violation is that each trip to the past makes it her future, that is, the trips violate sequentiality; and in regard to space, the violation is that the immediacy of the move from Maryland to Los Angeles suggests that these places coexist within the limits of her house, which violates separability. Neither is possible: slavery happened either in the past or it happened in the future, and her house is either in Los Angeles or in Maryland. Both cannot be true, real. It is improbable.

Unless, alternatively, one ignores the laws of logic for a moment and contemplates the possibility that Dana's travel is not spatiotemporal but material. That would violate Kant's definition of Time as a formal (pure) intuition—"in respect to all phenomena, consequently of all things which come within the sphere of our experience, it is necessarily objective”—but not his statement that “if we abstract our intuition of ourselves and all external intuitions [...] and consequently take objects as they are in themselves, then time is nothing.”[88] Such a move would require two further departures from the Kantian program: first, and most fundamentally, it would demand the release of *existence* from knowledge, address humans as existents, that is, as things *of* the world and not as things that experience the world, and vacate any concern with the in-itself (which he says does not concern knowledge) of anything, including humans; and second, it would demand the release of matter from form, which for Kant is what is in play in knowledge. Released from modern philosophers' preoccupation with avoiding having to ask about the relation between *determinacy* and *finality*, as well as from their reliance on *formality* and *efficacy*, matter does not have to be submitted to the laws or forms of logic. If one agrees with Kant, matter (if it is anything other than phenomena already comprehended by the pure intuitions of space and time) is of no interest to (and hence is also not contingent on) determinative (and, I add, interpretive) thought and its conditions of possibility, in particular the *I Think*.

88 Kant, *Critique of Pure Reason*, 31.

CHAPTER 3
“a foreign language”

> "What's the use of saying all that? And how can you be married to him?"
>
> "Rufe, how'd you like people to call you white trash when they talk to you?
>
> "What?" He started up angrily […]. "I am not trash!" he whispered. "You damn black …"
>
> "Hush, Rufe." I put my hand on his shoulder to quiet him. […] "I didn't say you were trash. I said how'd you like to be called trash. I see you don't like it. I don't like being called nigger either."
>
> He lay silent, frowning at me as though I were speaking a foreign language. Maybe I was.
>
> "Where we come from," I said, "it's vulgar and insulting for whites to call blacks niggers. Also, where we come from, whites and blacks can marry."
>
> "But it's against the law."
>
> "It is here. But it isn't where we come from."
>
> "Where do you come from?"
>
> —Octavia E. Butler, *Kindred*

Name-calling never went away. Though now, if explicit, it is called stereotyping and profiling. If not explicit, when what is used as an insult is a description of the effect of the injury—in phrases such as "welfare queen," "gangbanger," "deadbeat dad"—it is called "racial code." Dana could have told Rufus about how different things are where/when she comes from, but she knows that they are not that different. It is not easy to say how, but it does, however, happen that blackness functions as an indicator of an economic and juridical situation. A high percentage of black residents in a neighborhood indicates that the cost of housing there will be lower than in one with no or few black families. High incarceration rates work the same way, but in the other direction; a black population will show a higher percentage of persons incarcerated under indicators such as location, age group, income, or educational level. Dana wondered if it were indeed true that the language she was speaking was foreign; even if it was true, it made it no less astonishing that no white person back in the mid-1970s seemed to realize that how things were for black folk had to do with how things were then/there in the southern United States in the 1830s.

How different was it really? she asks herself. Perhaps it makes a difference that she knows that she can tell Rufus not to use the N-word. What else? Enslavement, incarceration—what is the difference? The amount of evidence of the extent of the control the criminal justice system has over the black population in the United States is overwhelming.[1] In 2019 the unemployment rate among black Americans (6.2 percent) was almost double the national average (3.6 percent).[2] Statistics tell only half of the story, and, in doing so, they become part of the problem. How to correlate the number of lashes a person's ancestor received 190 years ago with their likelihood of being unemployed in July 2020? Or being in the criminal justice system? Or dying of COVID-19? The difference, as Dana knows, is that then/there Rufus and other Owners would rather not exercise their right to kill or let a Slave die; they would rather have them working in the field than immobilized by too many lashes—though sometimes it was worth it for one of them to lose a few days of work rather than let a clear breach go unpunished. The difference: a police officer does not think twice before shooting to kill a black person, whereas then/there the overseer had to take into account the Owner's economic needs before maiming a slave.

With the abolition of slavery, it became no longer legal to buy, sell, or hold a black person as chattel; however, perhaps Dana even wondered if that meant that the Owner passed on to the United States (its state and city governments) his/her authority to employ total violence as a mechanism for subjugation. Here/now the state has no interest in repairing the economic dispossession generated through enslavement, and it seems to have no need for its black citizenry to uphold its authority[3]—for

1 For instance, as the NAACP registers, "one out of every three Black boys born today can expect be sentenced to prison." "Criminal Justice Fact Sheet," NAACP, accessed June 9, 2021, https://naacp.org/resources/criminal-justice-fact-sheet.

2 Bureau of Labor Statistics, U.S. Department of Labor, "Unemployment Rate Unchanged at 3.6 percent in May 2019," *Economics Daily*, June 12, 2019, https://www.bls.gov/opub/ted/2019/unemployment-rate-unchanged-at-3-point-6-percent-in-may-2019.htm?view_full.

3 The United States derives its authority from liberty, the very principle that did not involve its black population until (well)

neither self-interest nor legitimacy plays a role in regard to the position of black persons vis-à-vis the state. If racially defined *authority* is over life and death—the liberty (right) to buy a person and kill them—and if it only operates in combination with an economic or an ethical demand, and if the ethical demand is racially defined, then all that is left is economic interest. If the state has no economic use for the black person—other than as incarcerated labor—then there isn't really a reason for keeping alive those not yet caught by the criminal justice system, is there? If she thought that way, most likely Dana would not have liked to. So many black persons were thinking that way in California in 1976.

What was it that Dr. King wrote about the "solution to poverty"? "Guaranteed income"? That was in his book *Where Do We Go from Here?*, published in 1967, a year before he was assassinated. That was after the uprisings in Watts and Detroit, that was after it had become obvious that freedom alone was not enough, that freedom—as black persons had known for about one hundred years—could never be enough. Perhaps Dana would also have wondered if Malcolm X would agree with her interpretation. He too cried for freedom. Not freedom that was given—for him freedom given is no freedom at all. Perhaps, like Stokely Carmichael (later Kwame Ture) and Charles Hamilton, he too knew that there is no real freedom without economic self-determination.[4] The Black Panther Party for Self-Defense declared, "We want freedom," but also, "We want an end to the robbery by the capitalists of our black community," and, "We want an immediate end to police brutality and murder of black people."[5] That was also in 1967. Perhaps now Dana understands

---

nearly two hundred years after the Declaration of Independence, when one recognizes that the Voting Rights Act of 1965 also did not provide a guarantee of enfranchisement.

4 Kwame Ture and Charles V. Hamilton, *Black Power: The Politics of Liberation* (New York: Vintage), 1992.

5 See Jeremy Vernon, "The Black Panthers' 10-Point Program," Black Power in American Memory, April 18, 2017, http://blackpower.web.unc.edu/2017/04/the-black-panthers-10-point-program/.

how the police and capitalists are linked. She didn't nine years before. Existing then/there with Rufus, as his property, being treated like a slave, Dana glimpsed the reasons why the police were the new overseer and the prison the new plantation. If blackness = captivity, if the captive's only legal act is to create wealth for the captor, refusing to produce wealth or no longer doing so must be a crime: to be black and free is to rob whites of the wealth they might extract from you.

Is that the reason why Dana found herself back then/there? Was she born captive even if her year of birth was 1951, less than two decades short of the centennial of Juneteenth? Or was it because she and Kevin had moved into a house, their house, her first valuable property? If existing in the 1970s as a black person in the United States is still to exist as property—and police brutality is just the most dramatic (because definitive) reminder that one's life belongs to someone else—then it is no longer the Owner but the State that now claims a life-and-death authority over black persons. If not even the right to vote assures the protection of black lives by the state, what to say about acquiring property? What is Dana's inheritance? What does it mean to have Rufus and Alice as ancestors? What have they left her? What does she owe (to) them? Rufus left her the impossibility of ignoring the prospect of poverty. Alice left her the certainty that the surrounding wealth, including the house she had just moved into, had been possible because of the labor beaten out of Slaves then/there. What else? Is it possible to exist in the world without always being reminded of this double inheritance—the one that took everything away and the one that remains in everything that was taken?

However these questions are answered, regardless of how they are formulated, Dana, like other descendants of Slaves, knows them all too well, perhaps because she is never allowed to forget that this double inheritance is not a paradox. It is not nonsense. Having everything taken away and yet remaining in everything that has been taken is a long way of saying that this is an unpayable debt. "Slave labor" is the flesh and blood of capital because labor is nothing more than the transference of that which composes flesh and blood, the elemental components of everything, any and each possible and actual existent. Until our descriptions of existence take this as the point of departure, critical descriptions of the global political architecture will presume that everything that matters originated in and reflects post-Enlightenment white Europe. Since anything can be traced back there, these descriptions will be unable to account for how much that which matters only does so because it is but the materialization of what has been extracted from everywhere else.

“racial capitalism”

> As a material force, then, it could be expected that racialism would inevitably permeate the social structures emergent from capitalism. I have used the term “racial capitalism” to refer to this development and to the subsequent structure as a historical agency.
>
> —Cedric J. Robinson, *Black Marxism*

> Racism is, thus, not only a problem for blacks who are obliged to suffer it. Nor is it a problem only for those sections of the white working class and those organizations infected by its stain. Nor can it be overcome, as a general virus in the social body, by a heavy dose of liberal innoculation. Capital reproduces the class, including its internal contradictions, as a whole—structured by race. It dominates the divided class, in part, through those internal divisions which have racism as one of its effects. It contains and disables representative class institutions, by neutralizing them—confining them to strategies and struggles which are race-specific, which do not surmount its limits, its barriers.
>
> —Stuart Hall, “Race, Articulation, and Societies Structured in Dominance”

If blackness operates as an economic indicator, it is not only because it recalls juridical authority—as in the State’s decision to segregate, to exclude, to allow expropriation, and to incarcerate, though all of these have economic consequences. If blackness returns economic dispossession, it is because it refers to coloniality and slavery as juridico-economic contexts. And, that being the case, the Colonial (as the political setting for the Slave as well as the Native) must be relevant for comprehending what the operating of this tool of the racial tells us about the workings of State Capital in the global present. That most critiques of Capital do not take this operation of blackness into account, as I have indicated, signals something akin to the blind spot, the mark of departure discussed in the previous chapter. If the blind spot left by a fourfold departure lagged virtually unnoticed in the *ethical* substratum of the figure of Subjectivity, here I find it inscribed in the *symbolic* (social-scientific) assembling of Capital as a totality (an internally ordered unity), which requests both the expected determinative procedures (operated by Labor as a Category) but also (historically presented) delimitative statements that produce, respectively, its inner and outer layers. The source of much of the difficulty in addressing racial subjugation resides in precisely how Marx assembled the concept of capital under the nineteenth-century episteme. Let me highlight two aspects. On the one hand, much like the interpretive versions of the analytics of raciality, which disavowed their determinative inheritance but kept (un-critiqued) its main product (racial difference) as datum or residuum, interpretive versions of historical materialism also disavow determinative (scientificist) approaches. However, on the other hand, the interpretive versions of historical materialism retain the Category of Labor as the determinative tool, which assures unity to the concept of capital, without considering how its elevation to this role as a scientific tool could be related to the extra-scientific aspects, such as juridical and ethical ones. Before tracing the latter and more significant aspect to the original presentation of the historical-materialist text as a symbolic (social-scientific) arsenal, I situate it in regard to how this inherent demand for unity troubles interpretive historical-materialist attempts to address racial subjugation—resulting in the writing of the Racial (and its referents) as anterior and/or exterior to the conditions of existence encompassed by Capital.

Why it is so difficult for the historical-materialist text to comport racial subjugation as an object of analysis may become less elusive if it is tackled at a metaphysical moment, that is, in terms of the demand for unity made by Labor's overall explanatory function. To do so, I return to conversations that started in the 1960s and 1970s that directly dealt with how racial subjugation rendered unity an especially difficult demand to identify because it is a given requirement for determinative approaches and interpretive versions of historical materialism. I approach these conversations through Stuart Hall’s and Cedric Robinson’s classic engagements with historical materialism’s limited (critical) capacity to deal with racial subjugation. Though it could be said that Hall’s position is hopeful, that it bets on the possibility of reconciling the demands of the interpretive regime, and Robinson’s is not, their approaches do share some crucial characteristics. For one thing, both advance a critique of Marxism’s inability to grasp racial subjugation, whether as a critique of its ideological workings or as a descriptor of politically situated (culturally differentiated) collectives. They also agree that racial subjugation is intrinsic and operative in the modern liberal capitalist architecture but does not quite fit within its framework, owing to aspects interior to or constitutive of the historical-materialist text. When considering these factors, both recall the presumption of *unity*, which, confronted with the demand to address the Racial, becomes a problem. Each, however, delineates the problem in a distinct domain: Hall’s “formal” approach emerges in his mapping of the relevant literature, in which he distinguishes between two modes of describing the social (structures and categories); in Robinson’s “historial” approach, it appears in his tracing of the separate trajectories of two emancipatory traditions, namely Western European and Afro-American.[6] Evidently, both approaches successfully describe the problem within the limits of their choices, with respective consequences: for Hall, this incapacity is due to the fact that each concept, Capital and the Racial, corresponds to a distinct modality of subjugation that becomes a problem (under the demand for unity) for the investigation of postcolonial political contexts where both modalities operate; Robinson renders it

6 “Historial” is a term Nahum Chandler employs to capture W. E. B. Du Bois’s rendering of African American historical experience, as “one that must be made, or always, originarily, remade, anew.” Chandler, *X—The Problem of the Negro as a Problem for Thought*, 34.

an effect of the scientific determinative role of the Category of Labor (and the whole framework it sustains) and the fact that historical materialism's critical scope does not reach its own cultural conditions of emergence. In short, for Hall, reconciling the Racial and Capital as concepts only becomes a problem in postcolonial social conditions, which is solvable with an analytical framework that yields a hybrid totality of sorts; in Robinson, the analytical unity performed by Labor's limited (determinative) task provides a partial account of capitalist social conditions. What interests me, however, is that when advancing these arguments both interpretive thinkers expose how the difficulty in addressing racial and colonial subjugation has to do with historical materialism's own constitution as a political/symbolic (social-scientific) arsenal—which only admits these modes of subjugation as anterior or exterior to capital.

In *Black Marxism*, Robinson takes on the problematic of economic reductionism, and argues that Marxism fails to account for the workings of "racialism" because the latter constitutes its conditions of emergence. The classic study offers a powerful deployment of the sociohistorical approach to the understanding of (historical) self-consciousness. Of relevance here, for Robinson, is the ignored fact that racialism's hold of Western European consciousness since feudal times remained operative in capitalism's economic arrangements and the celebrations of "rationalism" and "scientism." Hence, Robinson conceives of consciousness as the crucial (historical) element for the conditions of emergence and operations of Marxism (as a radical social theory) and how "racialism" (as a social organizing principle) operates within it.

There are two sets of corrections. On the one hand, there are the limitations of privileging the economic, and the related issue of the dismissal of culture, as well as the significance of "historical consciousness" for "class consciousness," which becomes more evident in Marx's and Engel's (but also later in Lenin's and Luxemburg's) dealings with the national question. From this interpretive perspective, Robinson advances two arguments relevant to any consideration of how the racial and the colonial function with/in capital. First, there is the twentieth-century question regarding the possibility of revolution in general, and outside Europe or North America in particular. Tackling it as a problem posed by the determinative core of historical materialism, and placing the problem of unity at the level of theoretical construction and separability (between what falls under the economic and what falls under the symbolic), Robinson notes that Marxists missed the fact that "the consequences of the hegemony of capitalism, that is, the social and political reactions to capitalism have seldom held to those contracted by a logic bound by the 'laws of capital.'"[7] Second, beyond calling attention to the significance of the historical (cultural), which is crucial to his racial critique of historical materialism, this perspective also support Robinson's identification of another radical tradition outside Europe, as well as a Black Radical Tradition that is coetaneous with slavery and colonialism. His interpretive proposition consistently places the foundations of this Black Radical Tradition in African culture and not in slavery or post-abolition social conditions.[8] Historicity also explains how the Racial figures under Capital, as he argues that a consequence of racialism's operations in "Western conceptions of society" was that it would "both as ideology and actuality [affect] the class consciousness of workers in England."[9] That cultural/ideological aspect has analytical consequences in terms of the assembling of the concept of capital.

On the other hand, Robinson highlights the crucial error of restricting "slave labor" to the moment of "primitive accumulation," that is, to "some 'precapitalist' stage of history," hence not

---

7 Cedric J. Robinson, *Black Marxism: The Making of the Black Radical Tradition* (Chapel Hill: University of North Carolina Press, 2000), 62.

8 Robinson, 2.

9 Robinson, 3. In Robinson's usage, racialism, one of the "ordering ideas that have persisted in Western civilization," refers to "the legitimation and corroboration of social organization as natural by reference to the 'racial' components of its elements. Though hardly unique to European peoples, its appearance and codification, during the feudal period, into Western conceptions of society was to have important and enduring consequences." Robinson, 2.

a part of capital's self-constituting processes.[10] The mistake of the materialist interpretation of history (as a "dialectic of capitalist class struggles") was, according to Robinson, Europe's self-conception, a historical fiction, which ignored both geographical (colonial expropriation of labor and lands) and historical (feudalism's racial beliefs) determinants of capitalism.[11] Robinson's typical interpretive approach focuses on historical (cultural) elements, which leads all too quickly to considerations of anteriority and exteriority.[12] For instance, Robinson's argument regarding the anteriority of racialism relies on it being an "ordering idea," an organizing (ideological or cultural) principle inherited from precapitalist Western European culture that focuses on physical differences. Not racial difference but racial differentiation is, for him, what is *anterior*, that is, a fundamentally European practice insofar as its political activation is concerned.[13] In any event, the

---

10 Robinson, 4.

11 "Capitalism was less a catastrophic revolution (negation) of feudalist social orders than the extension of these social relations into the larger tapestry of the modern world's political and economic relations. Historically, the civilization evolving in the western extremities of the Asian/European continent, and whose first signification is medieval Europe, passed with few disjunctions from feudalism as the dominant mode of production to capitalism as the dominant mode of production. And from its very beginnings, this European civilization, containing racial, tribal, linguistic, and regional particularities, was constructed on antagonistic differences." Robinson, 9–10.

12 Incidentally, my argument here appears similar to Robinson's. Regardless of whether it is or not, the most relevant difference might be the fact that mine is not an interpretive but a figurative move. I am not interested in framing blackness in terms of self-consciousness, Subjectivity, or another interpretive figuring of the *transparent I*, or even as an *affectable I*. I am interested in how blackness can collapse the totality that is capital and open the way for a more complex account, not so much of economic extraction and expropriation, but of political subjugation in general.

13 Robinson's argument is similar to Robert Park's and Oliver Cox's, and is close to Foucault's. What these three have in common is that they do not attend to how the scientific rendering of the notion of race has rendered it a modern signifier, with effects that go beyond ideological ones, precisely because it is inscribed in the liberal institutions and constructs ruled by universality.

problem of unity is raised and resolved with the Racial being adequately placed in its moment, namely, the symbolic. Labor, the leading tool in the historical-materialist arsenal, retained its capacity to assemble capital as a unity, but it no longer accounts for the kind of historical subjects (self-consciousness) it yields, because that requires the deployment of the Racial in order to capture both class consciousness and black (and Indigenous) self-consciousnesses.

Taking a different route by primarily addressing the limitations of the historical-materialist theoretical edifice instead of its historical (cultural) conditions of emergence, Hall's classic 1980 essay "Race, Articulation, and Societies Structured in Dominance" provides a mapping of the theorizing of "racially structured social formations,"[14] in which he identifies an "economic" and a "sociological" tendency. Each, he argues, has a "logic" identified with either the category of class or the category of race.[15] On the one hand, there is the approach that "take[s] economic structures and relations to have an overwhelming determining effect on the social structures of such social formations,"[16] including its symbolic (ideological or cultural) moments, where "racial distinctions" operate. On the other hand, in the sociological tendency "race and ethnicity as specifically social or cultural features" are the focus. At the core of this discrepancy is the question of accounting for how racial difference organizes postcolonial contexts and explains two of its distinguishing economic traits, namely (past) slavery and

---

14 Stuart Hall, "Race, Articulation, and Societies Structured in Dominance," in *Black British Cultural Studies: A Reader*, ed. Houston A. Baker Jr., Manthia Diawara, and Ruth H. Lindeborg (Chicago: University of Chicago Press, 1996), 16.

15 I would frame such a distinction in terms of the difference between the determinative and the interpretive episteme. Hall's framing of the problem of unity suggests that much; however, he frames his review of major works on the issue in terms of the then classic theme of whether the economic is the sole determining moment, if it is the determining factor in the last instance, or if other dimensions also play a determining role in the constitution of capital.

16 Hall, 17.

(present) underdevelopment.[17] By using the social categories of class and race, and not the economic Category of Labor, to distinguish these approaches, Hall signals how the presumption of unity raises a problem in regard to racial subjugation, which interpretive historical-materialism thinkers take as related to the appropriateness not of its determinative procedures and tools but of the scope of capital as an economic concept.

Addressing the problem of unity directly, with separability operating in the delineation of the *empiricum*, Hall's analysis of the literature takes it as indisputable that the Racial and Capital, as concepts, refer to distinct political architectures, with the former being directly related to the Colonial. Hence, he approaches the abovementioned discrepancy through a mapping of the debates about whether the historical-materialist framework applies to postcolonial political contexts.[18] Hall's concern is primarily what could be called an adequate, non-economicist, non-reductionist, complex historical-materialist approach, one able to account for how racial and ethnic elements operate in (post)conquest, (post)colonial configurations.[19] He finds Gramsci's and Althusser's formulations of the thesis of the "relative autonomy" of the "superstructural" (ideological or cultural)—with its "specific function in securing the conditions for the extended reproduction of capital"—promising in terms of supporting a theory of racism "capable of dealing with both the

17 At stake here are the difficulties in reconciling the two most important conceptual frameworks available for explaining the workings of capital in the (post)conquest and (post)colonial settings of the Americas, the Caribbean, and South Africa. Hall, 18.

18 Though this seems an archaic debate, as will be discussed later, it remains central in current left approaches to the racial (as it works through cultural difference), which insist in rejecting its significance to the analysis of global capital, dismissing it as an ideological tool of neoliberalism or a leftover of premodern social arrangements.

19 That is, it focuses on "the emergent theoretical problem of an articulation between two modes of production, structured in some relations of dominance," which he terms "the more generative new theoretical development in the field, affecting the analysis of racially structured social formation." Hall, 33–34.

economic and the superstructural features” of postcolonial contexts.[20] Expectedly, for his is also an interpretive enterprise, the issue of the determination of self-consciousness is not directly addressed in Hall’s effort to approach racial subjugation as premised on the “historical specificity of racism” while remaining within the conceptual and theoretical field of historical materialism.[21] Instead, the problem is posed as one of complexifying the original presentation of the historical-materialist framework while at the same time giving racism enough explanatory room (within the economic structure and the symbolic superstructure). If read in the context of the Sociology of Race Relations discussed in the previous chapter, it is not difficult to see how the interpretive (“sociological explanation”) remains dominant in Hall’s solution. Here, however, it is in terms of the class structure, which is complexified owing to the coexistence and articulation with (in postcolonial societies) a precapitalist symbolic moment, that is, Racial (ethnic or cultural) forms.

Nonetheless, in Hall’s interpretive solution to the problem of unity, the Racial remains *exterior* to the economic moment. Through the notion of social formation, it is kept in its proper, relatively autonomous (symbolic) place, where, in the guise of racism (as a cultural or ideological mechanism), it facilitates capital accumulation by creating divisions within the proletarian class. In other words, while capital’s reproduction of class—and

---

20 Hall, 48, 50.

21 Hall’s instructions:

> One must start, then, from the concrete historical “work” which racism accomplishes under specific historical conditions—as a set of economic, political, and ideological practices, of a distinctive kind, concretely articulated with other practices in a social formation. These practices ascribe the positioning of different social groups in relation to one another with respect to the elementary structures of society; they fix and ascribe those positioning in ongoing social practices; they legitimate the positions so ascribed. In short, they are practices which secure the hegemony of a domination group over a series of subordinate ones, in such a way as to dominate the whole social formation in a form favorable to the long-term development of the economic productive base. (Hall, 52–53)

its internal contradictions—is "structured by race," the latter remains exterior because, among other things, it is "not present, in the same form or degree in all capitalist formations: it is not necessary to the concrete functioning of all capitalisms."[22] In short, racism becomes a historical (Colonial) residuum that facilitates capital accumulation in the (post)colonies.

Taking different routes, Robinson and Hall indirectly deal with the problem of unity (inherent to any object of analysis conceived as a totality or a system), which is among the most general twentieth-century problems of the historical-materialist text inherited from the determinative episteme. Things become extremely complicated and elusive because the presumption of unity would require that a proper historical-materialist approach to racial subjugation integrate the concepts, such as the Racial and Capital, each referring to a different kind of unity of multiplicity—qualitative or quantitative, respectively. From the same starting point, the assumption that racial and cultural difference constitutes a datum/residuum extraneous to modern liberal-capitalist polity, each assembles a highly sophisticated way out of the muddle by highlighting a distinct aspect of the historical conditions of emergence (Robinson) and the theoretical architecture (Hall) of historical materialism. They seek to identify why historical materialism cannot comprehend racial subjugation and support racial emancipatory projects (Robinson) and how it could provide an appropriate account of the economic dimensions of racial/global subjugation (Hall). Nevertheless, this attempt is sabotaged by guiding assumptions that raise the problem of unity, as they imply that what is under investigation is part of an order (which is composed of minor orders) whose internal differences can be ascertained with the application of the principle of identity, which carries the force of necessity. Basically, these guide post-Enlightenment studies of the social under the assumptions that (a) *social* phenomena, like natural phenomena, are diverse and accessible (and follow the law of specification, which gives separability a metaphysical

22 Hall, 53.

aspect) to the Understanding and are always already determinable by it. Since the social has been defined primarily as the moral dimension of collective existence—whether through the historical or the social-scientific renderings of the concept of the cultural—specific forms of consciousness are presumed, and “material conditions” (institutions, practices, etc.) actualize and produce this particular consciousness, which is yet to be determined. And (b) finding such forms would provide the key for bringing about social transformation, including the revolution and the end of racial subjugation. A double gift of post-Enlightenment thinking, which instituted the symbolic moment by postulating both the possibility of *comprehending* Nature (which in the nineteenth century would also include the Human) through the (scientific) unity of the conceptions of the Understanding and the postulate that humans (as figured by the notion of culture, as in Hegel’s spirit of a people) find (historical) unity expressed in their “material conditions.” Both of these assume the *I Think* as the fundamental epistemological (Nature/*world*) and ontological (Human) figure, and in doing so, they also assume a *formal* (given by concepts) *or final* (given by principles) *identity/equality* between Nature/*world* and the Human mind.

What I am highlighting is that the problem of unity, which haunts but never reveals its full outline in historical-materialist considerations of racial subjugation, derives from the metaphysical assumption that what can be comprehended shares in the same form (formality) or purpose (finality) as that which does the comprehending, in this case, the tools of reason, as they operate in scientific or historical signification. If a unifying category or principle, a *conceptum*, is not found or turns out to be insufficient, as Hall shows in the case of historical-materialist economic orthodoxy, the move has been either to search for a more comprehensible concept or to assemble an image of the social that supports the operations of disparate and at times contradictory principles. Either way, what is not questioned is the presumption of unity—presented scientifically or historically—and the corresponding unifying concept or principle that captures it. For, as Hall’s effort indicates, these cannot reconcile race (refigured as an interpretive device) and class (in its determinative guise) in a coherent realization of the presumption of unity—and identify the one and only conceptum (function) or datum (empirical descriptor) that governs and specifies the manifold that is collective existence.[23] While there too it leads to problems, the presumption of unity leads to comparatively fewer problems in interpretive frameworks in which the Hegelian rendering of totality presumes the operation of one principle that actualizes in every one of the individual components of the manifold, thereby constituting them as one transcendental self-actualizing (qualitative) unity of multiplicity.

To be sure, the demand for unity does not present itself as a problem for Marx's original presentation of the historical-materialist text. For this symbolic arsenal is constituted through determinative procedures that suture its entrails and the delimitative statements that set aside everything that falls under the Racial as economically undetermined because juridically distinct from what falls under Capital. Put differently, historical materialism's inability to grasp racial subjugation can be better appreciated if one attends to both the determinative procedures and the delimitative statements that circumscribe the domain comprehended by the economic concept of capital. The demand for unity in the post-Enlightenment episteme can be met through a postulation of specificity or identity (qualitative) or through an explanation through equality (quantitative).[24] When deployed

---

23 Even the interpretive versions of the notion of class by Hall's contemporaries and intellectual partners E. P. Thompson and Raymond Williams (all three were founding members of the *New Left Review*), neither of which he cites in his piece, would not resolve this difficulty because, as Robinson evaluates, in regard to the original presentations of the historical-materialist text, they also ignore that the notion of race is a European cultural artifact. See E. P. Thompson, *The Making of the Working Class* (New York: Vintage, 1966); and Raymond Williams, *Marxism and Literature* (Oxford: Oxford University Press, 2009).

24 This allows for an appreciation of the itinerary of the racial in the interpretive regime, in particular how, as discussed in the previous chapter, its transformation into a (moral/cultural) datum/residuum rendered it an irrelevant (at worst) or supplemental (at

in the assembling of a totality, determinative procedures and delimitative statements rely for their validity and intelligibility on the principle of identity (for the latter) and equality (for the former). It is well known that Marx deployed the determinative tools and procedures of scientific reason to produce an account of the capitalist mode of production as a unity, a totality, a function of the Category of Labor—a description of how it allows for the figuring of the *equality* of distinct things. In the case of delimitative statements, the ones that spell out what is qualitatively specific to capital, these have called attention to those critical thinkers who highlight how the historical-materialist text is a specimen of modern thought and/or culture.[25] In this chapter, I will map these two moments of Marx's assembling of the totality that is Capital in order to prepare the stage for the wounded captive body in the scene of subjugation, for it to reflect on Capital and, as blacklight, for it to tear the symbolic membrane of the concept of capital and push its ethical charge in a presentation of the general law of value from which she shatters the intrastructure of post-Enlightenment thinking and expounds the cooperations of the ethical and the economic moment of its political architecture.

Setting the stage for the *wounded captive body in the scene of subjugation* to do her work will take a great deal of preparation, perhaps even more than in the previous chapter, because it will take pinpointing the lines along which she can break the

best) political category. This also indicates, of course, that what most call Eurocentrism emerges in the division of labor among the social sciences as they were instituted in the nineteenth century under the determinative regime and as a response to the interpretive orientation—which would become dominant.

25 In addition to its similarity with Robinson's analysis, my argument here is in line with Gayatri Spivak's reading of Marx, as will be discussed later in this chapter. What distinguishes mine is how I position the wounded captive body in the scene of subjugation as exposing the operations of the juridical and the ethical in Marx's assembling of the economic—she opens up the possibility for thinking of labor (from) without the constraints of necessity and its onto-epistemological pillars and descriptors.

historical-materialist text apart. This preparation includes the commentary in this section on how Robinson and Hall deal with the problem of unity in tandem with the separability it presupposes and reproduces vis-à-vis twentieth-century interpretive approaches that consider historical materialism's incapacity to comprehend racial subjugation. The second preparatory step, in the next section, deals with how determinacy and sequentiality operate in twentieth-century versions of historical materialism that return to the theme of primitive accumulation. After considering the operations of these onto-epistemological pillars in an attempt to resolve the intractability of the Racial and the Colonial, I locate the wounded captive body in the scene of subjugation at the core of the formal construct (the equation of value) through which Marx provides an account of the efficacy of labor as a material (productive) and scientific (analytical) force. There, as *she* appears in that which living labor needs to be applied for capital accumulation to ensue, where the ethical appears as the sole source of economic value, she once again returns the juridical to where it is said to not belong and, in doing so, allows for the contemplation of what becomes thinkable when the entire edifice sustained by necessity crumbles.

"tangle of political violence"

> One concerns the commodity market and the place where surplus value is produced—the factory, the mine, the agricultural estate. Regarded in this light accumulation is a purely economic process, with its most important phase a transaction between the capitalist and the wage labourer. … The other aspect of the accumulation of capital concerns the relations between capitalism and the non-capitalist modes of production which start making their appearance on the international stage. Its predominant methods are colonial policy, an international loan system—a policy of spheres of interest—and war. Force, fraud, oppression, looting are openly displayed without any attempt at concealment, and it requires an effort to discover within this tangle of political violence and contests of power the stern laws of the economic process.
>
> —Rosa Luxemburg, *The Accumulation of Capital*, quoted in David Harvey, "The 'New' Imperialism"

After attending to Rosa Luxemburg's statement that the mechanisms of primitive accumulation, the "tangle of violence and contests of power," are "often hard to determine," with a simple "yet" David Harvey both engages and dismisses the place of these mechanisms in the analysis of Capital *proper*. Agreeing that primitive accumulation is ongoing, he proceeds, "Yet it is omnipresent in no matter what historical period." To be sure, this statement sets up his point that the deployment of these "violent mechanisms"—supported by the State—"picks up strongly when crises of overaccumulation occur in expanded reproduction, when there seems to be no other exit except devaluation"; that is, the "tangle of violence" operates when capital accumulation as usual cannot go on.[26] Almost imperceptible in this gesture, which rehearses Marx's writing of primitive accumulation as a sort of economic "state of nature," is how it also recalls perhaps the most intractable aspect of determinative knowledge, which is the presumption of unity (within genus or species), which demands that concepts and categories neatly and flawlessly comprehend, that is, determine the diverse aspects, of datum or the empiricum manifold they were deployed to comprehend.[27] That demand, which Luxemburg's quote indicates, is especially difficult to meet in regard to situating what Marx called "the so-called primitive accumulation" concerning the totality determined by

26 David Harvey, "The 'New' Imperialism: Accumulation by Dispossession," in *Socialist Register 2004: The New Imperial Challenge*, ed. Leo Panitch and Colin Leys (London: Merlin Press, 2003), 75–76.

27 Hegel finds this a problem of "the treatment of concepts and of the moments of the concept in general, of the thought determination as forms that are at first different from the material and are only attached to it," which cannot attain truth. This is so because "as mere form, as distinct from the content, such concepts and their moments are taken in a determination that stamps them as finite and makes them unfit to hold the truth which is itself infinite. In whatever respect the true may otherwise be again associated with restriction and finitude, this aspect is the side of negation, of its untruth and lack of actuality, even of its cessation, and not of the affirmation which, as the true, it is." G. W. F. Hegel, *The Science of Logic*, trans. and ed. George di Giovanni (Cambridge: Cambridge University Press, 2010), 17–18.

the "stern laws of economic process," that is, early twentieth-century Capital. What I have in mind here is that the global regions where the "tangle of violence" prevailed were (like the others before) colonially subjugated to European powers, that is, under a modality of juridical domination through total violence.

Not surprisingly, Harvey attends, like Marx and Luxemburg before him, to "primitive accumulation" with the demand for unity in mind—determinative procedures (which suture) and delimitative statements (which outline) that effectuate post-Enlightenment onto-epistemological descriptors, namely determinacy and sequentiality, respectively—which recalls the similar gesture found in the classic presentations of the modern juridical domain. That rhetorical gesture, the tale of the end of the "state of nature," is the description of an anterior but atemporal state of nature, a "tangle of violence" from which rational individuals agree to leave by entering into a contract in which all consent to relinquish their total liberty.

Nearly one hundred years after Luxemburg's death, this economic version of the state of nature appears in Harvey's own rendering of primitive accumulation, safely placing it outside of the moment of proper capital accumulation. When discussing the process of "accumulation by dispossession"—with which he captures the ongoing "predatory practices of 'primitive' or 'original' accumulation within the long historical geography of capital accumulation"[28]—Harvey acknowledges that the "violent mechanisms" that have always been part of capitalism, namely colonial (and imperial) juridico-economic practices and structures, remain operative in the early twenty-first century.[29] Nevertheless his account, like Luxemburg's, presupposes the spatial exteriority of these new sites of capital. These predatory juridico-economic mechanisms, he argues, remain peripheral

---

28 Harvey, "The 'New' Imperialism," 74.

29 In "Marx's general theory of capital accumulation," Harvey argues, "'primitive' or 'original' accumulation has already occurred and accumulation now proceeds as expanded reproduction [...] within a closed economy working under conditions of 'peace, property and equality.'" Harvey, 76.

to the proper process of accumulation, as they are activated as part of historical and spatial "fixes"—"temporal" and "spatial displacements" facilitated by "financial and/or state institutions"—designed to address overaccumulation; that is, they are activated to prevent systemic collapse, resulting in devaluation, thereby explaining how capitalism has survived many crises over the course of its existence.[30] In short, Harvey's "accumulation by dispossession" renders a duality *geographically* (it mostly operates outside Europe and the United States, capital's place of proper reproduction) and *juridically* (it is facilitated by the State's use of its monopoly of violence), which expectedly does not trouble Marx's original assembling of the totality that is capital. For Harvey, accumulation by reproduction continues to rely on "wage labor" until the next crisis hits.[31] My point is: though Harvey is providing a theoretical account of primitive accumulation, his attempt is telling of what I find in the original presentation of the historical-materialist text, which is to keep the "tangle of violence" outside the determination of the proper functioning of capital in the very emphasizing of its juridical nature, that is, in keeping it in a domain separate from the economic, which is the one falling under the concept of capital.

Returning to Luxemburg: her recalling of primitive accumulation made sense within the larger context of deploying the Marxist notion of imperialism to modern nation-states' colonial ventures of the late nineteenth and early twentieth century.[32] At that moment, besides the theorizing of imperialism, there was also the related challenge of accounting for the roles of the state (directly addressed by Lenin) and of the nation and the cultural (directly addressed by Gramsci), in both the relatively newly

30 Harvey, 64, 63.

31 Insofar as it is an imperial practice, accumulation by dispossession results for Harvey, as primitive accumulation in the early twentieth century for Luxemburg, from political conditions (Harvey, 69). This, as we know, is part of the overall shift in the historical-materialist discourse to deal with the state (as Lenin did) and the nation (as Gramsci did) in the theorizing of capital.

32 Harvey, 76.

featured composite Nation-State in Europe and the emerging postcolonies of the Americas and (colonial) Empire in Africa, as well as in the newly acquired lands to the east after the defeat of the Ottoman Empire.[33] What has become of the historical-materialist text as we encounter it in the early twenty-first century reflects the many responses to such challenges related to determinacy (like primitive accumulation) and sequentiality (like the possibility of a communist revolution where capital's contradictions had not matured).[34]

None of these onto-epistemological pillars, or the presumption of unity they are designed to fulfill, as Robinson's and Hall's analyses show, render historical materialism incapable of comprehending racial subjugation. The concepts of the Racial and Capital are products of the nineteenth-century determinative regime. The problem results not so much from how the original presentation of historical materialism ignored how the colonial juridico-economic structures (slavery and conquest) participated

---

33 Nevertheless, even if it did not result in a reconfiguring of capital, the place of the new colonies was not lost to those organized in the struggle against colonial and racial subjugation across the globe. For Du Bois and other black Marxist intellectuals, Caribbean and African intellectuals, and militants, historical materialism offered a framework that both countered intrinsically conservative anthropological and sociological explanations for racial and imperial subjugation and served as a global platform for the presentation of their political project and revolutionary designs.

34 What the many versions of the historical-materialist text have not been able to account for is how, in addition to what Harvey calls, after Henri Lefebvre, "the production of space," the old and new European colonies were also involved in the processes of production and reproduction of capital taking place in Europe and North America. When elaborating on this proposition in the following pages, I am not focusing on the relations between colonial powers and the colonies or even on the actual relations and structures of the colonial context. All I am doing is trying to bring out how both modes of governance, the colonial and the liberal, are part of the post-Enlightenment juridical structures and mechanisms. Another part of this argument is how the racial, operating at the symbolic level, facilitates activations of the colonial (total violence) in a moment where it has seemingly vanished as a mode and infrastructure of governance.

in the accumulation of capital. Instead, it derives from how, as Glen Coulthard has recently recalled, the original presentation of historical materialism is determined by the formulation of labor—namely, "wage labor"—that has a quantitative (time) and a qualitative (liberty) aspect, both of which are (historically) specific to the historical (social) conditions it was designed to explain.[35] While as a category Labor obtains (scientifically) the presumed unity, it does as it is specified (as an economic category) by the principle of liberty in its ethical and juridical figurings—which provide the historical specificity of the "modern bourgeois society."[36]

When the *wounded captive body in the scene of subjugation* guides a re/de/compositional reading designed to unravel Marx's formal presentation of the general law of value, both the determinative and the delimitative statements that gather Capital as a totality. When confronted by *her*, both labor's efficacy (as productive activity) and formality (as an economic category) break apart, for she immediately recalls the colonies and "slave labor"—and in doing so, exposes how the ethical moment supports the determination of capital by the conceptum of labor. With that one movement—which I call *negativation*—she dissembles both the determinative procedures and the delimitative statements that assemble Capital as a totality, with both scientific unity and historical specificity.[37] More specifically, this reading of Marx's presentation of the general law of value—in chapter 7,

35 I am referring to how Coulthard recalls that Marx had no interest in the colonies beyond, as I also note, what the situation there could allow him to say about capital. See Coulthard, *Red Skin, White Masks*, 15.

36 Though it requires delimitations, the presumption of unity is also upheld in determinative frameworks. In these, the assembling of a totality requires the assignation of a category—in this case, labor—that determines each and every component of a set and constitutes them as a (quantitative) unity of multiplicity.

37 Let me recall again that Marx does not design capital as a Hegelian totality. This is a version of historical materialism that is attributed to Georg Lukács. Hence my references to totality retain its primarily quantitative meaning, and it is presented as an effect of the category of labor.

volume 1 of *Capital*—seeks to expose and depose the delimitative and determinative moves that hold this totality together, as they ensure necessity as the ground for the Category of Labor's determinative work. Though I mainly focus on Marx's formulations of labor in general—labor productive of (creating) exchange value—of central importance is how the juridical form of a contract (a referent of liberty) provides the organizing principle for describing properly modern capitalist "social conditions."

Negativation, the movement of this reading, takes three steps, which will be presented in this chapter. My first step is to describe Marx's formulation of labor as a determinative tool, the conceptum that provides the key for comprehending the various aspects of "modern bourgeois society" under the concept of capital. Second, after describing how a quantitative presentation of labor allows for the assembling of the key figure in the determination of capital as a mode of production,[38] the reading turns to Marx's comments on the colonies and "slave labor." Here I track the role of "social conditions of production" in the circumscription of capital, in its specification (or distinction), as an analytical gesture, which I call delimitation. For these comments show how the juridical forms of "wage labor" and private property—both referents of the ethical principle of liberty—are deployed to assemble Capital's membrane without which the claim for historical specificity (as a discrete point of the movement of history) would not hold. In other words, "wage labor" as a referent to a specific moment (social conditions of production) functions as a historical operator, a qualifier that delimits capital and appears in comments on "slave labor" and

38 According to Marx, "The equality of all sorts of human labor is expressed objectively by their products all being equally valued; the measure of the expenditure of labor power by the duration of that expenditure, takes the form of the quantity of value of the products of labor; and finally the mutual relations of the producers, within which the social character of their labor affirms itself, take the form of a social relation between the products." Karl Marx, *Capital: A Critical Analysis of Capitalist Production*, vol. 1, trans. Samuel Moore and Edward Aveling, ed. Frederick Engels (London: Swan Sonnenschein, Lowrey, 1889), 42.

the colonies, without bringing them within the scientifically determined totality. Instead, the "unpaid labor" that prevailed in the colonies remained without capital in the same way as the "predatory practices" that made the land on which they work available. By attending to delimitation, one does not find that which is outside of capital or its opposite, one rather finds that which is not economically identified or determined because it is not comprehensible by a quantitative category. What is delimited might as well be—and I will show how it indeed is—within capital. For limitation, the gesture's descriptor, refers precisely to that which remains undetermined,[39] that is, not that which is *not* (thereby determined as such) but that which is merely *non* (or in the sense I read in Fred Moten's ante-ontological).

Finally, my third step is the activation of the wounded captive body in the scene of subjugation, the ante-ontological black feminist poethical tool—that is, to use Moten's construction, the "ongoing present" of blackness's "common refusal"—to re/compose Marx's equation of value toward assembling another equation, one in which value loses (Human) "difference," along with its capacity to sustain total violence. What results from this dissolving of the outer and inner weavings that assemble Capital as a historico-scientific totality is a collapsing of the distinction between the Colonial and the Liberal polity, that is, through exposing "slave labor" in the very components of the exchange value of a commodity, where Marx says it cannot be. From there, the debris of what is still the most powerful set of tools for the critique of capital, the wounded captive body in the scene of subjugation reminds us that what is before us is not a simple task but a demand for the end of (the) *world* as we *know* it, that is, the restoration of the total value expropriated from the Slave and Native requires an image of *existence* that does not presume linearity and the onto-epistemological intrastructures and political architecture it supports.

---

39 An aspect of Kant's subcategory of limitation—which I will return to later in this chapter—is its correspondence to infinite judgments.

"All the slave's labour appears as unpaid labour"

> In slave-labour, even that part of the working-day in which the slave is only replacing the value of his own means of existence, in which, therefore, in fact, he works for himself alone, appears as labour for his master. All the slave's labour appears as unpaid labour. In wage-labour, on the contrary, even surplus labour, or unpaid labour, appears as paid. There the property-relation conceals the labour of the slave for himself; here the money-relation conceals the unrequited labour of the wage-labourer.
>
> —Karl Marx, *Capital*, vol. 1

Focusing on "slave labor" and "the colonies" imposes considerations of primitive accumulation, regardless of whether one wants it to or not, which is perhaps the most intractable theme that the demand for unity forces on the historical-materialist text. Both Luxemburg's rendering of primitive accumulation and Harvey's accumulation by dispossession offer little for a historical-materialist approach to racial subjugation precisely because of how comfortably they sit within Marx's own framing of the question(ing) of "the colonies" and their place in the production of capital. No matter if one is willing to throw out the proverbial baby (and render labor relations only one significant economic relation among many others)—it seems that for a while Marxist thinkers have been willing to do without the bathwater (economic determination in the last instance)[40]—if one is not willing to let go of the bassinet (the view that capital is primarily an economic formation), the conversation will continue to consist of endless returns to the original text, even if it has nothing to offer to the mapping of how the Colonial and

---

40 Though I am not focusing on relations in this exercise, I agree with Coulthard in that holding on to the concept of class as the only properly political category of the capitalist political architecture is to miss and fail to account for how capital has lived and continues to live off colonial mechanisms of dispossession. Not, however, as Harvey argues, by incorporating new sites, but by redeploying its tools of total and symbolic violence to further its control over Indigenous lands. See generally Coulthard, *Red Skin, White Masks*.

the Racial are constitutive of the post-Enlightenment political architecture. As I am experimenting in this chapter, such an approach must begin with unweaving the threads that hold Capital together. Toward doing so, I have designed a reading strategy that allows me to pursue the three registers of deployment of the conceptum of labor—the economic, the ethical, and the juridical—that gathers capital in Marx's original presentation of the historical-materialist text.

With the guidance of the wounded captive body in the scene of subjugation, my reading cuts through this historico-scientific totality precisely because, as indicated in the previous section, it cannot but recall the threads of the "tangle of violence" that Luxemburg states conceal the "laws of the economic process" that determine capital. Luxemburg's thesis on primitive accumulation is helpful because it is an attempt to adjust the account of capital to accommodate Imperialism in the early twentieth century. That move is exemplary of how historical materialism can only deal with the "predatory practices" that have been so crucial to the emergence and workings of capital, which obtains its global nature from the outset through a re-elaboration of an aspect of the historical-materialist text that does not fundamentally alter the labor/property pair at its core.[41] In her account of how "the colonies" constitute sites of primitive accumulation governed through total violence, Luxemburg manages to maintain the integrity of capital as a totality through a separation of proper capitalist production and reproduction from primitive accumulation, or "the travails by which the capitalist mode of production emerges from a feudal society."[42] This she accomplishes with the deployment of cultural difference as a datum. In her account of the second phase of colonialism, which she names imperialism, she draws from the then current anthropological descriptions of

41 Like Harvey, Luxemburg found that primitive accumulation never ceases to take place: in order to appropriate the means of production and labor power to create a market, capital relies on the state for the deployment of total violence and extreme taxation.

42 Rosa Luxemburg, *The Accumulation of Capital*, trans. Agnes Schwarzschild (London: Routledge Classics, 2003), 345.

the "others" of Europe, in particular the term "natural economy," under which she categorizes "feudalism" as well as "primitive communism" and "patriarchal peasant economy."[43] That is, her articulation of primitive accumulation combines two specimens of determinative knowledge, namely the historical-materialist text and the analytics of raciality, rather coherently, as the the products of the latter enter into the analysis as a datum. This move allows for conceptual innovation, even if it is limited, for it must keep the constitutive separation between what is to be determined through the thesis of capital accumulation that attends to what is interior to proper reproduction and what is anterior (now racially and/or geographically presented) as part of primitive accumulation.

As I said before, the task here is to re/de/compose the original presentation of capital by identifying how labor and property function in its composition as a totality. Doing so has consequences that open up a discussion that goes beyond its significance for a critique of the critique of capital. I am aware of the possibility but have no intention to foreground or preempt these consequences; I simply ignore them here. All I am doing, in short, is reading the statements that assemble capital as a (formal-historical) totality. Fortunately, because this totality is held by a given juridical form of the relation between labor and property, and because (as Marx, Luxemburg, and Harvey concede) capital has from the start always relied on a "tangle of violence" and "predatory practices," the wounded captive body in the scene of subjugation—as a referent of both the labor-property relation and the "tangle of violence"—is an excellent guide for the unraveling of capital. After reading Marx's statement, in a text that precedes *Capital*, that labor is the proper analytical tool for the scientific description of capital, that is, the Category of Labor, which is a determinative tool of knowledge, I proceed with a reading of how Marx specifies that which labor explains, that is, of statements that establish what does not belong to that totality. In other words, the delimiting statements that provide the

43 Luxemburg, 349.

outline of that totality by stipulating what in contemporaneous and linked sites of economic activity and kinds of labor—namely, the colonies and "slave labor"—renders irrelevant empirical ("in reality") and/or analytical (categorial) statements on Capital.

"labour as such"

> Indifference towards any specific kind of labour presupposes a very developed *totality* of real kinds of labour, of which no single one is any longer predominant. As a rule, the most general abstractions arise only in the midst of *the richest possible concrete development, where one thing appears as common to many, to all*. Then it ceases to be thinkable in a particular form alone. On the other side, this abstraction of labour as such is *not merely the mental product* of a *concrete totality of labours*. Indifference towards specific labours *corresponds to a form of society in which individuals can with ease transfer from one labour to another*, and where the specific kind is a matter of chance for them, hence of indifference.
>
> —Karl Marx, *Grundrisse* (italics added)

Far away, and apparently exhausted, are the debates on subsumption, determination in the last instance, and even overdetermination.[44] And while the Global South/Global North pair has replaced core/periphery in common language, world-systems theory seems to have become part of today's everyday vocabulary. Few seem to remember that Immanuel Wallerstein intended the concept of the "world-system" to describe a totality of sorts.[45]

---

44 I will not cover these debates here; my discussion of Hall's and Robinson's interventions earlier in this chapter gives a sense of what I find relevant in these debates for the analysis of racial subjugation.

45 Major works that have developed these concepts include: Immanuel Wallerstein, *The Modern World-System: Capitalist Agriculture and the Origins of European World-Economy in the Sixteenth Century* (New York: Academic Press, 1974); Andre Gunder Frank, "The Development of Underdevelopment," *Monthly Review* 18, no. 4 (1966); and Fernando Henrique Cardoso and Enzo Faletto, *Dependency and Development in Latin America*, trans. Marjory Mattingly Urquidi (Berkeley: University of California Press, 1979).

It remains, however, almost impossible to begin a conversation with most contemporary left European thinkers about the relations between the Colonial, the Racial, and Capital that does not stop at some version or another of the "tangle of violence" and primitive accumulation. When asked why, the only answer I can concoct, which may already have been anticipated, is that it is due to a combination of the pervasiveness of the racial dialectic in the interpretive "common sense" and historical materialism's lack of capacity to address colonial/racial/global subjugation.

As long as it is ignored and remains unchallenged how the historical-materialist text and the arsenal of raciality were both assembled under the determinative regime and have been refigured under the interpretive regime, both will maintain at their core the foremost post-Enlightenment ethical figure, the *transparent I*, intact. For these and other reasons that are important but perhaps too lateral to mention, I turn to the wounded captive body in the scene of subjugation and her capacity to challenge both Harvey's geographical separation and Luxemburg's anthropological separation between that which is an expression of the "laws of the economic process" and that which is a "tangle of violence." Precisely because she figures labor and property in the mode of governance characterized by total violence, as Marx and Engels describe the colonial juridico-economic modality, here too she can fracture the mirror effect (of the *transparent I* figured as "wage labor") that renders capital a ("mental" and "concrete") totality. Without the pretension to come up with a new reading of Marx or the commitment to not misread him, I can start from anywhere. My choice is the famous third section of the introduction to *Grundrisse*, "The Method of Political Economy." Here I am interested in how Marx describes capital as a totality and labor (labor as such) as the simple economic category that, in the "modern bourgeois society," acquires universal interpretive (historical) and determinative (scientific) primacy.[46]

---

46 For a similar reading of *Grundrisse*, see Carol C. Gould, *Marx's Social Ontology: Individuality and Community in Marx's Theory*

What I do in this and the next section is pursue that which determines and that which delimits capital as a *totality*.[47] Using the term totality signals that I am reading Marx's analysis of capital as an application of what he calls "the scientifically correct method," the one that, instead of starting from the population (approached as an abstraction), would "move analytically [...] from the imagined concrete towards ever thinner abstractions" and the "simplest determinations," and from there returns to the population "not as the chaotic conception of a whole, but as a rich totality of many determinations and relations."[48] The concept of capital constitutes an exemplar of such totality since it is "the all-dominating economic power of bourgeois society," as it determines (explains) other economic concepts and kinds of production; it is "the starting-point as well as the finishing-point" of the analysis.[49] Unarguably, while capital names the interpretive-determinative (historical-social-scientific) totality Marx describes, it is both historically and scientifically contingent on another economic category, namely labor. For, as Marx instructs in the quotation that opens this section, the category that David Ricardo proposed as "wealth-creating activity" and Adam Smith further expanded as *the* productive activity (regardless of the particular kind of labor), becomes both the historical descriptor for "the modern bourgeois society" and the scientific key to it as well as to the others that preceded it. "As a rule," Marx instructs further, "the most general abstractions arise only in the midst of the richest possible concrete development, where one

---

of Social Reality (Cambridge, MA: MIT Press, 1980). The similarities primarily regard the view that the *Grundrisse* spells out the method employed in the assembling of capital and that such method writes capital as an analytical totality.

47 I know that by using the term totality I risk being brought into a number of debates and competing readings of Marx. But let me repeat again what I've said above: I am not invested in providing a corrective or innovative interpretation of Marx.

48 Karl Marx, *Grundrisse: Foundations of the Critique of Political Economy*, trans. Martin Nicolaus (London: Penguin Books, 1993), 100.

49 Marx, 107.

thing appears as common to many, to all."[50] In short, labor is the economic category that captures both modern bourgeois society as a specific historical moment and unity (the arrangement or order of relations) and the specific operations of the other economic categories under the capitalist mode of production.

Of interest here is how Marx assembles labor as a determinative tool—that is, as a scientific category that figures necessity, formality, and efficacy, and also describes a particular societal form. Reading Marx's formulation of labor as the key category, that is, the conceptum that comprehends capital as a totality, I identify its operations in four dimensions, namely metaphysical, onto-epistemological, existential, and ethical:[51] (a) *metaphysically*, there is a relocation of (historical) necessity from the (Hegelian) transcendental (figured as self-productive reason) to the material (figured as need); (b) *onto-epistemologically*, the thesis of the universalization of labor—which accords with Locke, Smith, and Ricardo—inscribes it in the unfolding, dialectical movement of material history;[52] (c) *ethically*, productivity is an attribute exclusive to human labor and, as such, it signals liberty, while its universalization (the irrelevance of particular kinds of labor) signals equality; finally, (d) *existentially*, as is proper to determinative constructions of the social, labor is relevant insofar as it is collective activity and plays a role in the configuration of actual conditions of existence.

Necessity and efficacy are deployed, implicitly or explicitly, in each of these operations of labor as social form. Expectedly,

---

50 Marx, 103, 104.

51 The key here is that, for Marx, labor creates capital: "Capitalist production is not merely the production of commodities, it is essentially the production of surplus-value. The laborer produces, not for himself, but for capital. It no longer suffices, therefore, that he should simply produce. He must produce surplus-value. That laborer alone is productive, who produces surplus-value for the capitalist, and thus works for the self-expansion of capital." Marx, *Capital*, vol. 1, 517.

52 Marx's view of labor as *the* productive activity differs from Locke's, Smith's, and Ricardo's, as he explains in the *Grundrisse* and *Capital*. For example, see Marx, *Grundrisse*, 103, 550.

necessity governs Marx’s analysis of bourgeois economic activity the same way it does knowledge production (Kant) and historical production (Hegel): in Kant, it is formal, an attribute of propositions; in Hegel, it is Final, the End and Essence that is Spirit; in Marx, it is material necessity, in the sense of being that which the Human (as a singular or multiple entity) would not exist without. Hence, insofar as necessity renders labor (which is productive in causing an effect upon things it is applied to) in the guise of efficacy, we find that, in the same way that necessity mediates the relations between the object and subject in knowledge (through pure intuition), it mediates, in economic activity (as a human attribute to work on things given by nature), the relations between Capital and labor and labor and Nature. Further, another transformation operating in Hegel’s text—absent in Kant (because of formal mediation)—is the recognition that force (in the confrontation set up in the moments of negation and the negation of negation) is the element that gives the efficacy (relation of cause and effect) that propels Spirit’s self-development.[53] That confrontation, in Marx, turns into the defining relation of class antagonism, which characterizes a fully “developed” mode of production, becoming a descriptor of society. It is the internal propelling force (efficient cause) of historical development that leads to the vanishing of one mode of production as another emerges from its entrails.

What I find in Marx’s version of history as the dialectical movement is again how efficacy, as an onto-epistemological descriptor, secures necessity as grounds for its determinative statements. For it does not matter if the development of

53 Recall that for Hegel the movement of history is the self-actualizing moments of self-confrontation of Spirit through which it learns that what it sees as exterior—space, nature, etc.—is indeed an aspect of itself, which it then sublates. When introducing his “method,” Marx explicitly rejects Hegel’s “totality thoughts” (“the philosophical consciousness”), “for which conceptual thinking is the real human being, and for which the conceptual world as such is thus the only reality.” For him, as we know, society, human beings creating their own conditions of existence out of necessity, is the real subject of history. Marx, 101.

productive forces necessarily leads (*historically or actually*) to the replacing of one mode of production with another. What matters is the necessity (*analytical*) of a link between a specific mode of production and specific productive forces—a link given by the fact that the development of productive forces inescapably leads to the emergence of another mode of production. Put differently, that which in Newton's physics arrives at universal laws of motion here gives an account of the universality of material production in human history, that is, efficient causality governs the linear movement (development) of history in the same way as it does (develop) knowledge (in Kant's correction of Newton). Efficacy governs all renderings of labor as a conceptum: (a) *metaphysically*, the production of conditions of existence; (b) *onto-epistemologically*, universalization occurs because of the very process of material production that changes conditions of existence, leading to the disappearance of particular kinds of labor and forcing displaced and dispossessed individuals to sell their labor power; (c) *ethically*, the production of material existence is an expression of (natural) necessity whose capacity marks the Human (liberty), and the prevalence of "wage labor" marks the historical moment of (juridical) equality; and (d) *existentially*, universalized labor (as abstract human productive capacity) makes capitalist production possible and, therefore, it is a formalization of the Human as a historically (dialectical movement) and scientifically (categorial comprehension) determined collective, the one that is also the key to capital's destiny. Put differently, labor as a symbolic (scientific) tool comports with the other moments—productivity (economic), liberty and/as equality (ethic), and property and/as liberty (juridic)—of the post-Enlightenment political architecture. And thus it provides the key for deciphering the assembling of capital as a totality, because it is deployed to articulate what falls under the concept of capital in each of the above moments, that is, it signals both what is historically (specific to) and scientifically (determinative of) capital, that which renders it unlike any other mode of production. In Marx's framing of capital, labor operates as a *conceptum*, that is, at once an *economic* category (measure), an *ethical* signifier (the *idea* of the human's self-producing capacity, that is, self-determination or liberty), and a *juridical* form (as “wage labor”). This de/compositing of labor into its modes of operation as the category that sutures capital as a totality is crucial because it allows for the appreciation of the historical-materialist text’s inability to address racial and global subjugation.

“by supposing a primitive accumulation”

> The accumulation of capital pre-supposes surplus-value; surplus-value pre-supposes capitalistic production; capitalistic production presupposes the pre-existence of considerable masses of capital and of labour-power in the hands of producers of commodities. The whole movement, therefore, seems to turn in a vicious circle, out of which we can only get by supposing a primitive accumulation (previous accumulation of Adam Smith) preceding capitalistic accumulation; an accumulation not the result of the capitalistic mode of production, but its starting point.
>
> —Karl Marx, *Capital*, vol. 1

> *Not only the category, labour, but labour in reality has here become the means of creating wealth in general, and has ceased to be organically linked with particular individuals in any specific form.* Such a state of affairs is at its most developed in the most modern form of existence of bourgeois society—in the United States. Here, then, for the first time, the point of departure of modern economics, namely *the abstraction of the category ‘labour,’ ‘labour as such,’ labour pure and simple, becomes true in practice*. The simplest abstraction, then, which modern economics places at the head of its discussions, and which expresses an immeasurably ancient relation valid in all forms of society, nevertheless achieves practical truth as an abstraction only as a category of the most modern society.
>
> —Karl Marx, *Grundrisse* (my italics)

Excruciatingly tight, Marx’s assembling of capital as a totality does not allow for the kind of reversal and repurposing—here I have in mind moves such as Foucault’s refashioning of Kant’s rules (of cognition) and Chandler’s recuperation of Derrida’s desedimentation (to locate the para-phenomenological core of black thought)—that trouble the core of otherwise conceptually secure philosophical devices.[54] Seeking to get away with the obvious (because expected and always already dismissed) challenge designed in this book, it seems appropriate to start from a strategically naive question: How did Marx manage to keep the colonial context out of his assembling of capital? Asking this question, I am not suggesting that Marx should have integrated the colonial context or that he could have done it without impeding the assembling of capital as a totality. My argument here does not presume that an error has been made nor the perpetration of an unwarranted exclusion. As I said above, the construction is flawless, beautiful even. It is, however, a composition, an assemblage that, being so, can be re/de/composed. Arguably there may be many ways of doing so. For this exercise, I have chosen to focus on the outer layer (the membrane) and the inner weavings that support the concept of capital both scientifically (analytically) and historically—that is, capital as a totality (a singular ordered manifold) that can then be deployed (as an interpretive presupposition or an analytical tool) in the explanation of certain aspects of the post-Enlightenment political architecture. I will begin with the membrane, that outlining of capital's specificity—rendered in juridical and ethical terms—in statements on property and labor that Marx made when commenting on "the colonies" and "slave labor."

Reading *Capital*, we find explicit and implicit statements that comment on the colonial context—under the terms "the colonies" (conquest and settlement) and slavery (slave trade and slave labor)—with descriptions meant to convey why they do not fall under the concept of capital. This is consistent with the qualitative sense, because within every moment in the specifying of capital is the conceptum of labor, that is, a referent to particular *existential* conditions. Hence it is the postulation of capital's characteristic presentation of liberty and equality—namely, the

---

54 I make this observation regarding Foucault's recalling of the Kantian program in Ferreira da Silva, *Toward a Global Idea of Race*, 23–25. For an elaboration of Chandler's take on desedimentation, see Chandler, *X—The Problem of the Negro as a Problem for Thought*, 11–67.

pervasiveness of (free) labor and (private) property—that supports Marx's distinction between the Colonial and the proper context of Capital. While the relation between labor and property is conceptualized in *Capital*, descriptions of the Colonial highlight (but do not determine) the absence of such presentation of free labor and private property instead of the prevalence of total violence and the abundance of "public" lands. The "tangle of violence," the colonial juridical modality of subjugation, made the site of "the colonies" available for primitive accumulation, where massacres of Indigenous populations and kidnapping, trafficking, and enslavement of persons from the African continent ensured the appropriation of precious metals, making them available for investment. Instead of determining them, Marx compares "the colonies" (the pervasiveness of total violence, public lands, and "slave labor") to the liberal polity ("modern bourgeois society"), where private property and "wage labor" prevail, in order to highlight what is specific to the latter. Put differently, Marx's comments on "the colonies" render a qualitative explanation—that is, one where taxonomy (and its reliance on identity) rather than mathesis (and its operation of equality) is at work—in which the contrast between the prevailing property form and labor relations index historical (existentially and ethically) difference and, therefore, allow for the delimitation of capital's specific social conditions.

In reviewing Marx's comments on "so-called primitive accumulation," I identify two major statements, one regarding property and the other about labor. The first and perhaps most direct delimitative statement is the one that describes "the colonies" as a context where accumulation of capital cannot take place. When commenting on economist E. G. Wakefield's "colonisation theory,"[55] Marx disavows analyses that place them within the scope of capital with a distinction between two types of private property, each deriving from a particular mode of appropriation. First, there is private property of means of production, as found in "the colonies," which is characteristic of

55 Marx, *Capital*, vol. 1, 791.

precapitalist production, in which the owner is also a laborer; second, there is capitalist private property, "in which [means of production and subsistence] serve at the same time as means of exploitation and subjection of the labourer."[56] For this reason, Marx argues, the available lands in "the colonies" consisted in a problem for the emergence of capital, as their existence gave potential "wage laborers" the hope (and the reality) of becoming independent producers, as peasants in the "newly discovered" lands. There "the bulk of the soil is still public property, and every settler on it therefore can turn part of it into his private property and individual means of production, without hindering the later settlers in the same operation. This is the secret both of the prosperity of the colonies and of their inveterate vice—opposition to the establishment of capital."[57] Whether implicitly or explicitly comparing the Australian colonies with the European polities, supporting Marx's delimitation of what is properly capitalist are two different types of economic activities in connection to the juridical form of private property:[58] one, noncapitalist, where there is no separation for the proprietor between means of production and the laborer; and the other, capitalist, where there is a separation between the property owner and labor.[59] "There," in "the colonies," Marx counters Wakefield, "the capitalist regime everywhere comes into collision with the resistance of the producer, who, as owner of his own conditions of labour, employs that labour to enrich himself,

56 Marx, 792.

57 Marx, 794.

58 For a study of the category in the colonial context that complicates attempts at setting up a dichotomy between private property proper (bourgeois) and the colonial, see generally Brenna Bhandar, *Colonial Lives of Property: Law, Land, and Racial Regimes of Ownership* (Durham, NC: Duke University Press, 2018).

59 Again, in this distinction, the colonial mode of appropriation of value disappears in sequentiality (growth of private ownership of land over time) because, for Marx, it has been surpassed by capital. This is primarily an effect of determinacy, of how the historical-materialist category of labor transubstantiates colonial juridico-economic methods and practices for the expropriation of total value created by native land and "slave labor."

instead of the capitalist."[60] His procedure in this chapter is not one of theory building (which would require the establishing of an identity/equality) through the analytical (determinative) application of the conceptum of labor.

The second delimitative statement comments on private property in regard to "wage labor" when recalling that the laborers' ownership of their labor power is crucial to capital accumulation. According to Marx, Wakefield's description shows "the truth as to the conditions of capitalist production in the mother-country." For instance, it shows that ownership of the means of production is not enough to characterize capitalism, that "capital is not a thing, but a social relation between persons, established by the instrumentality of things."[61] Only a certain kind of "social relation," the exploitative "wage laborer"/capitalist relation, a mode of coming together for economic production, is capitalist. That is, it creates the conditions that are comprehended by the concept of capital. What Wakefield observed in "the colonies" was a situation in which the laborer could accumulate for herself because he remained possessor of his means of production; under these circumstances, labor does not produce exchange value and surplus value is not extracted. Nor is capital accumulated, because since she works on her own lands, the laborer in "the colonies" is a nonproducer of capital. In "the colonies," according to Marx, there has been no "expropriation of the mass of the people from the soil [that] forms the basis of the capitalist mode of production."[62] (Unfortunately I cannot comment here on the significance of this statement that actively erases the Indigenous populations who, rather than being expropriated and expelled from the countryside, were exterminated.) For this reason, they lack the historically distinctive prevalence of "wage labor" and, more importantly, of workers who are free and willing to sell their labor power at wages advantageous to the capitalist.[63] Even

60 Marx, *Capital*, vol. 1, 790.

61 Marx, 791.

62 Marx, 793.

63 What distinguishes capitalist production is that "it not only constantly reproduces the wage-worker as wage-worker, but produces

though they have the means of production, raw materials, and even wealth that could go toward "original accumulation," "the colonies" lack the determining relation of labor exploitation, which occurs under contract and involves juridically equal parties. For, Marx argues, money and commodities "are no more capital than are the means of production and of subsistence." To become capital, the context has to be configured so that there is a sharp distinction between the "owners of money, means of production, means of subsistence" and "free labourers, the seller of their own labour-power."[64] That did not prevail in the "tangle of violence," both the economic and juridical conditions that rendered these profitable.

Tracing Marx's outlining of capital (a specific manifold) as a totality through the deployment of the universality of labor as a historical aspect and analytical tool allows the identification of the nominal (descriptive) threads that sustain the qualitative (interpretive) distinction between a colonial and a liberal juridico-economic context.[65] Threads, we find, that are obtained by the category of labor as a conceptum (economic and juridical), when considered in regard to property and liberty. More precisely, as the two statements that open this section show, the best procedure for identifying how they enter the assembling of the "unity of the diverse" that is capital is to follow Marx's delimitations of productive (of capital) labor through its relation to the liberal (juridico-economic) form of private property. Not, however, in statements that establish what they are, what

---

always, in proportion to the accumulation of capital, a relative surplus-population of wage-workers. Thus, the law of supply and demand of labour is kept in the right rut, the oscillation of wages is penned within limits satisfactory to capitalist exploitation, and lastly, the social dependence of the labourer on the capitalist, that indispensable requisite, is secured; an unmistakable relation of dependence." Marx, 794–95.

64 Marx, 737.

65 According to Marx, this deployment is due to a historical process of dispossession, which creates the conditions for the encounter between capitalists (those who have benefited from it) and laborers (the dispossessed) in the market, where the latter come to sell their only remaining property—labor power.

each comprehends, but in those that relate how a given context or kind (which is always already present in its difference from another kind) of labor does not fall within what has been *determined* as capital.[66] Without the risk of reading one for the other, as Marx consistently deploys the main categories of his critique of political economy, it is possible to track his delimitation of these very categories through noting how the absence of a certain arrangement of labor and property renders the emergence of capital unviable.[67]

Reading Marx’s comments on the colonies, I find a delimitation, the weaving of the outer layer of capital, that is, a qualitative distinction that is not performed through the setting up of an opposition (A versus B) but that identifies, selects, and separates what belongs to the “social conditions” specific to capital from what does not—or capitalist from *non*capitalist. Worthy of attention here are the two reasons this qualitative distinction does not set up a dichotomy. First, because the “tangle of violence”—that is, the social conditions characterized by the total abundance of public lands and slavery—is defined juridically. That is, while

66 Not surprisingly, these are not statements that set up an opposition, as that would be incoherent, because Marx’s description of the process of history locates the conditions of emergence of a new mode of production in the very configuration of the preceding one. Much has been written about why and how conquest and slavery (do and do not) participate in the formation of capital. However, both debates regarding transition between and coexistence of different modes of production, relations of production, or relations focusing on how colonialism is a moment of primitive accumulation keep the Colonial as exterior or anterior to Capital proper—which is also how Marx treats it in *Capital*, vol. 1, chap. 33, “The Modern Theory of Colonization.”

67 What I am suggesting is that Marx’s arguments here are presented qualitatively, that is, from the assumption that the historical specificity of capital as a social reality resides in its particular mode of appropriation of labor (historical) and kind of property relation (juridical). Marx’s comments on the colonies and “slave labor” consistently highlight that the social context (the colonies) and kind of labor appropriation (slavery) differ from capitalist society in juridical terms, because “wage labor” and the prevalence of private property characterizes the latter.

economic production does take place in "the colonies" and the enslaved person is a kind of laborer, the original presentation of historical materialism does not provide clues as to how colonial economic production would fit into its general picture of modes of production. For instance, the nineteenth-century colonial context does not fit the description of either ancient slavery or feudalism, though it has traces of both. Second, and relatedly, it remains *undetermined* scientifically (without a corresponding economic mode of production) and *unspecified* historically (without a proper position in the temporal sequence of modes of production). Marx deploys labor and private property as the historical lenses for reading Wakefield's description of the colonial context. Lenses that, instead of magnifying that which would constitute a specific totality (colonial or liberal mode of production), focus on what in this colonial context is not comprehensible by how the categories of political economy describe them and how they are presented under capital. Simply put, by highlighting how the juridical ("social") conditions of production in "the colonies" do not enter into his analysis, Marx also delineates the historical specificity of capital as a totality.[68]

"as he buys his horse"

> The slave-owner buys his labourer as he buys his horse. If he loses his slave, he loses capital that can only be restored by new outlay in the slave-mart.
>
> —Karl Marx, *Capital*, vol. 1

If commenting on Wakefield's description of "the colonies" allows Marx to highlight the significance of the unavailability of public lands, his own references to "slave labor" indicate

68 In the sixth notebook of the *Grundrisse*, a discussion on Ricardo and the problem of constancy ends with a reminder that the "excerpts here quoted from Wakefield's *Art of Colonization* belong with the ones given above about the necessary separation of the worker from the conditions of property." Marx, *Grundrisse*, 564.

that concentration of land ownership is not enough for establishing one of the “essential conditions” for capital. What they do is emphasize that the requirement must be met that labor alone become the laborer’s private property for the realization of capital as a specific mode of production. Though the reference to distinct presentations of labor, as property (juridical) and as liberty (ethical), is crucial, these set up a comparison that involves “wage labor” and “slave labor” not as modes of the labor process but only as referents to their respective “social conditions” of production.[69] Put differently, in comments regarding “slave labor,” the underlying movement is toward indicating that it is not productive of capital and not about how it differs from “wage labor.” While the establishing of an identity/difference does take place, it is in the service not of composing a totality but of comparing in order to identify what does not belong in it (in this case, Capital). Here again Marx moves to outline capital through its delimitation, that is, the delineation of its boundaries through the presentation of (free) labor and (private) property in instances that highlight how “slave labor” is nonproductive of value (exchange value) that can be partially appropriated (surplus value). The nonsignificance of “slave labor” for capital is registered contemporaneously with—and within—the assembling of capital as a (quantitative) category that names the properly capitalist mode of production and reproduction of value.

Perhaps the most significant statement in the delimitation of “slave labor,” that is, in the assertion that it is not contributive to proper capital accumulation, is that the Owner realizes profit when he or she buys or sells a Slave. “The price paid for a slave,” Marx states, without recourse to an equation or function, “is nothing but the anticipated and capitalised surplus-value or profit to be wrung out of the slave.” Thus the enslaved laborer is like a horse or other agricultural instrument of production

69 Instances that suggest a comparison between “wage labor” and “slave labor” do appear in *Capital*; however, these are mostly metaphorical and refer to “slave labor” to convey the magnitude of wage-labor exploitation.

that—and here the delimiting occurs—insofar as she labors, is nonproductive labor. Moreover, he proceeds, "the capital paid for the purchase of a slave does not belong to the capital by means of which profit, surplus-labour, is extracted from him. On the contrary. It is capital which the slave-holder has parted with, it is a deduction from the capital which he has available for actual production. It has ceased to exist for him, just as capital invested in purchasing land has ceased to exist for agriculture."[70] If, as noted before, human labor alone is productive (value creating), if a Slave is a human being, why is it that her labor is not productive?

Underlying Marx's distinction between "slave labor" and "wage labor" are two descriptors, which I discussed previously, namely liberty (the ethical) and fungibility (the economic). There, in chapter 2, I underscored how, when paired with dignity, fungibility recalls the significance of the juridical moment of subjugation occluded in the racial dialectic. Here I find how this recalling of the juridical moment is what allows for a qualitative distinction that does not establish a dichotomy or equivalency precisely because each figures different juridical positions in regard to labor, which can be distinguished in terms of corresponding juridical forms: "wage labor" (contract) and "slave labor" (title). Both are implied in a quick but telling play on words: "As a slave, the worker has exchange value, a value; as a free wage-worker he has no value; it is rather his power of disposing of his labour, effected by exchange with him, which has value. It is not he who stands towards the capitalist as exchange value, but the capitalist towards him."[71] A twist that only makes sense if one recalls that, for Marx, "wage labor" alone is a producer of exchange value—her labor that she sells, must sell, to the capitalist. However, her value resides in her

70 Karl Marx, *Capital: A Critique of Political Economy*, vol. 3, *The Process of Capitalist Production as a Whole*, ed. Friedrich Engels (New York: International Publishers, n.d.), chap. 47, pt. 5, accessed December 12, 2020, https://www.marxists.org/archive/marx/works/download/pdf/Capital-Volume-III.pdf.

71 Marx, *Grundrisse*, 288–89.

capacity to sell her labor power, that is, her liberty. As for the Slave, she has exchange value only because she is a commodity; and under this condition, being fungible, even though human, she does not produce surplus value (because her Owner has the authority to appropriate the total value her labor yields). Why? Because she can't sell, she can't alienate her labor for a few hours of the day.

The key for this distinction resides in the first chapter of the first volume of *Capital*, where Marx explains the difference between exchange value and use value, noting that exchange value is realized in the market, whereas use value is realized in the household (consumption). Both "wage labor" and "slave labor" have use value—one as holder of productive activity and the other as instrument of production (like a horse or a piece of land). However, the use value of the Slave is realized at the moment of exchange in the market when she is bought or sold, while the use value of the "wage labor" is sold by her for a limited time in the factory, and is realized in the commodity when it is sold in the market. Delimitation here takes place in the implication that, once again, "slave labor" is a nonproducer of value because it only counts as a commodity, an instrument of production, that is, a use value in the private consumption of the household or plantation.[72] More explicitly, delimitation here occurs at the ethical moment because "slave labor" does not enter the market in a condition of liberty; s/he is not "the untrammelled owner of his capacity for labour, *i.e.*, of his person," "that as a free man he can dispose of his labour-power as his own commodity," which s/he sells to the capitalist whom s/he meets in the market "on the basis of equal rights."[73] Similarly, juridically, as a commodity whose use value is to work in the fields or the household, the Slave is property, like a horse or a

---

72 Interestingly, this construction of "slave labor" renders the colonies like a household economy and not a site of the production of capital.

73 Marx, *Capital*, vol. 1, 146–47 (italics in original).

piece of land—liberty as figured by private property does not apply to her, even if she is considered a person.[74]

What is at work here is perhaps the most crucial distinction in the delineation of capital as a totality. In Slavery, as use value, the Slave's labor is fundamentally unpaid work—that is, the product of her labor is totally (not merely partially) appropriated. In the Slave/Owner relation there is an appropriation of total value produced by the "slave labor," which disappears in the "property relations"—that is, in the Owner's title, or legal possession of the person of the Slave. That, however, does not enter Marx's considerations because it belies the conditions under which partial appropriation (exploitation or the appropriation of surplus value) is possible, that which allows for the *delimitation* of capital; it gives its (historical) specificity as well as that which (as abstract labor that translates into time) enables its (scientific) *determination* (the description of its order, the identification of its categories and relations). My point is that the distinction between "slave labor" and "wage labor" is qualitative, that is, it is an ethical delimitation ("wage labor" includes property of one's own person, that is, liberty) of capital at a specific historical moment, which does not have to be demonstrated because it is assumed—as postulated by Kant, Hegel, and others before and after—that post-Enlightenment European and North American "social conditions" constitute the moment of realization of the principles of universal reason. That this was so, in economic terms, is given by the degree of abstraction of actual

74 That is the case in the United States Constitution, in which enslaved persons are considered in Article I, section 2, regarding state representation in the House of Representatives: "Representatives and direct Taxes shall be apportioned among the several States which may be included within this Union, according to their respective Numbers, which shall be determined by adding to the whole Number of free Persons, including those bound to Service for a Term of Years, and excluding Indians not taxed, three fifths of all other Persons." The 13th Amendment supposedly annulled this statement. *The Constitution of the United States: A Transcription*, National Archives, U.S. National Archives and Records Administration, accessed July 1, 2020, https://www.archives.gov/founding-docs/constitution-transcript.

labor (not identified with any particular productive activity, craft, or workplace), the laborer's realization of her property over her productive capacity, and her ability to sell it in the market to the capitalist—that is, the social conditions marked by equality and liberty. I will return to this distinction in the next section because it is key for tracking the participation of "slave labor" in the accumulation of capital.[75]

Let me close this section with a comment on "method," that is, my use of delimitation to describe Marx's statements on "the colonies" and "slave labor." Basically, delimitation is a manner of reading statements that, instead of providing an interpretation of their content, attends to how these perform their function, which is to distinguish between what falls under a particular concept (as opposed to that which is determined by a given category) and what does not fit under (negative) and exceeds (infinite) it (which is not the same as what contradicts it, its negation). As such, it is a tool for reading otherwise. Instead of the predication of the relevant economic concepts—in this case "wage labor" and (private) property, both of which are signifiers of liberty and equality in the modern text—I focus on the nonspecification of the Colonial as a political configuration in descriptions of its economic conditions (the violent appropriation of land and the prevalence of "slave labor") designed to indicate that it does not fit under the concept of capital. Note that here "otherwise" means not a position but a direction of reading. I could have just as well read Marx's comments and set up an opposition between the Colonial and the Liberal context, in which private property prevails, in order to identify how Marx distinguishes one from the other, and from there move on to reproduce two totalities.

---

75 "In slave-labour," Marx argues, "even that part of the working-day in which the slave is only replacing the value of his own means of existence, in which, therefore, in fact, he works for himself alone, appears as labour for his master. [...] All the slave's labour appears as unpaid labour. In wage-labour, on the contrary, even surplus labor, or unpaid labour, appears as paid. There the property-relation conceals the labour of the slave for himself; here the money-relation conceals the unrequited labour of the wage-labourer." Marx, *Capital*, vol. 1, 550.

That would be an interesting and perhaps even necessary theoretical exercise, but it is not what I am after here. All I will do, given the orientation of this exercise, is to track known but key statements on both "the colonies" and "slave labor" to expose how, for Marx, they are uncomprehensible with/in the totality that is capital because they lack the historically specific juridical and ethical features, and not because they fall under a distinct mode of economic production. For capital is historically specified, delimited by labor, as Marx repeatedly says, under certain "essential social conditions" in which it takes the (juridical) form of private property and the (economic) form of commodity; as such, it is specific to the liberal polity, for it refers to the principles of liberty/equality (juridical/before the state) and equality/liberty (economic/in the market), respectively.

What appears when these outer threads unravel, in particular the labor/(private) property pair, is precisely the outer lines of the totality of capital that expose how this in/distinction between the economic and the ethical scene of value, which is mediated by the juridical form of private property, operates in the historical-materialist text. Again, I do not intend to show that Marx does not count "slave labor" as part of the accumulation of capital or prove that he should have done so. Historical materialism cannot remain intact after a confrontation with the Racial. For one thing, raciality immediately renders plain the liberal (ethical-juridical) basis of Marx's assembling of capital as a totality; that is, that liberty is historical materialism's guiding principle for assembling capital as a historically specific moment. Until it is acknowledged that for the historical-materialist text and the liberal text (and the current political discourses that draw from either or both of them) equality presupposes liberty—that is, "wage labor" comes into a condition of equality in the market because the market is (first and foremost) free to sell it as any other commodity over which it has a claim as private property—colonial and racial subjugation will remain intractable. And critical accounts of the political architecture of the global present will therefore at best remain useless to the colonially and racially subjugated, that is, to global subjugated persons and populations.

"Nonpeople rented for a few hours, a few days"

> I was working out of a casual labor agency—we regulars called it a slave market. Actually, it was just the opposite of slavery. The people who ran it couldn't have cared less whether or not you showed up to do the work they offered. They always had more job hunters than jobs anyway. [...]
>
> Getting sent out meant the minimum wage—minus Uncle Sam's share—for as many hours as you were needed. You swept floors, stuffed envelopes, took inventory, washed dishes, sorted potato chips (really!), cleaned toilets, marked prices on merchandise ... you did whatever you were sent out to do. It was nearly always mindless work, and as far as most employers were concerned, it was done by mindless people. Nonpeople rented for a few hours, a few days, a few weeks. It didn't matter.
>
> —Octavia E. Butler, *Kindred*

"Nonpeople rented for a few hours," as a statement, does not give much away without the preceding description of what it was like to be casual labor. "Nonpeople" gives everything away once it is read along the negative statement at the end of the passage: "It didn't matter." What matters? Black Lives Matter—the solitary call of millions, billions, of black persons in the United States and the world over, at this moment, as I write this sentence—is being answered by millions of other persons. Whatever days of confinement and fear of a never-seen-before deadly virus (SARS-CoV-2) and the disease it causes (COVID-19) have played in this response, it is taking place. Nowadays. As I am writing this, thirteen days after George Floyd was lynched by a police officer in plain view of pedestrians and other officers, eighty-four days after Breonna Taylor was shot dead in her bed by police officers. Today. These days. And it seems now for many more days to come, Black Lives Matter will continue to matter. To many, and perhaps to many more. How it does or should matter to all will not become comprehensible until there is a thorough account of how the modern ethical moment has been delimited and determined in texts that render black life/death an economic and juridical matter.

Who is to guarantee that the racial dialectic will not encompass any thorough account of the economic and environmental processes behind (the so-called root causes of) the underlying conditions that make COVID-19 more lethal to black, Latinx, and Indigenous peoples in the Americas than to white and Asian Americans. Until Black Lives Matter matters timelessly, it will not matter how many voices, in unison, chant that it does. For the most part, my speculative exercises are thought experiments that seek to expose and dissolve the political/symbolic tools that render black death a matter of necessity. Enacting procedures designed to unthink—that is, to expose how necessity and its onto-epistemological descriptors (formality and efficacy) and pillars (separability, determinacy, and sequentiality) enter the constitution of accounts of racial subjugation and capital accumulation—I unleash blackness's capacity to render otherwise, to track a way that renders it impossible to articulate a coherent account of the juridico-economic basis of racial subjugation or the ethico-symbolic basis of capital accumulation. Toward the same effect, in the previous chapter, I activated the wounded captive body in the scene of subjugation as a tool for dislodging the sutures of determinacy as it operates in the still prevailing account of racial subjugation—the racial dialectic. My task there was simple. A re/de/composition that takes place rather quickly, because when blackness refers to the wounded captive body in the scene of subjugation it immediately recalls juridical domination, and in doing so, it clouds Subjectivity's *world*, which can no longer stand before it as an (interior/temporal) first person or pure consciousness, and must contend with its own reflection of the post-Enlightenment political architecture, which is no longer transparent, but which instead reveals its juridical, economic, ethical, and symbolic outlines.

When radiating the intensity of the wounded captive body in the scene of subjugation, blacklight fractures the image of the political subject, which postcolonial theorist David Lloyd finds outlined in Kant's subject of the aesthetic. There, he shows, the political subject as a thing of representation indexes a position of enunciation that is at once ethical, juridical, economic, and symbolic—precisely the figuring of the *transparent I* that would rule in the post-Enlightenment political architecture, in the interpretive regime.[76] Designed to trouble this arrangement, the wounded captive body in the scene of subjugation casts blacklight into the space between determinative and reflective judgment, thereby unleashing blackness from the hold of the Understanding. When doing so, she dissolves the exterior membranes and interior threads of capital through a movement that begins by dissolving the very construction of cultural and racial difference as datum, which ensures the coherence of the totality, by returning the total violence to the symbolic violence of (scientific and historical stages of) modern representation. While this operates primarily in the moment of reading, in the engagement with the onto-epistemological features that disappear with "slave labor" through its juridical position as property, the wounded captive body in the scene of subjugation invites a contemplation of what it would take to undermine the empire of necessity. After working out necessity, that is, after dissolving both the discursive device (the racial dialectic) that returns violence to blackness and the determinative gesture (the equation of value) that equates ethical and economic value to liberty, she deftly undermines the presumption of unity that governs the Kantian image of existence (the ordered world or Nature)—that is, the metaphysical presupposition of Husserl's natural attitude and pure consciousness as well as of Du Bois's two "worlds" and of the tools of scientific reason.

"A price for European hospitality"

> Refugees should be reassured of their safety, but it should also be made clear to them that they have to accept the area of living allocated to them by European authorities, plus they have to respect the laws and social norms of European states: No tolerance of religious, sexist or ethnic violence on any side, no right to impose onto others one's own way of life or religion, respect of every individual's freedom to abandon his/her communal customs, etc. If a woman chooses to cover her face, her choice

76 David Lloyd, *Under Representation: The Racial Regime of Aesthetics* (New York: Fordham University Press, 2019).

> should be respected, but if she chooses not to cover it, her freedom to do so has to be guaranteed. Yes, such a set of rules privileges the Western European way of life, but it is a price for European hospitality. These rules should be clearly stated and enforced, by repressive measures (against foreign fundamentalists as well as against our own anti-immigrant racists) if necessary.
>
> —Slavoj Žižek, "We Can't Address the EU Refugee Crisis without Confronting Global Capitalism"

From its title, Žižek's 2015 piece on the "refugee crisis" seemed to grasp the workings of cultural difference for what they are—which is not, as he claims elsewhere, merely an ideological weapon of neoliberal capital designed to (again) divide the working class.[77] It seemed he might have stretched the totality a little and taken a bird's-eye view of global capital. It seemed so, but not for long. He opens the article by acknowledging that refugees are risking their lives by crossing the Mediterranean Sea, fleeing countries torn by the wars of global capital—conflicts about control of access to or distribution of prized minerals that build and fuel our electronic gadgets. Five paragraphs into the text—if not counting the uninspired reference to an African "heart of darkness"—he is reined in by the classical "primitive accumulation" or "accumulation by dispossession" argument, even if, reluctantly: "it is clear that the rise of these 'failed states' is not just an unintended misfortune but also one of the ways the great powers exert their economic colonialism."[78] To be sure, he does seem to try to stretch the conceptum of labor. Much like his reference to "economic colonialism" (as if there has even been one that is not economic), however, his diagnosis of a "new slavery" ("right here, within our house"), which he finds

77 For this argument in regard to multiculturalism, see Slavoj Žižek, *The Fragile Absolute, or Why Is the Christian Legacy Worth Fighting For?* (London: Verso, 2000).

78 Slavoj Žižek, "We Can't Address the EU Refugee Crisis without Confronting Global Capitalism," *In These Times*, November 2015, http://inthesetimes.com/article/18385/slavoj-zizek-european-refugee-crisis-and-global-capitalism. Subsequent Žižek quotes are from this source.

"a structural necessity of today's global capitalism," does not prevent him from repeating the fascist anti-immigrant argument that refugees crossing the Mediterranean are "possessed by a certain dream"—not a right, as established in international refugee law—of "not only proper food and medical care but also the transportation to the place of their choice." This argument is to be expected given the overall patronizing tone of the text. Unexpected, however, is how he proceeds to state that "protection of one's specific way of life is in itself" not a "proto-Fascist or racist category." That statement, which breaks what he calls a "Left taboo," opens the way for his demands for juridical (European-wide state-like law enforcement as administrative) measures—as exemplified in the quote above—to ensure that refugees do not violate the European (which is an unabashedly white) "way of life."

How to read Žižek's statement? A generous reading finds it articulating the racial dialectic but not Foucault's "discourse of race" (or its transcription as "state racism"). After all, he is calling not for the eradication of refugees but for their control, in a statement that rehearses the classic version of the thesis on primitive accumulation. I will not comment on the articulation of the racial dialectic because his statement concerning "the protection of one's specific way of life" is unequivocal and unsophisticated to the point of inviting the question of whether he was just waiting for an opportunity to say what follows it. Regarding the latter, I will not go beyond saying that, as mentioned above, he uses the term "economic colonialism" and names the hyper-exploitation of refugees "new slavery" without considering the conditions under which their labor becomes available to be exploited to such an extent, which has to do with the current dynamics of capital, as he says, and also with the centuries-old fact that capital has accumulated not only through the exploitation of "wage labor" but also through the expropriation of lands and labor in the places from where those he would like to offer conditional hospitality come.

What interests me is not so much the content but the form of Žižek's statement, because it gives away so much about the inability of contemporary left theorizing to consider how raciality operates in—because it governs—the political architecture of the global present as well as the radical reconfiguring of the political (at the level of thinking, of the concept) necessary for it to be possible. The statement itself is telling: "The protection of one's specific way of life is [not] in itself a proto-Fascist or racist category." It is not a justification or an explanation; that is, it is not an affirmation but a negation, a rejection of an accusation that, however, does not have a subject. As such, it presupposes a universal (protection) that is denied as a species of another universal (political category). Along with other signifiers of transparency, such as Europe and the (not failed) states of these two universals (and the authority carried in this kind of predication), the statement arrogates universality, but not the determinative kind. It is an interpretive statement—in which "one" could easily have been replaced by "my" (the first-person possessive), which reeks of phenomenological sentiment in the double reference that "one's way of life in itself" recalls both the lifeworld and its essence while appealing to common sense in its generality (the use of "one" ensures that). This kind of generality, subjective generality, is precisely that which Kant attributes to aesthetic (reflective) judgment. That is, it is a call to the racial common sense that, as Lloyd describes, is an effect of how the theorizing of aesthetics produces its own rendering of racial difference and, in this case, in the delimitation of the Human as a "subject of representation."[79]

My point is: although Žižek uses the words colonialism and slavery, and dedicates a significant part of his text to non-Europe, all that he articulates is the fundamental difference between the affectable racial other (the African and the Indigenous) and the proper political (European) subject, the one whose mental apparatus is prepared to entertain the showings of universal reason, that is, the proper subject of representation at all levels—aesthetic, practical, scientific, and even economic. This is the worker whose labor exploitation counts in the accumulation of capital precisely because, as Žižek states in the opening of

79 Lloyd, *Under Representation*, 152.

the piece, unlike the "new" slaves (refugees), he enjoys freedom. This anthropological distinction, which serves as the basis for Žižek's appeal to the state-like figure of the European Union to activate the law (not right) and unleash its mechanisms for law enforcement (not legal protection) to curb the immigrants and their pathological practices and beliefs, only makes sense to (goes unnoticed by) those who agree with him. Here again the image of the "tangle of violence"/state of nature refers to something that is not necessarily the past but yet somehow prior to capital's juridico-ethical (social) conditions, which now is attached to refugees and the (former) colonies from where they come.

Left thinkers of today, much like Marx and Luxemburg, redeploy the image of the state of nature as they consistently and comfortably rewrite the Racial and the Colonial, whether as datum or residuum, as anterior or exterior to the post-Enlightenment political architecture.[80] Like Badiou, Žižek misunderstands how the Colonial and the Racial have always been and remain integral to the functioning of capital, and assumes that the total and symbolic violence that produces the figure of the Racial/Cultural Other of Europe has no juridical or economic or ethical relevance for what unfolds in the global present. In Žižek's text we find (a) a repetition of Marxism's disavowal of the juridical and economic relevance of coloniality and raciality, and (b) a reflective repetition of the racial dialectic, which results in an appeal to state protection (which sounds like self-preservation [of one's way of life]), which again (c) returns total violence to the racial "other," in this case hailed in their cultural difference. As Lloyd has showed, the racial operating at the level in/as "common sense,"[81] as the index of subjective universality, is constitutive of modern representation, and is therefore integral to the global political architecture.

---

80 For an exception, that is, an interpretive reading of Marx's thought that allows for the consideration of coloniality and raciality, see Massimiliano Tomba, *Marx's Temporalities* (Leiden: Brill, 2013).

81 Lloyd, 88.

For this reason I find that as long as interpretive figurings of the Subject, which are guided by *homo historicus*, continue to ignore its operations as *homo scientificus*, such dimensions will remain unreachable. Because, as argued in the previous chapter, the Racial is constitutive of the figuring of Subjectivity that distinguishes the interpretive regime. (I am actually more wary of quick dismissals of the Subject and embracing the object, which does not expend enough time, considering the consequences derived from the fact that they are co-constituted.)[82] For the radical charge is to expose and undermine the political workings of the symbolic (scientific and historical), which is something the wounded captive body in the scene of subjugation does. While radiating as blacklight, she returns total violence, thereby disturbing the neat ethical arrangements that occlude the juridical element that is operative in black subjugation. Toward activating her, I prepared the terrain by attending to labor and property as the threads that outline capital's scientific unity. There I also tracked the delimitative statements that establish capital's historical specificity, that is, Marx's assertions that, in spite of the existence of accumulated wealth, means of production, free laborers, and capitalists, the absence of a labor market renders it noncapitalist. My next step in preparing the grounds for her activation is to trace Marx's assembling of the inner threads that gather capital as a scientific totality.

82 "For Badiou and his students," for instance, "relinquishing a position of superiority, authority, or mastery over things or humans is a gesture sufficient to release the subject from its immanent context and to extricate the subject from that which has been made available for thinking—object and Other. In other words, announcing the possibility of knowing without the presupposition of correlation, as in the position delineated by Quentin Meillassoux, is enough to liberate 'objects' from the meanings and functions attached to them in the moment of naming; or announcing the appearance of a subject that is related to nothing but the event (Badiou) is enough to liberate its 'Others' (those whom Badiou derides for holding on to cultural difference) from the meanings and functions attached to them in the moment of naming." Ferreira da Silva, "Fractal Thinking."

“The secret of the expression of value”

> By the general law of value, if the value of 40 lbs. of yarn = the value of 40 lbs. of cotton + the value of a whole spindle, *i.e.*, if the same working time is required to produce the commodities on either side of this equation, then 10 lbs. of yarn are an equivalent for 10 lbs. of cotton, together with one-fourth of a spindle. In the case we are considering the same working time is materialised in the 10 lbs. of yarn on the one hand, and in the 10 lbs. of cotton and the fraction of a spindle on the other. Therefore, whether value appears in cotton, in a spindle, or in yarn, makes no difference in the amount of that value. The spindle and the cotton, instead of resting quietly side by side, join together in the process, their forms are altered, and they are turned into yarn; but their value is no more affected by this fact than it would be if they had been simply exchanged for their equivalent in yarn.
>
> —Karl Marx, *Capital*, vol. 1

Let me turn to Marx’s original presentation of the historical-materialist text, which still focuses on the economic category of labor as delimited by the juridical form of private property. Here I will look into two other aspects of the conceptum that identify and determine capital as a specific mode of economic production, namely labor’s qualitative (as particular substance) and quantitative (as universal measure) moments of operation. More precisely, I am interested in what makes it possible to capture labor in such a way that, in the assembling of capital as a totality, labor is both (a) scientific: its efficacy is capturable by the infallible determinative procedures that cannot but yield necessity, that is, mathematical demonstration; and (b) ethical: its efficacy, defined as a specifically human capacity, as a production of value (efficacy), manifests liberty as it transforms what is given into something according to a plan (finality, that is, purpose or end). Neither of these aspects of labor is specific (historically) to capital; they are, however, determinative of capital when translated economically as (c) labor’s capacity to yield value greater than its own cost (more than the wage paid), or (d) what it yields during a certain time (owing to mechanization). Precisely what renders the last two statements possible holds the secret of the expression of value, that is, time. What renders time's function in the historical-materialist text important to my task here is how it mediates labor's ethical and scientific renderings that, in turn, expose the former as the thread that can unravel the inner sutures of capital.

Time, the ontological dimension modern philosophers deployed when protecting Human specificity—the horizon of purposiveness and self-determination as signified by liberty—plays such a crucial role because, if it had not translated the expenditure of human labor into the production of commodities, it would have been difficult for the original presentation of the historical-materialist text to hold its own in the post-Enlightenment determinative episteme. For one thing, it is because Marx equates labor to time that it functions (*formally*) as universal measure, a modern category that has the same degree of abstraction as money, yet with an attribution of efficacy as a capacity to transform matter (productivity). To be sure, labor's determinative capacity is also contingent on Marx's deployment of time as an abstract measure in a manner not dissimilar to Newton's deployment of time in the description of the movements of the universe.[83] Much can be said about how time operates ontologically and epistemologically in Marx's original presentation; here, however, I focus on its fundamental epistemological role. For while it figures prominently in the version of the general law of value presented in volume 1, chapter 7 of *Capital*, *time* is epistemologically and ontologically active in the equal or equivalence (=) sign in every appearance of the equation of value, but in particular in volume 1, chapter 1 of *Capital*. Epistemologically, that is, attesting to the scientific character of the original presentation of historical materialism,

83 In Newton's equation of motion, time operates as the abstract (universal) determinant of the relations (distance or position, for instance) between bodies, and allows for the description of how these change; in Marx's equation of value, time is also an abstract (universal) determinant of relations, but in this case it allows for a description of how labor power changes the qualitative elements in production (raw materials and instruments) into something that can be captured quantitatively (as money).

time (the means for equivalence) provides labor’s mediation of the cotton and the spindle on the one hand and the yarn on the other. The “magnitude of this value” of abstract labor in the commodity, he states, is a quantity measured “by the quantity of the value-creating substance, the labour, contained in the article. The quantity of labour, however, is measured by its duration, and labour-time in its turn finds its standard in weeks, days, and hours.”[84] In short, the time expended in the production of commodities accounts for their being exchangeable (fungible) in spite of their distinct use values.

Time is the secret of the expression of value because it carries the abstraction of labor to both sides of the equation—the value of the cotton = the value of the yarn, only because time (as labor time) operates in the equal (=) sign regardless of the specific kinds of tasks that are necessary for making the cotton available and transforming it into the yarn. Furthermore, in this operation, time (the measurable abstract time that obtains labor’s production of exchange value) also nullifies the participation of “the colonies” and “slave labor” in the creation of capital. For, as I discussed previously, these lack the basic characteristic that gives the labor market a significant number of free and dispossessed persons who, in order to satisfy their needs, are to sell their labor time for a wage. Without the social time difference—as labor—between the wage paid and exchange value (determined by the average social labor time), there is no way to ascertain how labor produces capital. That is why “slave labor” in the colonies does not count: there is no quantitative basis for differentiating between “slave labor’s” yield and the Owner’s profit. It cannot be measured. Every hour, minute, second of “slave labor” belongs to the Owner; it is used by the Owner, as a tool, an instrument of production. Only what is dis-countable, when measured as time, has exchange value, that is, produces capital.

Both as a quality shared by labor and its products and as a quantity that measures labor, which is accumulated in commodities and is equatable to money, time does the heavy

84 Marx, *Capital*, vol. 1, 5.

lifting in the assembly of the concept of capital. It obtains the properly capitalist relation of production (which is specified as partial appropriation)—and it functions in the determination of capital as a particular mode of production because it is an abstraction that translates labor into money. In the account of the production of exchange value, time functions in two ways: (a) as a scientific tool (as indicated above), a quantity (a concept and abstract measure), the social labor that Marx chooses as determining a commodity's *exchange value*; and (b) as an ethical referent, in that it could only become a universal measure for exchange value when "all kinds of labour are equal and equivalent, because, and so far as they are human labour in general, cannot be deciphered, until the notion of human equality has already acquired the fixity of a popular prejudice."[85] Equality plays this role only as a descriptor of how the laborer and the capitalist enter the Market, that is, on equal terms as seller and buyer. However, it does so as an index of liberty, which is the first and defining attribute of "wage labor" because, without the freedom to dispose (the ownership) of her labor power, the laborer cannot enter the Market and sell it. For private property (of one's own labor) is the distinctive aspect of the capitalist mode of production precisely because the laborer owns nothing but her labor power. The fundamental (qualitative) contradiction (opposition) between two kinds of Owners, of means of production and of productive capacity (labor), distinguishes capitalism as a historical moment. What I am proposing here, in other words, is that, in the original presentation of the historical-materialist text, the principle of liberty—as figured by both the juridical form of private property and the economic notion of equality—refers (economically) to the expropriation of land and the means of production that rendered laborers without the means of production, therefore forcing them to sell their labor power to those who concentrated those means, and (ethically) to the fact that these laborers could do so because they owned (juridically) their own labor. Beyond being an abstract referent to the

85 Marx, 29.

ontic thesis of human equality, then, time's ethical significance refers to the figuring of liberty—in the self-producing figuring of the *homo historicus* as *homo laborens*.[86] Despite the "material" point of departure and determinative profile at the core of the original presentation of historical materialism, Marx's remains the Hegelian figuring of the *transparent I* in the scene of representation.

Because it is the measure of labor, *time* is also the component of the equation that captures its capacity to *create* value. For it is labor applied over time that performs the transformation of forty pounds of cotton and the value of a whole spindle into forty pounds of yarn. "Human labour-power in motion, or human labour," Marx postulates, "creates value, but is not itself value. It becomes value only in its congealed state, when embodied in the form of some object. In order to express the value of the linen as a congelation of human labor, that value must be expressed as having objective existence, as being a something materially different from the linen itself, and yet a something common to the linen and all other commodities."[87] Furthermore, although the exchange value of a commodity is nothing but accumulated (congealed) past labor (or dead labor), it does not count in the value that is created. Only labor in motion, living labor measured, captured by/as time, that is, living labor accumulated in *that* yarn—in the duration of "labour time necessary for its production"[88]—creates economic value, therefore rendering it exchangeable with other commodities of the same value. That accumulated labor—insofar as only a fraction of it is anticipated to go to the worker for her reproduction in the form of wages—also produces/determines capital: whatever fraction of the value of a commodity is left after the value of labor and

86 Or, as Marx puts it: "What distinguishes the worst architect from the best of bees is this, that the architect raises his structure in imagination before he erects it in reality. At the end of every labour-process, we get a result that already existed in the imagination of the labourer at its commencement" (157).

87 Marx, 19.

88 Marx, 24.

the value of the means of production is discounted enters the (re)production of capital.

Though it is crucial for labor's function in the assembling of capital, its role as a scientific category (quantity) and an ethical referent (liberty), this double operation of time speaks to the composition of the equation—two terms united/separated by an equal/equivalence (=) sign: forty pounds of yarn = the value of forty pounds of cotton + the value of a whole spindle. And it speaks to the composition of the yarn only because it is there to capture its composition (working time). Therefore, working time as a measure of the labor expended in the creation of the yarn tells us nothing in regard to what is specific to labor under capital. Certainly, a partial and partisan reading (attending to labor's ethical and scientific functions as mediated by time after commenting on its scientific-historical significance as presented in the introduction to the *Grundisse*) already gives a sense of what is involved in *negativation*, that is, the anti-dialectical effect of the wounded captive body in the scene of subjugation when she shines from within Marx's formalization of the economic scene of value.

"the fundamental conditions of capitalist production"

> Free labourers, in the double sense that neither they themselves form part and parcel of the means of production, as in the case of slaves, bondsmen, &c., nor do the means of production belong to them, as in the case of peasant-proprietors; they are, therefore, free from, unencumbered by, any means of production of their own. With this polarisation of the market for commodities, the fundamental conditions of capitalist production are given. The capitalist system presupposes the complete separation of the labourers from all property in the means by which they can realise their labour. As soon as capitalist production is once on its own legs, it not only maintains this separation, but reproduces it on a continually extending scale.
>
> —Karl Marx, *Capital*, vol. 1

"Free labourers," which do not count as "means of production," are the sine qua non for the emergence and continuation of capital as a historically specific mode of production because they alone create capital, that is, they transform the value embodied in raw materials, instruments of production, including past labor power itself, into a new value, that is, into commodities. Or put differently, the delimitative statement reads: *"slave labor" is nonproductive (and doesn't yield surplus value) because it is "unpaid labor" mediated by the title/property and not the contract/property juridical relation*. The delimitative statement—*"slave labor" is negative (non) in respect to the production of exchange value or it does not belong to the set that is productive of exchange value*—that immediately deauthorizes any attempt at considering "slave labor" as a reproducer of capital does not establish that it does not create value in general. For, according to Marx, the labor process is creative regardless of its social conditions of deployment. If both statements belong in the original presentation of the historical-materialist text, it might be relevant to consider what renders both of them true. Let me bring them together in a different way: *any labor is creative, but only free (wage) labor creates capital*. My motivation is, as said from the outset, to erase this distinction, that is, to dissolve this specification. This I will do in two steps. First, in this section, I attend to the second part of the assertion—*only free labor creates capital*. Again, I am not interested in challenging, correcting, or improving this; all I will do is de/compose it in order to expose the various components that enter into the assembling of capital, which include both the ones that enter into the movement of determination and the delimitation that secures it as a totality.

The argument that *delimits* the capitalist mode of production relies on the articulation of two kinds of necessity: first, the "natural" conditions that make the expenditure of labor power necessary, that is, human beings must apply their sweat and bodily constituents in order to produce for their own subsistence; and second, the social (juridical and economic) conditions—liberty and/as equality—that Marx argues are "essential" for the appropriation of surplus value. My move here is to consider both of them simultaneously and to submit the thesis that while (a) the necessity of natural conditions is given metaphysically and existentially in the statement that labor is as crucial for social existence as language, (b) the necessity of the social conditions is given onto-epistemologically; that is, Marx is a post-Enlightenment thinker who presumes that when/where he was writing was the most developed stage of the trajectory of the Subject of History, which, for him, is not Spirit but Society.[89] Both are presupposed in Marx's descriptions and formalization of his "general law of value." Here, however, I am only interested in the second kind of necessity. The onto-epistemological basis of the equation gives away the secret behind the secret that is time. For it recalls that which cannot appear in the equation (the general law of value, as presented in volume 1, chapter 7 of *Capital*) but that came through previously in Marx's statements of delimitation, that is, how liberty both circumscribes (delimits) and sutures (determines) capital. On the one hand, as the determination of creative (human) labor as private property, time expresses how the juridico-ethical notions of liberty (including in the guise of equality) rule the original presentation of the historical-materialist text. On the other hand, liberty (self-determination as self-production, i.e., *homo historicus* as *homo laborans*) inhabits the equation as the quality of the component, that is, labor, which, equated with time (also itself the figuring of liberty), renders the equation possible. In sum, liberty, in the guise of time and equality, guides the abstraction of labor (at once its individualization and alienation) as it allows Marx to apprehend it as/in time.[90]

---

89 In a way, this follows from Cedric Robinson's argument that Marx is a Eurocentric thinker. The only distinction is that I find Marx's Eurocentrism in his being a post-Enlightenment determinative thinker whose statement in the unfolding philosophical conversation tries to resolve the double task of describing human conditions as ruled by universal reason and the protection of Man's singularity.

90 "The equality of all sorts of human labour," Marx argues, "is expressed objectively by their products all being equally values; the measure of the expenditure of labour-power by the duration of that expenditure, takes the form of the quantity of value of the products of labour; and finally, the mutual relations of the producers, within which the social character of their labour affirms itself, take the form of a social relation between the products" (42).

Let me further specify my approach to how the ethical operates through/in the conceptum of labor. Labor as/in time—not as material (potential and kinetic energy) capacity nor as intellectual (training, specialization, experience, etc.) ability—exudes the principles post-Enlightenment philosophy arrogated to its own historical moment: liberty and/as equality, which, as noted previously, participate in labor’s determination of capital in its ethical (as freedom to sell one’s labor power) and economic (as the abstract equality of labor capturable by time) renderings. In short, labor as/in time, living labor, like an agent of Spirit, infuses capital because it is the abstraction that permits the transformation of the mechanism for the transfer of matter energy (labor) into property (labor power), which is itself a commodity that can be bought and sold in the Market in an agreement in which the seller and the buyer enter as economically but not juridically or ethically differentiated, that is, as free and equal persons. Consistently, according to Marx, that contractual relation provides the grounds for the properly capitalist relation of production (capitalist and laborers), its juridical form (contract), and the very existence of capital as such. The primal scene of capital—which evokes the “moment” of the signing of the “social contract”—is the meeting of the *free* (property-owning) capitalist and the *free* (of any other property but his labor power) laborer in the market:

> Labour-power can appear upon the market as a commodity, only if, and so far as, its possessor, the individual whose labour-power it is, offers it for sale, or sells it, as a commodity. In order that he may be able to do this, he *must have it at his disposal, must be the untrammelled owner of his capacity for labour, i.e., of his person*. He and the owner of money meet in the market, and deal with each other as on the basis of equal rights, with this difference alone, that one is buyer, the other seller; both, therefore, equal in the eyes of the law. The continuance of this relation demands that the owner of the labour-power should sell it only for a definite period, *for if he were to sell it rump and stump, once for all, he would be selling himself, converting himself from a free man into a slave, from an owner of a commodity into a commodity*. He must constantly look upon his labour-power as his own property, his own commodity, and this he can only do by placing it at the disposal of the buyer temporarily, for a definite period

> of time. By this means alone can he avoid renouncing his rights of ownership over it.[91]

For the ethical operator, liberty, that marks this relation to prevail, that is, for the laborer's labor power after meeting the capitalist in the market—where equality rules—to remain "his own property" (this condition of liberty distinguishes creative labor), their relation is mediated by a *contract* through which both agree on the price and duration of the labor the capitalist will have at his disposal. This is so because, as we saw in the delimiting statements, the worker who cannot dispose of labor as her property does not produce surplus value, which is the difference between its price (price of labor) and its yield (value created by the labor). For Marx, the Market, the kernel of the liberal polity, is the locus of the original encounter—even as he points to the capitalist mode of production's "illusions as to liberty."[92] The Market is an "essential [historical] condition" for capital.

Highlighting the ethical operating within is crucial to the dissolution of the economic scene of value, because to it belong the delimitative statements that describe why "slave labor" is irrelevant to the accumulation of capital. For one thing, looking at both moments of analysis, the one that attends to the *necessary* social conditions (dispossessed laborers and property-owning capitalists) and the one that attends to the *historical* (ethico-juridical) or "essential" conditions (the market as the site of actualization of liberty and equality where laborers and capitalists meet to engage in a relation mediated by contract), the totality may be disassembled and Capital's context expanded beyond its necessary and historical conditions.[93] Instead of merely

---

91 Marx, 146 (my italics).

92 Marx, 551.

93 By making these distinctions, I am not stating that the "wage laborer"/capitalist relation is not historical—in the sense of emerging in a given moment. What I am highlighting is how the same circumstances are described in two distinct ways: on the one hand, as logically necessary and, on the other, as historically contingent. Each addresses the same main characters, "wage laborer" and capitalist, but from a different perspective. See Dale

economically (ontic labor pure and simple) and *scientifically* (as an *economic* category) determined, the consideration of Capital would also attend to Marx's recalling of labor's *ethical* ("free labor") and *juridical* ("wage labor") aspects, which are crucial to its delimitation, that is, to establishing what is noncapital and what is constitutive of it and constituted by it. Now, this figural presentation of capital does a few things at once. Most importantly, it refers to what does not fall under it but is opposite to it, which comes out of Marx's delimiting without necessarily setting up an opposition. This is so because of the second most important thing: it shifts in register from the historical distinction between a juridical modality corresponding to capital (the liberal) and another where capital's "essential conditions" do not prevail (the colonial). While Marx assembles the totality that is capital in the economic register, and takes the others as "essential conditions" but not determining ones (capital production occurs not in the

W. Tomich, *Through the Prism of Slavery: Labor, Capital, and World Economy* (Oxford: Roman & Littlefield, 2004), for a version of the argument that "in Marx's conception, categories are at once historical and logical" (19), and for the case that, in the *Grundrisse*, one finds a presentation of the method employed in the analysis of *Capital* (21). When assembling his argument regarding how slavery participates in capital accumulation, Tomich chooses to privilege the historical over the logical in order to "overcome the theoretical fragmentation that has characterized the treatments of slavery." His project "is not to simply add slavery to an already given and completed concept of capital," but "to rethink the totality of relations of capital in a way that is inclusive of slavery and diverse non-waged relations." In doing so, he goes "*against the grain of Marx's classical theoretical presentation* in order to reincorporate into the field of analysis those 'historical contingencies and disturbing accidents' that were eliminated in the process of abstraction" (28; italics in original). Tomich's move here is to assemble a theoretical framework in which "production appears as an intrinsically social and historical process," that is, one in which social relations "are taken to be constitutive of specific, historical conditions of production" (28). His is an ambitious and well-performed effort of conceptual innovation, which he calls theoretical-historical, and which accounts for slavery by expanding the description of capital to give weight to the "world market" and the "international division of labor" (30–31).

market but in the factory), he defines the totality's outer layers through statements on labor and through the notion of private property, which belies the ethical and juridical aspects. This is given explicitly but en passant in a comment (also quoted above) on the wage form: "All the slave's labour appears as unpaid labour, In wage-labour, on the contrary, even surplus labour, or unpaid labour, appears as paid. There the *property-relation* conceals the labour of the slave for himself; here the *money-relation* conceals the unrequited labour of the wage-labourer."[94] Lightly but effectively, this comparison granted by concealment does its own concealing through the terms *property* and *money*, which places the Slave/Owner relation juridically (as it is mediated by property) and the "wage laborer"/capitalist relation (unquestionably) economically (as it is mediated by money). This is an important distinction, because presupposed (concealed) here is also that the latter relation is mediated juridically through a contract, that is, in that moment the "wage laborer" and the capitalist are transparent to each other as effected and presupposed by the concept of equality (before the law).

What I did above was to consider the "essential" (social) conditions with the intention of returning labor to what it is—that is, the raw material of production. However, for now, as I said before, I am still accepting Marx's thesis of labor as the sole creative element in what falls under the notion of the economic. In the next section, I advance this thesis that lifts determinacy ("necessary conditions") as I move to re/de/compose the formalization of economic value, attending to the raw materials that enter into production. Instead of reading the moments of the post-Enlightenment political architecture—that is, the juridic, economic, ethic, and symbolic—through Capital, which has been the usual strategy that always gets stuck in the problem of unity, this figuration reads Marx's assembling of the totality that is capital along the lines of Robinson's (discussed earlier in this chapter) and Spivak's readings of Marx (on which I comment later this chapter) as a specific (liberal) presentation of them.

94 Marx, *Capital*, vol. 1, 550 (my italics).

How this is done follows as a set of questions, each giving a description of capital that maps onto the post-Enlightenment political architecture: (a) economic category (creates that which is sold in the market); (b) juridical relation (labor, insofar as it is creative of commodities, involves two parties, whose relations are not familial or communal but juridically mediated); (c) ethical (insofar as it refers to human expenditure of potential energy, labor in modernity also carries a certain representation of human uniqueness); (d) symbolic (as a scientific concept, labor explains how wealth is created, accumulated, concentrated, or shared). Another way of reading this composite is by taking each of these moments as an entry point through which blacklight is shed on the totality’s defining form, namely the equation of value; in doing so, one can suffuse the very concept of capital and bring to the fore some of the otherwise unnoticeable features of its composition.

“the cotton and the spindle” + $sp = v$

> While the labourer is at work, his labour constantly undergoes a transformation: from being motion, it becomes an object without motion; from being the labourer working, it becomes the thing produced. At the end of one hour’s spinning, that act is represented by a definite quantity of yarn; in other words, a definite quantity of labour, namely that of one hour, has become embodied in the cotton. We say labour, *i.e.*, the expenditure of his vital force by the spinner, and not spinning labour, because the special work of spinning counts here, only so far as it is the expenditure of labour-power in general, and not in so far as it is the specific work of the spinner.
>
> —Karl Marx, *Capital*, vol. 1

When tracing the delimitation of productive (wage) labor, that is, the statements that write “slave labor” as exterior to the totality that is capital, I highlighted how this irrelevance is stated (not theorized) and supported by references to the juridical form of property title and the total violence it authorizes. Marx’s delimitation of capital can be transcribed into the statement: *“slave labor” is nonproductive (of surplus value) because it is juridically figured by the title/property and not the contract/property relation.* Yet another way of saying the same thing is: *"slave labor" does not enter into the determination that sutures capital as a totality, that is, as a specific mode of production characterized by the contractually mediated appropriation of value.* Or, alternatively, it could be said that *the value created by "slave labor" (because rendered by total violence) cannot be comprehended by the concept of capital because the latter is delimited by labor (under contract) and determined by labor (as time).* Regardless of how this delimitation is presented, it remains implicit that "slave labor" (vis-à-vis capital) is not only non-determining of but also undeterminable by it—because the enslaved person's labor power is not measurable by time, it is not equivalent to money. Further, when tracking the determining operations of labor as an economic category, that is, of the labor form, I highlight how time, as it captures labor expenditure (which in the equation is signaled by the equivalence of "="), enables the move that marks the departure of the original presentation of historical materialism from Political Economy. As I said before, I do not have the pretension of correcting Marx's text nor am I committed to (saving) it (from itself).

Re/de/composing Marx's text allows me to avoid setting up a dichotomy of "wage labor" versus "slave labor." An unhelpful setup, this dichotomy already organizes Marx's account of capital through his reference to the "essential [social] conditions" that contain capital in the liberal polity. In any event, what attending to determination and delimitation as two moments of assembling capital allows is to return to the economic scene, to production, where capital is both expended and created. While there I can try to activate *undeterminable* "slave labor" by focusing on that in which Marx locates its irrelevance for capital accumulation, that is, the raw materials and instruments that living labor transforms into capital.

When de/composing the equation of value in the previous pages, I focused on that which ensures its presentation as a scientific statement under the determinative episteme, that is, the equal (=) sign through which "working time" both hosts and exposes labor's determining role as an ontic, epistemological, juridical, and ethical operator. Here, in this third moment, negativation suspends labor's juridical and ethical functions as *wage* (or *abstract* or *universalized*) *labor* and tracks its workings as labor "pure and simple," that is, as creative (*material*) capacity. Let me first recall how *abstract labor* refers to ethical and juridical operations; the equivalence (10 lb. yarn = 10 lb. cotton + ¼ spindle) and the *labor time* expended in the production of cotton no longer counts as an efficient (living or dead productive) force. Entering the equation as a raw material, the social labor time (recalling that tending cotton in the plantations and extraction of gold or iron ore was a collective activity that extended into and across different continents) expended in the production of use value, that is, cotton, it disappears in the "capitalist process of production" of the yarn, that is, when it is considered as the production of surplus value.[95] After the commodity cotton is

95 Let me recall how Marx does it. He begins with the assumption that "the value of each commodity is determined by the quantity of labour expended and materialised in it, by the working-time necessary, under given social conditions for its production." He then proceeds to "calculate the quantity of labor realised" in "10 lbs. of yarn." This requires the consideration of the raw material (10 lb. of cotton), which costs ten shillings (here "the labour required for the production of the cotton is already expressed in terms of the average labour of society"); to that he adds the "wear and tear of the spindle which [...] amounts to the value of 2s." With the hours of labor expended in the production of cotton and the hours "required to produce the quantity of gold represented by twelve shillings, we have here, to begin with, two days' labour already incorporated in the yarn." When explaining the equivalence in the equation ("40 lbs. of yarn = the value of 40 lbs. of cotton + the value of a whole spindle"), which means that "the same working time is required to produce the commodities on either side of this equation, then 10 lbs. of yarn are an equivalent for 10 lbs. of cotton, together with one-fourth of a spindle," or "the same working time is materialised in the 10 lbs. of yarn on the one hand, and in the 10 lbs. of cotton and the fraction of a spindle on the other." What it means is that even though the spindle's and cotton's "forms are altered, and they are turned into yarn," the values of the cotton and spindle are "no more affected by this fact than [they] would be if they had been simply exchanged for their equivalent in yarn." Or put differently: "The labour required for the production of the cotton, the raw material

of the yarn, is part of the labour necessary to produce the yarn, and is therefore contained in the yarn. The same applies to the labour embodied in the spindle, without whose wear and tear the cotton could not be spun."

At this point, one can conclude that the labor time necessary for the production of the raw materials and instruments of production enter into the value of the commodity. Perhaps anticipating such a hasty conclusion, after attending to the conditions that assure that "the values of the means of production, *i.e.*, the cotton and the spindle, [..] are therefore constituent parts of the value of the yarn"—namely, that they "become yarn" and that "the time occupied in the labour of production" does not "exceed the time really necessary under the given social conditions of the case"—Marx moves to consider "what portion of the value of the yarn is added to the cotton by the labour of the spinner." Here is the crucial shift, as Marx recalls that the labor of the spinner is not to be analyzed in the same way as the labor process, which he looked at "as specifically different from other kinds of productive labour." Instead, he says, "we consider the labour of the spinner only so far as it is value-creating, *i.e.*, a source of value," that is, abstract labor, as identical to any other kind of labor ("cotton planting, spindle making"), and he recalls that "solely by reason of this identity [... they] are capable of forming the component parts, differing only quantitatively from each other, of one whole, namely, the value of the yarn." When considering abstract, quantifiable labor, which is "necessary under the given social conditions," everything changes. When labor is treated as "the expenditure of labour-power in general," which is transformed in the process "from being motion, it becomes an object without motion; from being the labourer working, it becomes the thing produced."

The next step is that raw material and the product itself "appear in quite a new light," too: "the raw material serves now merely as an absorbent of a definite quantity of labour," in which "it is in fact changed into yarn, [..] because labour-power in the form of spinning is added to it." He adds: "But the product, the yarn, is now nothing more than a measure of the labour absorbed by the cotton." What about the labor, cotton planting, that creates the cotton? Before he gives us more elements for considering this question, Marx takes a detour in which he considers the capitalist being disappointed when adding up the cost of elements acquired for the production of the yarn and the price of the yarn, and realizes that they are the same. Hence Marx's next move is to consider the difference between the "value of a day's labour-power" and the value of "the past labour that is embodied in the labour-power and the living labour that it can call into action, the daily cost of maintaining, and its daily expenditure in work"—that is, the difference between "the exchange-value of the labour-power" and its "use-value." The significance of this is that the value of the labor power and the value it creates "are two entirely different magnitudes; and this difference of the two values was what the capitalist had in view, when he was purchasing the labour-power." For the capitalist purchases "the specific use-value which this commodity [labour] possesses of being a source not only of value, but of more value than it has itself."

Though Marx does not address it directly, here one gains a sense of how "slave labor" disappears before entering the equation, which is that "the seller of labour-power, like the seller of any other commodity, realizes its exchange-value, and parts with its use-value." Not because the labor of the slave has more value than itself, but because, at one end, the slave does not take part (as an *equal*) in the relationship of exchange (change of *title*); she is only what is exchanged and, at the other end, the slave is not *free* to dispose of her labor power in a relationship of consent (*contract*). In any event, Marx returns to the equation not taking into account the difference between the exchange value and the use value of labor power. What he shows is that the laborer works twice as many hours as the price she charged for her labor power, and these extra hours are absorbed in the yarn: "There is now materialised in this 20 lbs. of yarn the labour of five days, of which four days are due to the cotton and the last steel of the spindle, the remaining day having been absorbed by the cotton during the spinning process." Since "the value of the yarn is 30 shillings," and the "values of the commodities that entered into the process amounts to 27 shillings," Marx instructs, "a surplus-value of 3 shillings has been created. The trick has at last succeeded; money has been converted into capital."

What happens to "slave labor" then becomes evident in the distinction between the two modes of considering labor: if, as the "labour-process, pure and simple," the qualitative aspect is of interest, that is, it "produces use-values," while "as a value-creating process" it becomes distinct, and "the same labour-process presents itself under its quantitative aspect alone." "Here," Marx instructs further, "it is a question merely of the time occupied by the labourer in doing the work; of the period during which the labour-power is usefully expended. Here, the commodities that take part in the process, do not count any longer as necessary adjuncts of labour-power in the production of a definite, useful object. They count merely as depositaries of so much absorbed or materialised labour; that labour, whether previously embodied in the means of production, or incorporated in them for the first time during the process by the action of labour-power, counts in transformed by the living labor of the spinner, it has no significance for the exchange value of the commodity because what counts is the free living labor that transfers the attributes of the raw material and the instrument of production and the laborer into the newly created use value. More importantly, the commodity cotton—and the labor hours embodied in it—play no part in the reproduction of capital because its process of production does not generate surplus value.[96] The transformation of "money into capital" occurs when the amount of labor time paid as a wage is less than the amount of labor time embodied in the commodity produced. For surplus value is the relation between the "value of labor power" and the "value that labor creates"—that is, the specific use value of labor, as a commodity, is to create a "value greater than its own."[97] Through this analytical move, which is sustained by the mere statement that labor is productive under particular social conditions—that is, the liberal polity—Marx's equation disappears the creative capacity of "slave labor" and "the colonies" into/as raw material.

That being the case, and given that I have already mapped the functions of labor and described how, though they are necessary for the assembling of capital, that is, contingent on the demand for its unity (the holding together of all the economic spheres), all I need to do now is to activate two of them—labor's ontic and epistemological functions—and recompose the

---

either case only according to its duration; it amounts to so many hours or days as the case may be." From this Marx makes yet another distinction between two aspects of production: on the one hand, "as the unity of the labour-process and the process of creating value, [it] is production of commodities," and "on the other hand as the unity of the labour-process and the process of producing surplus-value, it is the capitalist process of production or capitalist production of commodities." Marx, 166–79.

96 The significance of cotton to industrial capital cannot be overstated. Secondary-school textbooks—at least the ones I studied back in Brazil—introduce the Industrial Revolution by referring to the mechanization of cotton spinning in the later eighteenth century. For a more advanced account, see Sven Beckert, *Empire of Cotton: A Global History* (New York: Alfred A. Knopf, 2014).

97 Marx, *Capital*, vol. 1, 217.

equation of value accordingly. On the one hand, I keep Marx's description of labor as a creative activity, which he grasps as such because the (self-determined) laborer has the control, determining the process and its outcome, that is, its efficacy and finality (purposiveness).[98] Nothing more, no other component of the equation of value shares this attribute. On the other hand, I also retain time's function as a measure that translates labor expenditure, thereby permitting the expression of the value of a commodity as an effect of the application of labor. Everything else—that is, the functions that become apparent in Marx's delimiting statements, which are the ethical and juridical aspects of labor that portray "the colonies" and "slave labor" as non-determinable of capital—is ignored. With that, it is possible to re/compose the equation of value in a way that brings out how "slave labor" participates in capital accumulation.

Marx's equation of value, as described volume 1, chapter 7 of *Capital*:

20 lb. yarn =	20 lb. cotton + ½ spindle [4 workdays] +	1 workday
(30 shillings)	(24 shillings)	(6 shillings)

As mentioned before, when explaining the equation, Marx considers a couple of scenarios. Here I am interested in the last one, in which he disaggregates the *y* value of the yarn (thirty shillings) into *c* (the value of the raw material and instrument of production) and *v* (the value of labor/wage). In this calculation,

98 Let me quote David Lloyd's comment on this sentence, in which he highlights how this is the core of Marx's idea of alienation: "Isn't this just what Marx's understanding of the alienation of abstracted labor under capitalism refutes, this notion that under such productive relations labor is 'free' and therefore determines its end: instead, the wage laborer loses the end of her labor in the product that is alienated from her as a commodity owned by the capitalist. This stalls the dialectic of emancipation he embeds in the labor process in general. Not that he abandons the figuration of *homo laborans* or the dialectic, just that the problem with capitalism is its appearance as an 'alien power that dominates the worker.'" I absolutely agree with him.

Marx finds that the capitalist retains three shillings (of the six created in a working day) as *sp* (surplus value), which is the value created by "wage labor" when expended in the production of the yarn. How to decompose this equation? The first move is to de/compose the value of the commodities other than "wage labor" (yarn, cotton, and spindle), because these are determined by it.

My de/composition yields three versions of the equation of value. The first version considers *labor pure and simple* (regardless of the juridical situation of the worker). (Incidentally, this version of the equation also acquires "wage labor.")

Equation I – yarn:

$c + v + sp = y$

Here *c* is the value of the means of production (instruments and raw materials), *v* is the value of labor/wage, *sp* is the value produced by labor minus value of labor, and *y* is the value of the commodity.

Equation II can then be written in two ways:

(a) $c + v + tv = y$ (b) $c + tv; tv = v + sp$

The latter versions consider "slave labor" and are similar but with one difference. Since there is no surplus value because, as Marx recognizes, "slave labor" is thoroughly unpaid labor, *sp* is replaced by *tv* (total value). Let me begin with version (b) because it is Marx's. Since there is no wage stipulated, no value of the work to be discounted from the value of the yarn, "slave labor" counts as part of the cotton, a raw material and/or instrument of production—that is, it is included in *c*. My version, (a), keeps the value of the worker in the equation because it acknowledges that the body of the "slave laborer" is expended (materially, that is, a transfer of potential energy) in the production of the cotton, not as raw material or an instrument of production, but as that which makes possible the transfer of the potential (and other forms of energy) from instruments of production and raw material—that is, "slave labor" cannot count as part of *c*.

When delimiting capital, Marx states that, because of its juridical status, as property the Slave counts as an instrument of production (a Thing, commodity, or tool). However, he also notes that "slave labor" is performed under the "brutal lash" of the Owner. In chapter 2, I located the wounded captive body in the scene of subjugation to challenge phenomenological and other interpretive reframings of the *transparent I* as Subjectivity, as she shows the political (juridico-economic) conditions of possibility for the *transparent I*’s expression. At the same time, because such expression is contingent upon her figuring as both *exorbitance* (total violence) and *absence* (whatever marks her interiority cannot be expressed in the language of transparency), she holds the key for unraveling Subjectivity and the *ethical* scene of value it sustains. Here again, in the *economic* scene of value, she is trouble. For insofar as she is a Human (laborer) transforming raw materials and other means of production—and if one accepts Marx’s view on productive labor—through the expenditure of her body into commodities (sugar, cotton, etc.), the Slave is living labor. As such, she has creative capacity, and is thus not a Thing; that is, she counts as more than an instrument of production.

My point here is that, on the positive side of the accumulation of money (to be turned into capital) enabled by slavery, there is something that is not a surplus (*sp*) but *excess* (*x*)—$x = sp + v$—that which is not registered in the classic historical-materialist account of capitalist accumulation. This excess is the value of the Slave’s labor (still considered as labor time) embodied in the cotton that is retained by the Owner. (However, this transference, it should be noted, is not exhaustive: while the product of one’s labor can be appropriated, labor—the productive capacity itself—cannot. For the logic of the liberal formulation of labor and property at the core of historical materialism, insofar as it is an intrinsic attribute of humans, has it that labor itself [productive capacity] is not alienable. What the worker sells, for instance, in the historical-materialist account is not labor power but labor time, or a certain duration of expenditure of her labor or “vital energy.”)[99] Moreover, the excess (*x*) retained by the Owner corresponds to the economic deficit attributed to the descendants of enslaved persons—which I call *negative*

99 See, for instance, Marx, *Capital*, vol. 1, 146, 151.

accumulation—that the tools of raciality have transubstantiated into a natural deficit.

When the analysis of capital attends to both modes of appropriation of labor, it is no longer ludicrous to demand the return of the total value yielded by the Slaves' labor and the Natives' lands. For one thing, it redefines the economic dimension of racial subjugation, as this can no longer be explained as the effect of unbecoming "prejudices," "beliefs," or "ideologies," or as a mode of control of labor that remains exterior to capital (per Quijano), or as a cultural (or ideological) construct that represents non-Europeans as nonhumans (per Wynter). Foregrounding both juridico-economic (colonial) and symbolic (racial) violence, the analysis of racial subjugation begins, for instance, with the acknowledgment that not only were emancipated slaves dispossessed of the means of production, of the total value created by that of their ancestors, but they were also comprehended by a political/symbolic arsenal that attributed their economic dispossession to an inherent moral and intellectual defect. From an economic point of view, it is thus possible to reconsider the post-slavery trajectory of black populations as one of an accumulation of processes of economic exclusion and juridical alienation—slavery, segregation, mass incarceration—that have left a disproportional percentage of them economically dispossessed. Now, the *negative* here has ethical significance (because labor in Marx's rendering is also significant) as well as economic consequences because, again, labor is quantifiable as time. *Negative accumulation*, otherwise an oxymoron, perfectly describes the colonial as a (juridico-economic) modality and the operations of the racial as a symbolic tool in the post-Enlightenment political architecture. For what slavery as a modality of expropriation has produced is an economic subject who, like Dana, owns minus (−) productive capacity because the total value yielded by her labor has been appropriated by the Owner and nullified by the critique of capital that disappears her as raw material.

"whether under the slave-owner's brutal lash, or the anxious eye of the capitalist"

> As the taste of the porridge does not tell you who grew the oats, no more does this simple process tell you of itself what are the social conditions under which it is taking place, whether under the slave-owner's brutal lash, or the anxious eye of the capitalist, whether Cincinnatus carries it on in tilling his modest farm or a savage in killing wild animals with stones.
>
> —Karl Marx, *Capital*, vol. 1

My procedure here may approximate Gayatri Spivak's reading of Marx in which she tracks the foreclosure of the "other of Europe" with the figure of the "native informant," that is, "a mark crossing out the impossibility of the ethical relation."[100] When tackling Marx's version of Europe's self-narrative, she reads the *Economic and Philosophical Manuscripts of 1844* and *Capital* (volumes 1 and 2) in order to expose how Marx's "Asiatic Mode of Production" (AMP) refers to a difference that is not that which organizes the totality that is capital (class) and the movement of history—that is, the dialectic. Her crucial move is to consider AMP an index of a difference,[101] which she retrieves from Marx's attention to the "notion of 'value form'"—that is, just before he engages in the core of theory, the pivot toward the determination of capital.[102] What she finds in Marx's brief reference to AMP is his "exigency of accounting for difference,"[103] which is figured in his earlier work, the *Economic and Philosophical Manuscripts*, in the distinction between Species-Being and Species-Life. The significance of this distinction, she claims, is that it refers to a "difference between need and making that means not only the

100 Spivak, *Critique of Postcolonial Reason*, 6.

101 "The Asiatic Mode of Production is the name and imaginary fleshing out of a difference in terms that are consonant with the development of capitalism and the resistance *appropriate* to it as 'the same.'" Spivak, 79 (italics in original).

102 Spivak, 71.

103 Spivak, 79.

possibility of exchange, but also the possibility of a surplus accessible to further exchange (or use)."[104] Though she does not name it as such, her procedure (reading AMP with Species-Life) also grasps a moment of delimiting the totality that is capital.

My tracings of Marx's comments on the colonies and "slave labor," as I have mentioned, also identify statements that delimit rather than determine. What is described falls under something (social conditions) that can be qualitatively (juridically) distinguished but is not quantitatively (economically) distinguishable (as a mode of appropriation of labor and means of production) from capital. Similarly, the difference refers to distinct modes of operation of property—"the colonies," which have too much public property; the Slave, who herself is a piece of property, and (as Spivak shows) the Asiatic Mode of Production, which applies to communities "without property in land."[105] To be sure, Spivak's registering of this differentiating recalls post-Enlightenment racial mappings of the global space—such as Herder's, Hegel's, and Cuvier's—which consistently limited the actualization of self-consciousness to the European space as a result of a uniquely European historical unfolding. This makes sense because she explicitly states her interest in their versions of the narrative of European "cultural identity."[106] What I find similar in her finding that AMP is a mark of an exclusion, of "the outside of the feudalism-capitalism circuit," is that, like "slave labor," it remains undetermined (quantitatively) even though it is separable (qualitatively) in terms of specific (imagined or observed) social conditions of production.[107]

Certainly, my tracking of delimitations of the colonial ("the colonies" and "slave labor") could be read in the same way, as

---

104 That "desire to theorize the other" is no longer active in capital, "when human self-conscious activity (Species-Being) appears in the value-form"; as such, "it shows itself capable of producing value in excess of what is needed to sustain being-natural in Species-Life (subsistence)." Spivak, 79 (italics in original).

105 Spivak, 80.

106 Spivak, 6.

107 Spivak, 83.

an attempt at identifying an exclusion (that may or may not be a constitutive one). Linguistically, the statements I commented on were exclusionary, in the sense that Marx explicitly says that "the colonies" are not sites for capital accumulation and that "slave labor" does not yield surplus value. Formally, however, the naming of a difference, which allows a separation on the basis of the principle of identity, does not signal an exclusion. More importantly, I did not identify a track that leads to the setting up of an indirect dichotomy, which is the move Spivak makes when (correctly) resolving the otherwise anomalous reference to AMP in Marx's distinction between Species-Life and Species-Being.[108] However, my tracking of Marx's delimitation captures a similar gesture, in which I find what Spivak calls Species-Life presented as a version of the "state of nature." The similarities stop there. Not only is my misreading not deconstructive, identifying delimitations is just one part, the first, of a three-part exercise.

What follows is a reading that seeks to dissect the totality that is capital. After tracking delimitations, I leave the historical (social conditions of production) and move to recompose the scientific (general equation of value) figuring of the scene (of production) of exchange value. But this move is disingenuous, because I am accepting premises that will be disowned in the next chapter. Most important is the thesis that privileges labor's efficacy (as cause and purpose)—with all the implications concerning extraction, intervention in regard to humans and nonhumans—that is, the idea that human labor alone is creative. However, I also violate the historical-materialist text because I focus on the raw material instead of labor. But instead of focusing on the cotton or the spindle as referents (the embodiment) of the Slave's creative capacity or material efficacy, I focus on labor itself, that is, on the material capacity (transfer of the potential energy) that is the Slave's body. Earlier, I deployed the poethical (de/compositional) tool of blacklight to expose how

108 According to Spivak, Marx's description in the *Grundrisse* figures an individual "who is still only defined in terms of Species-Life rather than Species-Being" (80).

"the colonies" and "slave labor"—as material efficacy—enter into the production of capital. Here I explore its other capacity, which is to de/compose at the molecular and atomic levels: I shed blacklight on the equation of value to make the cotton shine. Under blacklight, thrown over the equation of value in order to highlight the cotton, "the colonies" appear as sites of production, and "slave labor" as the creator of value. Beginning with the function of labor as a scientific category, and working through the other three, I re/compose the determining and delimiting statements that allow Marx to assemble the totality that is capital under the guidance of questions that, instead of figuring labor as a *conceptum*—with functions that ensure and sustain the totality that is capital—address it as a component that is both a singular part and expression of all that enters into the scene of production as described in Marx's formalization of his general theory of value.

My point of departure is simple, since the main distinction of "slave labor," that which disqualifies it as producer of surplus value, is the juridical relation that defines it as an ethico-economic figure, that is, title/property. Everything else, it can be argued, all other categories are applicable, but in particular labor pure and simple. Hence instead of the labor form, I begin and stay with labor pure and simple; that is, the labor process, the "expenditure of vital force," remains the same, regardless "of the social conditions under which it is taking place," as Marx noticed.[109] In Marx's rendering of the equation of value in volume 1, chapter 7 of *Capital*, "the colonies" where "slave labor" creates under the "brutal lash" enter into the equation as cotton (raw material). Certainly, as discussed earlier, the turn in the argument is not dissimilar to Marxist-feminist arguments concerning the elision of reproduction and, with it, domestic labor from Marx's account of the production of value.[110] Perhaps

---

109 Marx, *Capital*, vol. 1, 164.

110 See, for instance, Leopoldina Fortunati, *The Arcane of Reproduction: Housework, Prostitution, Labor and Capital*, trans. Hilary Creek (Brooklyn, NY: Autonomedia, 1995).

the most obvious difference would be the fact that I am not, as I have said repeatedly, setting up an adjustment of the historical-materialist text that would make it amenable to a contemplation of the Colonial ("the colonies" and "slave labor") as integral to the totality that is Capital. Hopefully, my move in the previous section already showed that this exercise is primarily a re/de/composition of leading critical descriptions (such as the racial dialectic and the original presentation of historical materialism) of the global political architecture by stirring up (what is most relevant on) its grounds.

In Marx's equation, I find that the *total value* yielded by the material capacity of the *bodies* of Slaves laboring on the *lands* of Natives in North (US cotton plantations) and South America (Brazil's iron-ore mines)—both *expropriated* through the violent methods and practices characteristic of colonial juridical modality—vanishes into/as *raw material*. The "slave labor" expended in planting and harvesting cotton seems to count only as *raw material*—a thing (natural subject of labor) that has "been filtered through previous labor"—which under capitalist production becomes "an absorbent of a definite quantity of [living] labour."[111] Because the Owner expropriated the *total value* yielded by her labor on expropriated Native lands, the *ethical principle of self-determination (in its juridical expression as liberty)*, which equally encompasses worker and capitalist in the *juridical form of the contract*, explains why "slave labor" does not count in capital accumulation. Since I have already traced how Marx deployed the colonies and "slave labor" to outline the totality that is capital and to describe how the categories of labor and (private) property are articulated within it, and lined by time, all that is left to do now is undo this assemblage by bringing the wounded captive body in the scene of subjugation into the scene of (exchange) value production.

If we follow Marx's comments on "slave labor," we learn that it appears as unpaid labor because that is what it is. However, we can begin with the simple statement that "slave labor"

111 Marx, *Capital*, vol. 1, 158, 170.

is unpaid, if only in regard to the relation between the Slave and the Owner. As a commodity that has the capacity to produce commodities, such as cotton, the labor of the Slave was paid a few times—to the trader in the place of kidnapping, the shipper, and the seller in the (Slave) Market. In the moments before the Slave's labor is applied to the cultivation of cotton—in Mississippi, for instance—she has generated a profit for many, a profit that traces back to her birth and early moments of fostering by her mother somewhere on the African continent. What I am highlighting here is that, if we begin with the singularity of the labor applied in the production of cotton that enters into the equation of value, we find that the first scene is not that of exchange between free persons in the Slave Market. Instead, we begin where labor (material capacity) is held—namely, the body and the persons and land that nourish it. And after Slavery's primal scene of violence (kidnapping) made a person born on the African continent into a commodity who can produce commodities as well as other producers of commodities, this person's labor power has never stopped being profitable, in that her material capacity (that is, every atom and particle that compose her body) is what is sold, not the person.

What this re/de/composition of labor does is to challenge labor as a conceptum, its apprehension as a symbolic and, in particular, *scientific* and *economic* category. In terms of its function as a descriptor of economic activities, the adjustment here is simple. Instead of considering labor ontically as the movement performed by a human—which Marx then states is translated into time—I am considering labor as the material capacity (transference and transduction of potential energy) every existing thing hosts, because it is simply an expenditure of its quantic *elementa*. Insofar as this capacity is a component of the scene of (re)production, it participates as that which performs—as Marx says—the *transference* of the (potential and mechanical energy) constituents of the lands and waters of "the colonies" where the cotton was planted and the instruments (including animals) were employed in the planting, care, and harvest of cotton bolls. With cotton as the Slave's and the conquered land's potential energy, animals also enter into the creation of yarn, along with the material capacity of the laborer employed in its production and of everything and everyone that generated and maintained the laborer's body.

Once labor is no longer qualified as "power" (that is, as having mechanical efficacy), even if it remains an economic category, it no longer plays a determinative function—once it becomes a component whose application facilitates the transfer of material capacity, that is, of the potential energy of other components that enter into the production process. It follows that the distinction between types of labor in terms of *juridical* forms (free labor and "wage labor") no longer holds. Because once labor is described in this way—as pure and simple transfer of potential energy or material capacity—the creative becomes the same as transference, and the very process of re/de/composition happens regardless of design (final purpose) or drive (efficient cause). What comes to the fore (insofar as the distinction between "wage labor" and "slave labor" is concerned) as both are appropriated is a difference given by the mode of appropriation.[112] Relatedly, the *ethical* function of labor is radically displaced in this move, because once labor is described as a material capacity (re/de/composition of potential energy) and not a mental ability (end, design, motive, or drive), it is not only the distinction between "free labor" and "slave labor" that no longer matters but the distinction between labor, raw material, and instrument of production as well. All three—along with everything else (solid, liquid, gas, or plasma) that enters into the production of the yarn—directly or indirectly enter into the creation of the yarn, whether through transference of potential energy (labor)

---

112 Elsewhere I have proposed to keep Marx's term "exploitation" to refer to the appropriation of surplus value or partial value. *Exploitation*, the appropriation of part of the value created by labor, also specifies the social (juridical) conditions for "capitalist production": the capitalist appropriates a value created that is above the wage the worker receives, as established in the *contract* of the sale of his/her labor power for a given period of time. I proposed the term expropriation for the appropriation of total value and labor value, under total violence, that takes place in the case of "slave labor." See Ferreira da Silva, "Unpayable Debt."

or internal kinetic energy (*calor*),[113] which everything transfers into the environment all the time. What results from this peeling off of labor's functions is an emptying of labor as a scientific category, because without the presumption of the other three moments, this category does not hold. Perhaps another way of saying it is that social-scientific concepts, and that includes the racial—because the modern notion of the social came to encompass all four—consistently attend to the four moments through which I have figured Marx's presentation of labor in his assemblage of capital. Now that labor has been returned to its basic, raw definition as material capacity, it is possible to re/compose the equation of value by including the value created by enslaved laborers working on Virginia's or Mississippi's cotton plantations on conquered (Indigenous) lands.[114] Negative accumulation, from this point of view, no longer seems an oxymoron. For it is about not only Slaves and their descendants having (−) productive capacity but whatever was created carrying material components of their bodies. What has been accumulated as capital is the infinite self-energy of the elementary particles that compose their bodies. Not in the form of determinable labor time but as that which is not determinable in the product, the excess (x) expropriated material capacity under the brutal lash, that is, the total violence that the wounded captive body in the scene of subjugation cannot but recall.

***

The conceptum of labor must grasp liberal "social conditions" —that is, the ethical and juridical structures of liberty—if it is to have any explanatory (determinative) significance.[115] Not surprisingly, the body of the worker—which he states is expended in the

113 *Calor* is a term for heat (transfer of internal kinetic energy) used in thermodynamics. It is the root of everyday terms such as calorie.

114 Mississippi and Virginia were major centers of cotton production in the antebellum US South.

115 Marx, *Capital*, vol. 1, 156.

application of labor power—plays no significant role in Marx’s totality. By returning to physics’ definition of labor (potential energy), I moved to recall the materiality of labor but—and I hope it is evident—not to make a case for the body’s vitality or (however figured) self-determining aspect. My move here targets both figurings of the *transparent I* that are consistently repositioned on whatever is chosen to challenge the former and its supremacy. Turning to physics has a rather prosaic twofold objective. On the one hand, it was designed to counter how labor as an economic and epistemological operator is released from the body and rendered an alienable property. This transformation is enabled by equating time and labor to another abstract entity, namely money. For profit—money that is always already capital—is nothing more than the difference between the value created by *living labor* (exchange value), the value of raw material and instruments, and the value of labor (use value). On the other hand, this turn also helps to release labor from the grip of the category of property in both its juridical and its economic forms. Time operates subtly here, because the move is directly related not to the capitalist’s ownership of the means of production but to the laborer’s ethico-juridical capacity (liberty) to sell his or her labor. That is, this effect is hosted in the juridical form of the contract, the capitalist agreement to pay a certain wage (which will be less than the value produced by labor) in exchange for the worker to apply her labor for a number of hours at the factory. In sum, the contract signals that the laborer is dispossessed, but for the ownership of her labor power.

An unexpected effect of Marx taking the body in its efficient (mechanic) and not functional (organic) aspect is that, once labor, the category, is stripped from the para-analytic demands to express the liberal polity, its juridical and ethical functions come to the fore. Both juridical forms and ethical principles are of utmost importance in the delimitation of the totality that is capital. For the title/property labor relation brings something that Marxists, to this day, would rather keep outside of the totality that is capital, namely total violence. At first it may seem the lack of liberty that defines the enslaved laborer would be a deterrent; however, a more careful consideration shows that the mode of appropriation of labor, which I call expropriation, as part of the "predatory practices" of "the colonies," signals something that threatens to distort the abstract totality. Further, the Native lands where the cotton was grown enter the value of commodity as "the universal subject of human labour," which provides "things which labour merely separates from the environment," without juridical mediation.[116] The production of cotton took place in the political (juridico-economic) architecture—*the colony*—where total violence rules, both actually and potentially. Under the owner's "brutal lash," enslaved workers in Mississippi's and Virginia's cotton plantations applied their material capacity (transferred their potential and internal kinetic energy)—that is, the *labor* and *calor* it took for planting and picking the cotton—to Native lands (expropriated at gunpoint and through the spread of deadly disease) and to the tools and animals used to create the cotton used in the production of yarn by English living labor.[117]

---

116 Marx, 158.

117 See Luxemburg, *Accumulation of Capital*, 350. However, unlike Luxemburg, I do not think of the colony as the frontier of capital. Instead, as Bartolomé de Las Casas, C. L. R. James, and Frantz Fanon have described, the colony is a modern juridico-economic structure designed and managed by European thinkers and policy makers. I am thinking here of John Locke's role in the writing of the Fundamental Constitutions of Carolina in 1669, which were characterized by unmitigated violence.

Resting on these pillars of separability, determinacy, and sequentiality, the thesis of coloniality, the tools of raciality, and the historical-materialist arsenal transubstantiate colonial expropriation into datum or raw material. Namely, the alteration takes place at the deepest level as the result of juridical domination because of the "matter," as either a residue of a previous category (temporally) or a natural occurrence (empirically). Consequently, the task becomes to design procedures capable of reversing this process. Ignoring determinacy and sequentiality, my contribution here consists of figuring capital as a juridico-economic architecture that involves the two modes of governance—the colony and the polity—that were assembled and consolidated over the past approximately four hundred years. Each mode of governance assures different modes of appropriation of land and labor, respectively, through a legally binding agreement or the threat and employment of violence (conquest and slavery). Further, each refers to distinct modes of appropriation of value as mediated by a particular juridical form—contract and title—which allows for its particular mode of use of labor for the reproduction of capital. In “wage labor” there is appropriation of the partial value created, which I will call exploitation, under legal obligation; in “slave labor” there is appropriation of the total value created, which I will call expropriation, under violent coercion.

CHAPTER 4
“where flesh joined with plaster”

> I could feel the knife in my hand, still slippery with perspiration. A slave was a slave. Anything could be done to her. And Rufus was Rufus—erratic, alternately generous and vicious. I could accept him as my ancestor, my younger brother, my friend, but not as my master, and not as my lover. He had understood that once.
>
> I twisted sharply, broke away from him. He caught me, trying not to hurt me. I was aware of him trying not to hurt me even as I raised the knife, even as I sank it into his side.
>
> [...]
>
> He lost his hold on my hand for a moment, but caught my arm before I could get away. [...]
>
> I pulled the knife free of him somehow, raised it, and brought it down again into his back.
>
> This time he only grunted. He collapsed across me, somehow still alive, still holding my arm.
>
> —Octavia E. Butler, *Kindred*

Ending Dana's travails back in her house in Los Angeles, without the arm that Rufus held, Octavia Butler leaves us with several questions: Was having his life saved by her, and the final scene of total violence, his trying to rape her, in any way relevant to what became of his life and Alice's life? Did Dana's presence affect what would have become of the Weylins' Slaves had she not been there/then at all? How was her presence/existence resolved by those who stayed behind, who existed in that moment? None of these questions matters, to be sure. Whatever happened then, and what came to pass in Dana's existence upon her return without a limb, is relevant not because of what one can learn, but because of what considering such questions suggests as a method for making sense of existence without the intrastructures of modern thought. At every moment, on all occasions, as long as she existed in antebellum Maryland—including while she was tortured, taught slaves to read, or resisted Rufus's attack—Dana could not but figure as "female flesh ungendered" without and against the protections of patriarchy or any of the liberal (ethical and juridical) protections in that moment in the United States, and for this reason she was a threat to both. The wounded captive body in the scene of subjugation, by recalling *life*—in the ethical scene (as a person without dignity) and in the economic scene (as labor without productivity)—renders flesh both ethically and economically *negative*, that is, $\infty - \infty$ or corpus infinitum.[1] For this reason, she presents more of a threat to the mode of thinking that both presumes and necessitates an image of existence obtained by identity and unity.

Because the overseer's lashes and the Owner's violating hands did land on her back, her body, her subjugation is rendered as something that happened. The wounds, healed and unhealed marks on her body, figure a juridical modality that both depended on and authorized her to be traded and raped for profit. Unavailable to the tools and procedures that require "access" to what is premised in Subjectivity, her body is standing or splattered on the ground, bleeding and weeping, her tears and blood mixing with the soil, being carried by ants, eaten by worms. Whatever happens to her body, to her person, however she responds to it, whatever she thought in that moment, will never be transcribed in the letters of the self, in the sounds of the subject. Any transcription will prompt the question of the message, will assume a response, will bring her into the subject's domain, where she by condition and definition had no place. And yet, anything and everything the Owner was able to acquire and accumulate was also partly her, chunks of her body (matter energy) materialized (converted) in each and every cotton boll. At every moment, wherever she was, under the heat of the sun or drenched by unrelenting rain, she was also always beyond and before everywhere (infinitely) but also anywhere/anywhen (immediately and instantaneously).

Labor that might as well be that which she is laboring on, that which her body becomes when it is applied in the effort to un/make, re/de/compose, enters into the constitution of that other thing, the cotton bolls, the stewed collard greens, the

---

1 Elsewhere I have employed Leibniz's plenum and Michelangelo Pistoletto's *canvas infinita* as descriptors of this rendering of ∞ (infinity). See, for instance, Denise Ferreira da Silva, "1 (life) ÷ 0 (blackness) = $\infty - \infty$ or ∞ / ∞: On Matter beyond the Equation of Value," *e-flux journal*, no. 79 (February 2017), https://www.e-flux.com/journal/79/94686/1-life-0-blackness-or-on-matter-beyond-the-equation-of-value/.

clean undergarments, the shack where she lives, or the houses her descendants may or may not be able to afford to own. That labor, her body in the cotton bolls, Marx tells us, does not count. It does not explain or create capital. It does transform, transfer, convert itself to what she is handling, touching, moving around. But because it is not graspable as a manifestation of her "will" or an effect of her "desire" or "drive," whatever she makes, whatever contains a piece of her is not to be counted as wealth. And yet she is right there. In that cotton boll, in that factory in London's East End, a child or a young woman uses up her body, moving the spindle, separating the threads, and both of them together—the captive body in the scene of subjugation and living labor—come together in the yarn. It is not only that her labor—the expenditure of her body—creates something that is then separated from her as an object of use and brought to the market to become a commodity. No, she is always there, within it, and never alone. That piece of fabric is also a singular composite that gathers the labor and the calor of everything found in the expropriated Native lands where the iron ore or gold was extracted or the cotton grown. From this tangible transduction alone—and not through the abstract translations operated by labor as a conceptum, in particular its translation as time that renders it measurable—it is possible to consider her person to matter both ethically and economically.

The subjectum, it turns out, is even less able to take on the wounded captive body in the scene of subjugation than the conceptum of labor. Her disruptive force resides in her charge being one that cannot be explained and thus remains incomprehensible. Unavailable and unattended, because whatever it would express is resolved as an effect of the brutal lash and the will and desire it expresses, she persists (as the lash itself signals that there is in/as her a will to tame and a desire to curb). It is just that the total violence—threatened and delivered—to crush what she, as a person, is assumed to possess also precludes any consideration of her as a thing of will or desire. This is the case precisely because the position, for which Subjectivity is the descriptor used to name the *transparent I*, requests the position the wounded captive body in the scene of subjugation is made to occupy and designate. In her non-presence during this occupation resides her ethical significance. Holding its secret, the captive body in the scene of subjugation, her wounded back turned away from conceptum and subjectum alike, hosts that which can dismantle their empire.

“hieroglyphics of the flesh”

> These undecipherable markings on the captive body render a kind of hieroglyphics of the flesh whose severe disjunctures come to be hidden to the cultural seeing by skin color.
>
> —Hortense J. Spillers, “Mama’s Baby, Papa’s Maybe”

When does thinking with blackness begin and stay with the wounded flesh? When the question(ing) of *world*, of existence is *known* (determined and delimited), it starts from exactly “where the flesh [is] joined with plaster,” or more directly, from where one acknowledges that the plaster (and every other material involved in the design and building) of a house, or anything that has any (economic) value here/now, is but a re/composition of the flesh, blood, bones, of the bodies of yesterday’s colonial figures, namely the Native and the Slave. From that origin without a beginning, which is also an end without an unfolding, thinking is released from the delimiting and determining gestures and devices that have supported modern thought for centuries. Without beginning with the need to account for how the mind and the body, or the mind and the soul, constitute two parts of one or more substances, and along with that, without the themes of exteriority and interiority, space and time, neither the *transparent I* nor his *world* need to emerge as themes. Nor is it necessary to avoid the question of why, and to devise so many ways of formulating the question of how, without allowing for the theme to become how everything that exists could, might, may, or will be a singular re/de/composition of everything else.

What if the wounded captive body in the scene of subjugation invites us to consider thinking that begins with the body in its singularity, at the level at which it is also not the same as, not identical with, but equally composed of that which makes up everything else that has, does, and will exist? Asking this question after Spillers's difficult and challenging proposition requests a consideration of what such thinking would entail. I am convinced that it involves both more and less than anticipated. It takes more than a redefinition of the categories of thought. It will take more than the coining of new words or the deconstruction of old ones. It will take, I submit, no less than interrupting the very process of Thought, which means releasing thinking from necessity and the onto-epistemological pillars and descriptors on which it rests, in order to maintain Man's uniqueness. Obviously I cannot pretend that I could even begin this process here. All I can do is close *Unpayable Debt* as it opened, which is by returning to the Kantian program to unleash an attack from its underside.

What if thinking began from a more complex description of existence, one which, in addition to the historical and the organic, also attended to its cosmic and quantic moments? What would become of cognition (sensation, imagination, Understanding) if it attended to both that which is in and figures spacetime and that which signals its beyond in the whole expanse of existence (the universe) in which there is no distinction between space and time because it consists mostly of what spacetime does not comprehend (theoretically and experimentally) but yet (observationally) affects it? From the cosmic level, the *I Think*, in its formal and historical constitution, as in *transparent (self-regulating) unity or (self-producing) identity*, dissipates in the spacetime instants in which it is at once not and no longer present; hence it cannot prejudge its capacity to know because it has no way of knowing whether or not there is an order, and even if there is one, it cannot rely on its categories to access it.[2] Without the presumption that

2 This is the case of dark matter and dark energy, approximately 27 and 68 percent of the universe, respectively. Neither can be described, explained, or calculated with precision, and they are postulated (said to exist) only because of the effects for which only the presence of matter or energy can be the cause. See experiments such as "SuperCDMS | Super Cryogenic Dark

existence—in the guise of Nature or *world*—is always already ordered (constituted by other smaller and larger ordered units) and comprehended by the *I Think*, its tools cannot even claim the capacity to delimit or determine. Even though the cosmic may be available to the senses via telescopes and probes, all that is known about it is transmitted as energy read through the electromagnetic spectrum, which translates information as amplitude and frequency that can be compared with what is already known. In the quantic moment, the *I Think* has no capacity to claim that its intuitions apprehend an already ordered world.[3] This is so for two reasons: first, because its *elementa* (wave-particles) are deeply implicated with all others in the universe in ways that escape sense perception; and second, because such connection is beyond the senses, the very first movement in knowing that sustains all other claims that apprehension is invalidated, as separability is the first pillar to crumble in the quantic moment.

That would render *time* irrelevant both to what has been and what is yet to come (the cosmic) and to what was already and what is also yet to become (the quantic). What the cosmic and the quantic moments do is not so much add other dimensions or levels to knowledge—this is not a matter of scale—but undermine the very bases of post-Enlightenment thinking, its pillars of separability, determinacy, and sequentiality, which transform events and existents into Nature or *world*. When thinking takes the moments that escape "experience" under consideration, the significant departure is not so much that they render the laws of logic (noncontradiction and identity) unnecessary, as those are still used in descriptions of phenomena in both dimensions.

Matter Search," SLAC National Accelerator Laboratory, accessed August 10, 2020, https://supercdms.slac.stanford.edu/overview.

3 What I am highlighting here is the fact that mathematical models are able to describe, explain, and calculate quantic and cosmic "objects." In the case of the former, they can actually lead to the creation of artificial things (like computers) that make use of their elements and processes. What cannot be done is to answer *finality* questions, such as *what* they are and *why* they act the way they do.

Of importance here is the fact that, while *epistemologically* useful, the tools of knowledge they support, the ones they validate, become *ontologically* relevant. The weird experimental findings of particle physics and the fact that only 5 percent of the cosmos is describable indicate that the tools of scientific knowledge cannot describe (define, interpret, or even observe) what exists and what happens in these moments. It is thus a stretch to call whatever they are "phenomena" since they do not fit into spacetime, because, for one thing, *they are*—in their presentation as matter or energy—spacetime, that is, *corpus infinitum*.

Only by attending to the *elemental*, I propose, in lieu of the metaphysical—that is, by abandoning the *universal* and the *transcendental*—is it possible to devise descriptors and maneuvers capable of dismounting the onto-epistemological pillars that support the reign of necessity. With *elementum*, I am moving to an anti/ante-Kantian reading of what Kant called the Thing (*das Ding*) by considering it in a materialist reading of Leibniz's plenum—that is, I am approaching the Thing as matter. Put simply, what I am proposing is a shift in the framing of that which concerns knowing, from the Kantian formal (*a priori*) to the material (*pars*). This substitution makes possible, among other things, the displacing of the theme of *identity/difference* (as given the principle of identity and the law of noncontradiction), through which necessity imposes separability in the descriptors of the existents and events, to return them with a presumed ordered unity. For what the focus on the *pars*, that is, on the elementary parts of which things are made (Aristotle's material cause)—*raw material*—provides is the possibility of displacing the sociological (moral) answer to Spillers's question of the possibility of material transfer in/through time, which would be, along the lines of Daniel Moynihan's thesis, that the transfer of the markings of total violence is a *cause/effect* of "black pathology."

Instead, a raw-materialist approach to the question would open the possibility for at least two sets of considerations: on the one hand, the one that focuses on the marked flesh and reads in it total violence deployed in order to extract total value; and, on the other hand, the one that focuses on the total value extracted, on its components (*pars*), and on what they have transduced or re/de/composed (into commodities, profit, capital, and more capital). For both to be thinkable two moves would be necessary: first, "the things of the world," emancipated from *time* and the categories of understanding, would no longer be addressed as phenomena; second, they would be considered without *space* at the level of the elementa that have existed since the unfolding of spacetime and also enter into the composition of all that has existed, does exist, and will exist. In short, existents and events considered not as separate entities but as deeply implicated *pars*, as elementa, as singular compositions, would regain their orientation toward the infinitum. This move, crucially, would not constitute a radical departure from the mode of thinking and the scales of time (the historical and the organic) that, not surprisingly, have become the basis for the deployment of identity in the writing of the human as object of knowledge, in both determinative or positive (scientific) and interpretive (historical) projects. Because, as Dana's story suggests, materiality takes many forms and works according to what these projects do, and we cannot merely wish away the organic and the historical, for their marks (as those of torture) constitute the *known* world in which we exist.

What becomes possible if thinking starts with the presumption of deep implicancy and infinity? My bet is that, in addition to being finally released from the imposition to comprehend, this image of existence would allow the Human to be released into the *world* to dissolve in/into/as everything with which it is already deeply implicated—everything in its deep implicancy with/in the expanse of spacetime and perhaps beyond. Not only will Dana's charge make sense (without postulating apprehension or seeking comprehension), but the demand it recalls will be the only acceptable "meaning" for justice. For how could she be continually summoned to that time-place to save Rufus's life? Why did she have to give up a limb to settle an unpayable debt? There was no agreement made by her or someone else on her behalf, that is, a contract, in verbal or written form. She just happened to be alive, to move into a house with her partner, her house—the house (which is her right to live there only when she wants) that cost her an arm. Reading the book today inspires black persons to consider how much more could become possible, or how much of what does become possible expresses that which never will be. Putting it another way: once all are aware that the world, this world, is a composite of so much of what never came to be and what never will be, Dana’s unpayable debt becomes everybody’s.

“literal and figurative emphases”

> This profitable “atomizing” of the captive body provides another angle on the divided flesh: we lose any hint or suggestion of a dimension of ethics, of relatedness between human personality and its anatomical features, between one human personality and another, between human personality and cultural institutions. To that extent, the procedures adopted for the captive flesh demarcate a total objectification, as the entire captive community becomes a living laboratory. The captive body, then, brings into focus a gathering of social realities as well as a metaphor for value so thoroughly interwoven in their literal and figurative emphases that distinctions between them are virtually useless.
>
> —Hortense J. Spillers, “Mama’s Baby, Papa’s Maybe”

If it is true that “the master’s tools will never dismantle the master’s house,” it is no less true that these very tools only operate within a context that presumes that an unyielding force ensures their supposedly lasting productive powers.[4] For if skin color has derived its onto-epistemological capacity of transmuting juridical and economic “effects” into moral (ethical) “causes,” there is no reason not to think that the juridic, the economic, the ethic, and even the symbolic (the moment in which raciality’s tools function) can only be conceived as such, as separate dimensions of

4 This is in reference to Audre Lorde’s famous statement as well as its many repetitions, which more often than not are meant to stop inquiry instead of unleashing the search for other tools. Audre Lorde, “The Master’s Tools Will Never Dismantle the Master’s House,” in *Sister Outsider: Essays and Speeches* (Berkeley, CA: Crossing Press, 2007), 110–14.

existence, because of how necessity sustains modern thinking through its onto-epistemological pillars (separability, determinacy, and sequentiality) and epistemological descriptors (formality and efficacy). Though all coalesce in the assembling of the symbolic moment, here I have focused on determinacy, primarily because of the hold it has had on the post-Enlightenment episteme.[5] Once determinacy found a comfortable place with/in sequentiality (I am referring here to Hegel's version of the dialectic) it did not take long for it to disappear in the terms and formulations of the scene of representation (the stage of interiority), only to be spotted in the moments when raciality is activated from within, and when the racial dialectic closes the circuit of explanation, keeping the juridical and economic out of consideration and the *transparent I* (in the interpretive episteme) protected in interiority. Because the arsenal of raciality cannot but expose how determinacy remains operative in the interpretive regime and works through its political/symbolic tools, its productive weapons, like blackness, have the capacity to demolish the latter as well as any term or formulation that presumes and predicates it.

When thinking begins without the *transparent I*, there is no more need to hold everything hostage as Nature or *world*, as the effect of a principle or law that would involve or resolve it in a knowable or thinkable totality, some kind of ordered world. As one of the master's tools, the racial dialectic is very efficient in its presentation of an order that, though benefiting those embraced by whiteness/Europeanness, never fails to attribute its operation to Nature (Kant's *a priori* laws), thereby giving contingent and emergent expressions of juridico-economic subjugation the unyielding force of necessity. Here the wounded captive body in the scene of subjugation, as a referent of value—in its literality and figurality—demands that the question be posed of by which means. That is, her marked body—which registers interiority as excess and opaqueness—raises the question of

5 This view of modern philosophy unfolding as a conversation frames Ferreira da Silva, *Toward a Global Idea of Race.*

how the interpretive figuring of the *transparent I* as a purely interior thing does or does not serve the master’s new needs.

The turn to the transcendental (with modifications) that supports this writing of Subjectivity, both beyond and before a world that cannot but reflect it, becomes no longer sustainable when the descendant of yesterday’s Slave sets out to describe her existence from the other side of subjectification, and in doing so fails to mirror transparent subjectivity. Instead, she mirrors the wounds that prevail in her absent family photo albums. Because she is not contemplated by the principles that sustain Subjectivity’s claim to transparency, she has no commitment to keep or destroy the world that mirrors it. All she does—whether she intends to or not, as intentionality (in Husserl’s terms) also has no business here (because she stands in the world and she is approached, along with everything else, as an object)—is to ask, if humans have been owned and traded like any other commodity, if they have been dissected and studied like any other object, what is the basis for “othering,” what has entered in the assembling of the place assigned to human “Others” in the world? This is not to signal exclusion but to ask for an engagement with the very onto-epistemological regime that created such positions of enunciation and reference, namely, I, Other, Nature, *world*, and everything everywhere in it.

My effort here, in case it is not explicit by now, is not to recall (and disavow) old dichotomies or set up new ones. The wounded captive body in the scene of subjugation brings a challenge to thinking that sits comfortably as a choice between two positions or as the positing of a contradiction and does not request a step back, away, or out of dichotomic thinking. She does not express the rules of production of a subject (its others and its abjections), she is not a discursive effect, she does not signal an aporia. When her body recalls wounds presumed in the blackness that tells of her condition as commodity and laborer, the captive body brings about juridical and economic considerations, not as a descriptor of specified or determined “social conditions,” but as one party of a juridical bind that gives the other party the authority to deploy total violence and in which the place assigned to her records fungibility, not dignity. That shift of registers does not set up an opposition, which would be possible if either the Human (the noble) lost its specificity (dignity) or the Thing (as commodity) acquired it, but if that happens, the latter would lose its exchange value (fungibility), that is, that which renders its equivalency to money.

A Human existing as a Thing, the wounded captive body in the scene of subjugation has this gift (perhaps what Du Bois meant by "second sight"?), which is a lack of concern with avoiding or resolving the constitutive distinction of the post-Enlightenment episteme. Without the transcendental, as we know, the philosophical figuring of the Human and Humanity—as the self-determined, self-producing *transparent I*—would not be sustainable, or even possible. More importantly, from the vantage point of this moment of the interpretive regime, without Hegel's version that interiorizes determinacy and renders productivity a necessary but violent moment of Spirit's self-actualizing movement, the *I Think*, the existing thing with a privileged access to transcendental Reason, would not be refigured in ethical terms, a need that haunted the moderns' self-description from early on. Inspired by classical physics, Kant's rendering of the transcendental retains the Cartesian *formal I*, and now includes the necessary tools (intuitions and categories) for apprehending and comprehending the world without becoming of it or one with it. This is what Hegel addresses with the presentation of the *transcendental I* (Spirit) and *world* (Nature), that is, the version of the ethical scene as the violent unfolding through which the former recognizes itself in the latter, which then becomes what it has always already been, a vanishing moment.

The wounded captive body in the scene of subjugation has nothing to do with this problem and the solution. Not solely a Thing—as the Owner's use of force is also meant to coerce her to show enjoyment, she is not a moment in the unfolding of the *transcendental I* (Hegel said that, as a Negro, she is an object of no-value). Not standing on either side, Human or Thing, hers is the position from which one can observe how the sides have been created in the first place. Hers is the position from which one can track necessity working through onto-epistemological pillars such as separability, the logical operations of the (categorical) principle of identity (and the law of noncontradiction), and the (hypothetical) principle of (efficient) causality. For this reason, her position also indicates why determinacy emerges as the defining gesture of modern knowledge, both because that was the authority of the divine author and ruler that the Human (as Subject) arrogates for itself and because that authority must rely on the same powerful force on which the former did, namely, necessity. Not solely Human, by definition a person without being presented as a thing of liberty, she signals the ethical scene obversely—no wonder the ease with which Hegel’s “actuality of the ethical idea,”[6] the State, kills black persons—she has no position in the world that mirrors the *transparent I* from which she was not even excluded because she was not even considered. Hers remains a no-go zone—no-*man*’s-land—for the tools and artisans of modern thinking.

Glimpses of it are offered by every report of a finding in particle physics or condensed-matter physics, or a new adjustment in quantum field theory or another theory, or a dark-matter experiment that seeks a response to the unanswered question, signs of a new physics, or merely to reconcile gravity with the standard model of particle physics. The critical insights have been explained and explored, with varying sophistication and transparency. Among the few sophisticated inroads into the onto-epistemological implications of the quantic, Karen Barad shows how the apparatuses of physics such as formalization—whether through measurement or categorization—“help constitute and are a constitutive part of what is being measured,” that is, “matter and meaning do not pre-exist, but rather are co-constitutive via measurement intra-actions.”[7] Barad’s notion of “ontological indeterminacy” is the first explicit philosophical deployment of quantum field theory and particle physics in the critical field of theoretical interventions. Though our approaches differ in

6 G. W. F. Hegel, *Outline of the Philosophy of Right*, trans. T. M. Knox, ed. Stephen Houlgate (Oxford: Oxford University Press, 2008), 232.

7 Karen Barad, *What Is the Measure of Nothingness? Infinity, Virtuality, Justice* (Berlin: Hatje Cantz, 2012), 6.

ways that will become more evident later in this chapter, Barad's ontological indeterminacy also recalls that position in which I find the wounded captive body in the scene of subjugation and from which I see her unleashing her capacity to unravel the interpretive episteme. Infinite and undeterminable (that is, at once all and nothing), everything possible and actual and forever virtual, an existent (elementa entering into the constitution of other things across spacetime, in spite of spacetime, and despite spacetime), she is neither Object nor Other—even if, as elementa, she composes today's dearest commodities.[8]

The wounded captive body in the scene of subjugation, her wounds that belie interiority, temporality, and transparency, hosts an image of existence that recalls elementa without needing them to be visible, palpable, provable. The image given by quantum physics, Leibniz's plenum or Michelangelo Pistoletto's *canvas infinita*, now seen not as the actualization of a divine design but as the perpetual re/de/composition of the elementa that emerged in the earliest moments of the universe and, ever since, have been reentering into the composition of everything that has existed, exists, and will come into existence. That is, not a world but, because it refers to any body, everybody's body, whichever, however, whatsoever, it, everything and anything, exists as *corpus infinitum*. And once existence is imaged as a corpus infinitum, everything else—I mean everything, including each and every one of the master's tools as well as the formulations, objects, and subjects they have created—is up for grabs.

Without separability and the local spatiality that provides determinacy (and its objects) and the unfolding temporality that provides Subjectivity (and its *world*), the terms, tools, and formulations of the post-Enlightenment determinative and interpretive moments are of no use. Historical materialism—both its determinative vein as designed by Marx and the interpretive versions,

8 If anything, as the phenomenon called quantum entanglement shows, one single particle that is a constituent of the letter *O* on my keyboard might just as well be entangled, immediately and simultaneously, with a particle in the tip of my hair or one composing a planet in a galaxy five thousand billion light-years away.

such as Lukács's, Gramsci's, and Althusser's—is perhaps the best example. If the original presentation was limited by determinacy, by the need to identify one, and only one, empiricum moment (the economic) and category (labor) that would determine and delimit the totality that is capital, the interpretive version had to deal with the (self-imposed) restrictions that resulted in the prevalence of the need to account for the superstructural (the symbolic in the guise of culture and ideology) that always left them threatened with dismissal as a departure from the original determinative presentation.

Today, we even find returns to formalism as such—like Badiou's version—which deride the interpretive without attending to how the formal has always sustained the historical-materialist framework both in Marx's inaugural (determinative) presentation (facilitated by biology) and in later interpretive ones, such as Sartre's (facilitated by phenomenology). Despite Oliver Cox's and Cedric Robinson's efforts to engage historical materialism with racial subjugation, their attempts required (like other interpretive ones) the articulation of the concept of the cultural to designate the superstructural element that facilitates or adapts capital to new circumstances. Perhaps the only exception is Fanon, whose deployment of historical materialism refused both the determinative requirement that labor be the defining category (by locating the peasantry as the revolutionary class in the colonial context) and the interpretive demand that culture be proposed as a fundamental and decisive political moment (which he countered by stressing how in the colonial context the racial structure is the superstructure).[9] What I am highlighting here is the fact that, as long as historical materialism's tools, formulations, and propositions render exteriority

9 Relevant here is Fanon's own seemingly determinative moment, that is, his considerations of mental illness as a crucial effect of colonial subjugation. Unfortunately, it is not possible to give it the attention it deserves here. All I can say is that it deserves to be examined in relation to how it is situated in the interpretive episteme and against the background of twentieth-century versions of historical materialism that were more explicitly interpretive.

(determinative) or interiority (interpretive), it cannot account for the political figure whose position undermines both as well as separates them. For the wounded captive body in the scene of subjugation does not request a form/law or principle/purpose that would provide the key to the assembling of any totality she explains. Instead, she signals how any totality, as well as the principles and concepts that would gather it, cannot stand when she and her wounds enter into the theater of thinking. Why? Because her juridico-economic condition of existence undermines the presumptive transcendentality in (both its Kantian/formal and Hegelian-Husserlian/empirical) formulations that sustain the figure that needs to be presupposed—the *transparent I*—in any strategy devised to build them (the totality and its principles and concepts).

Early and new critical texts, like historical materialism, also cannot withstand her charge. Here I am thinking of how the wounded captive body in the scene of subjugation halts any critical move that does not attend to how the position of enunciation of any political subject immediately obtains the arch form of the subject—the male, father, owner, husband—and as such renders her but fodder for the articulation of their (even if partial) authority.[10] That which is the case for critical racial interventions also plays out in gender-sexual interventions that fail to account for how the indicators of domesticity fail to signify the wounded captive body in the scene of subjugation as a woman and further her subjection (as Slave or the "black welfare mother") by signaling her moral failure to properly exercise the role of mother or wife. Because she cannot stand in the place produced by these categories—the image of the post-Enlightenment political architecture she calls on consistently removes her from it—she challenges that which occupies the position of power, of authority. There is no point in trying to reform the captive body and make her fit where she does not belong. Hers is a radical stance that is at once a demand for accountability or redress and a move to release existence from

---

10 Ferreira da Silva, "Hacking the Subject," 19–41.

the grips of the *transparent I*, to bring its world of knowledge to an end and clear the grounds for thinking beyond its limits. Her stance, in sum, insofar as it is confrontational, is *negativation*, namely, an enactment of *refusal*—refusal to die, refusal to comply, refusal to give up and give in—to which the mere existence of black persons here/now testifies.

If the unraveling of the racial dialectic performed by the wounded captive body in the scene of subjugation renders the master's tools inoperative, as they know nothing but the master's house and its inhabitants, a whole range of possibilities opens, including, but not reduced to, modes of engagement that further the disassembling of the master's tools and creative poethical tools that welcome other images of existence while the work of bringing about the end of the world we *know* is under way. Among the many possible ones, I explore the *figurative* as a modality of engagement that neither presumes nor demands data, meaning, evidence, or ground. Besides not conforming with the program of discovery, the figurative as an analytical modality of intervention combines the steps of critique with the procedures of the creative. For instance, my activation of blacklight in the reading of Marx's formalization of the general law of value (the equation of value) both exposes the shortcomings of the historical-materialist framework and outlines an approach to the analysis of the play of state and capital in the political architecture of the global present that does not remain prisoner of the limits of the determinative or interpretive regime. In doing so, this activation enabled the contemplation of an ethical program that has the only acceptable means for justice in decolonization (the restoration of the total value expropriated from Native lands and Slave bodies under total violence).

Further, the figurative hosts an image of existence, which does not anticipate unity and linearity but instead prefigures infinity and assumes a deep implicancy. That elemental stance allows for the imagination to move without the restraints of understanding because, as Barad describes, infinity and implicancy constitute the elementa that enter into the composition of everything that exists, actually, possibly, and virtually. Many approaches and perspectives can be designed from this point of departure. I have been considering two in particular. On the one hand, *fractal thinking* allows me to attend to the various interrelated dimensions at work in any particular thing or event from different perspectives: (a) *existentially* (quantic, cosmic, historical, and organic), (b) *politically* (juridic, economic, ethic, and symbolic), (c) *meta-analytically* (formal, final, material, and efficient), and (d) *elementally* (infinity, implicancy, figurality, and materiality).[11] Though it may be tempting to read fractal thinking as a 4×4 instead of a 4×3 reworking of the Kantian tables of judgments and categories,[12] this ungenerous reading would not be generative.[13] For one thing, the Kantian fourfold (the categories of the understanding) and Hegel's triad (the movements of the dialectic) are contingent on and yield linearity—which is what allows for the laws of logic (the principle of identity, the law of the excluded middle, and the principle of noncontradiction) to function in statements regarding what has actual (spatial and temporal) existence. Unfortunately, that which linearity facilitates is precisely that which renders senses such as "essential" identity, "unsublatable" difference, and "unescapable" (yet always desired) change. What the fractal offers is a mode of describing existence that, for instance, figures repetition—that

11 The best image to capture this arrangement is not the table but, as I indicate above, the fractal. I borrow the term fractal for two reasons: first, fractal describes most known solid matter that is not transparent but opaque, and while its patterns are repetitive, they are not smooth or linear or have any of the attributes associated with perfection or a perfect design; second, the repetitiveness of fractality is significant because it signals how much, as far as material existence is concerned, change does not matter. Furthermore, the preceding list of terms only identifies a few of a series of correspondences that could amount to as many possible arrangements as the four basic elementa (fundamental particles) thus far identified by particle physicists—these are of two types, fermions (quarks and leptons) and bosons (scalar and vector).

12 Kant, *Critique of Pure Reason*, 531, 544.

13 For one thing, if this is a table at all, if this can be seen as a classificatory scheme (which it is not), it's more along the lines of Foucault's Chinese encyclopedia (materiality is both a perspective and a sub-perspective) than of anything that derives authority from reason, in its subjective, universal, or transcendental figurations.

which seems to resist change (essential identity and unsublatable difference)—in such a way as to make it possible to attend to both at once, namely, the *how* of what appears to remain as change and the *what* of the how of what appears to remain as change.

When the Imagination no longer has to gather impressions (combine the many) to fit the Understanding’s few and rigid parameters, when it is left to its own devices, it can go about turning and twisting every tight knot, every neat table, every straight line. When the Imagination is released to go after, to work toward, to aid in the ethical search for the re/de/compositions that would not demand Dana’s charge be comprehensible but would allow the *unpayable debt* to be settled, that is, to be owned by those who ought to pay for it—then, and only then, in addition to knowing and repeating that the master’s tools cannot dismantle the master’s house, we will finally be in the position of not having to care about what they are or are not good for or able to do.

“ain’t I”

> Look at me! Look at my arm! I have ploughed and planted, and gathered into barns, and no man could head me! And ain’t I a woman? I could work as much and eat as much as a man—when I could get it—and bear the lash as well! And ain’t I a woman? I have borne thirteen children, and seen most all sold off to slavery, and when I cried out with my mother’s grief, none but Jesus heard me! And ain’t I a woman?
>
> —Sojourner Truth, “Ain’t I a Woman?”

The wounded captive body in the scene of subjugation releases existence from the grips of the *subjectum* by re/de/composing the *objectum* that cannot but reflect it. From the place where the conceptum of labor derives its meaning, she returns to the subjectum his incomprehensible violent grounds. Figured as *female flesh ungendered*, she exposes the arche-form or *arkhé*-form of the subjectum—the figure that hosts the colonizer/settler, the husband, the owner, and the citizen. The total violence that renders womanhood unavailable to her is the same that assures his enjoyment of liberty, as if it were not contingent upon the juridical and economic conditions that render the expression of other mothers' grief as noise. Nevertheless, she did/does cry, a cry that resonates now in distant galaxies and reverberates in each and every particle of everything that has come into existence since then. Resonating in every atom, every crack, every bit and piece that constitutes the world, echoing total violence, it reaches the world where it fractures the form of the subjectum along with its architectures. As she does so, whether through the scream or the laugh responding to the lash, she also escapes any attempt at capturing what that laugh or cry means, whether or not they mean what they seem to mean. Undeterminate because, as she figures the excess (of force) that renders her opaque, that which total violence cannot but yield also obtains a kind of in/distinction or in/difference that modern thought cannot stand. If the laugh signals compliance with the Owner's wishes, there is no way to know if it is her will (to do so) or a ruse to avoid further pain; if the scream signals the experience of pain, again, there is no way to know if she is feigning hurt to stop the punishment or if her scream is a plea to the Owner's mercy. Because it is always a response to the lash—not to a question, a request, or a demand—her laugh and her scream cannot but refer to the Owner's (juridical) authority to force her to comply, and to rape and/or kill her if she does not. But it can never be settled whether she did so (comply), much less if it was done of her own "will" or "desire," because his authority precludes her from having the two attributes modern philosophers only attribute to the Subject. To reiterate, because will and desire are the terms that distinguish the figurings of the Subject and Subjectivity—in the scene of regulation and the scene of representation—neither term is meant to correspond to her.

Laboring in the field under the Owner's (to use Marx's term) "brutal lash," the *female flesh ungendered* recalls the Subject's public and private claims and the separations that institute both. As a laborer in Mississippi's cotton fields, a use-value producer of exchange value that is extinguished even before she sets out to plow the field, she makes one wonder how is it that a piece of paper—a yellow sheet with some words and numbers in which she appears without name or place of birth—has such a capacity to nullify every bit of blood, flesh, and bone she exhausts as she moves up and down the field sowing or harvesting cotton bolls. Why not perceive her in her material capacity, that very transfer/transduction of the components of the soil and the plow to the cotton plant? What is it that her body lacks? Nothing really. For her body hosts the same potential and internal kinetic energy, that is, material capacity, as that of any other solid, liquid, or gaseous bit of matter. What she does not have, because she does not have the right (the property or title) over her own body and its capacities (to create and procreate), is the piece of paper (contract) that establishes that she and the owner of the land, its waters and animals, entered into an agreement on the same terms, as equal parties.

What I want to highlight here is that her position cannot be plotted in the dialectical image that postulates an end to Capital. The principle organizing the totality that capital both constitutes and explains is liberty—the capitalist contracting free labor in the market. Liberty (presented as the abstraction that obtains equality, that is, being equally free to sell in the market) is the principle that renders her out of Marx's assemblage of the totality that is capital. When commenting on labor, his chosen signifier is liberty. It must be so. Because if not, had he not placed slavery outside of *time* in the calculations of capital, her labor would have to enter, to count, to matter in the equation of value. And who knows the trouble that would bring him.

The wounded captive body in the scene of subjugation has no place in the plot, Marx argues. When she comes to the market, she comes as a commodity (a use value) whose exchange value is realized then and there only because the Owner possesses her and has the authority (the right as title) to use her as he does his horses and his house. In the triangle formed by capital, wage labor, and instruments of production, liberty places the first two in the same ethical region (which excludes the subjectum), while the last one consists of an objectum of production, that is, use value or commodity. Ethically, as a person that stands with the objectum, her position in regard to the capital/labor pair does not signal liberty (or equality, that is, that which unfolds from their exploitative relationship), nor does she figure the opposite; as a commodity, she does not have a place in the scene of value where these principles apply. Economically, as use value, equality applies to her as an exchangeable commodity, but as a human existent, her positions figure non-equality (as well as non-identity), that is, she does not belong to the set to which the notion of liberty applies.[14]

She figures the infinite possibility, actualities, and virtualities not comprehended in the totality known and knowable as capital, and yet she is defined by the same term that organizes it, that is, labor. For this reason, *female flesh ungendered* cannot but ask the question of labor's limits when considered mechanically. As motion in time, labor determines capital; it refers to the ethical and the mathematical principle (of equality) and the juridical form that obtains both, namely, the contract. Every rendering of labor in the determination of capital, every aspect of this conceptum—metaphysical, onto-epistemological, ethical, and existential—prompts the question of wherefrom it derives its explanatory power. Labor can only function as an accepted determinative tool because of its universalizing effect (which Marx reads as corresponding to equality), both onto-epistemological and ethical, which allows for its translation (shift of register) from a qualitative to the quantitative domain—when paired with time—and from there, to become both measure (of value) and measurable as productive of value. Without these, neither the existential nor the metaphysical operations of labor would be sustainable and, given that it is the conceptum supporting

14 Here Barad's intra-actions provide a basis for imaging what happens when social-scientific tools are deployed to comprehend the plenitude that is existence. The subtle but crucial difference is that the undetermined is not the "constitutive excluded," because it is not tied to what is determined and, as such, it is not one of the already named possibilities, such as a particle or a wave. What interests me is not the "exclusions" that are constitutive, but the fact that they are not so much excluded as not determined, that is, not even an option. Though apparently minimal, using the prefix "in-" instead of "non-" is a crucial gesture, one that is necessary for the consideration of the negative as infinite, instead of opposite.

the totality that is capital, Marx's critique of political economy would amount to very little.

If universal (wage) labor were to lose its explanatory capacity and become just a descriptor of social relations of production particular to a given spacetime moment (later eighteenth-century and nineteenth-century England), it would be possible to revisit the scene of subjugation and address it from its spatiotemporal location, namely "the colonies." There, where the wounded captive body in the scene of subjugation is submitted to the same lash as the horse she drives, working in the cotton field planted on expropriated Native lands, there, insofar as she is a means of production, she is indistinguishable from horse and land. However, there—as her material (potential and kinetic energy) capacity, as well as the horse's and the land's, is transduced into every bud of cotton grown and harvested on that land—she is not only use value but also transduction, a re/de/composition of all that the land has nourished. Here it is the excess: juridical authority, which her occupation, which the lash assures, and which also releases her from any easy reduction—as has been done over and over again, as Fanon recalls of Sartre—of her to a vanishing element in the trajectory of the *transparent I*. As we know, both self-consciousnesses enter equally (as consciousness in the moment of pure universality); the one only becomes the bondsman at the end of Hegel's lord-and-bondsman scene. Because she was bought as a Slave, as a commodity, she never confronted the Owner on equal terms in the life-and-death struggle. As Marx comments, the Owner can dispose of her as he wishes, but he will do quite a lot of calculation before he kills her. Since he cannot be without her existence, all he can do is rehearse a never fully realized/guaranteed—because impossible to verify—occupation and/or appropriation of her mind (will or desire).

The scene of subjugation is nothing but the attempt to overcome the other's will through the threat of total violence. However, because her will is not (juridically) free, by virtue of her condition as a Slave (presupposed unmediated self-expression), what the undeterminable wounded captive body in the scene of subjugation returns to the Owner is the reverberation of the excessive juridical authority he mistakes as the free exercise of his will. Juridical mediation robs both Slave and Owner of the Slave's compliance and, in doing so, prevents the Owner from being certain of her obedience as well as of his own dominance. Hence, all that is given in the scene of subjugation is the (actual and possible and virtual) *refusal* that occasions it. For that reason, because the subject with will (and understanding) is the one modeled after Kant's version of the Formal I—that is, the one figured in the post-Enlightenment juridical, economic, and scientific (symbolic) writing of the human—as a figuring of the excess (total violence) registered by the expropriation of the total value created by her labor, she undermines labor's work as a conceptum. For she recalls the racial event, that is, she reflects the Formal I in its constitutive violent relationship (thereby stripping it of formality), in which efficacy can never be ascertained because it cannot be decided that the lash (the cause) rendered a scream or laugh or silence (as its effect).

The wounded captive body in the scene of subjugation also threatens that which supports the subjectum's claim to exceptionality, as her wounds keep in plain sight the productive violence that moves Hegel to figure the transcendental subject as Spirit. From her vantage point, as a being owned in a context where to own something and to own oneself means to enjoy the highest position among all, none of the attributes of the subjectum warrants its universal claims. Without will or desire that can doubtlessly be ascertained to be hers (because it can always be attributed to the threat of the lash), as somebody's private property she challenges any attempt at establishing the authenticity of anything said to signal interiority. Further, a commodity among commodities, but also an object of both trade and labor—use value and value creator, or creator of value—her undeterminability extends beyond the signaling of the (ethically speaking) intractability (even stronger in the nineteenth century) of equating a person to a horse or to land. From the other side, the fungibility attached to the juridico-economic position that is the Slave also raises the question—which seems presupposed in abolitionist discourse—of whether dignity can be claimed by humans who torture other humans and horses as well. However, as Saidiya Hartman shows, the appeal to empathy would constitute another moment of subjection, as it supported or advanced the presumption of the availability of black interiority to being occupied, that is, fungibility extended to the place where dignity finds/founds its value.

What the failure of empathy (that Hartman describes) indicates but does not necessarily express—mostly because it takes some time for transparency to become the privileged ontological support for dignity and liberty—is the operation of self-determination through the Kantian rendering of free will and the utilitarian concept of self-interest.[15] Both center the individual as the primary ethical entity, though the former rests on self-determination of transcendental (pure) reason, while the latter does so along the lines of the early-modern principle of self-preservation. Both, however, achieve the same effect of moral devaluation of the wounded captive body in the scene of subjugation, as determinacy is the onto-epistemological pillar governing both versions of the modern ethical text. The wounded captive body in the scene of subjugation holds no mirror. A human among use values, her expressions of pain and pleasure are liable to suffer repression, and therefore she does not fully belong to the world of commodities. And as a trade object, a use value among persons, her presumed interiority is available for occupation, and therefore she does not fully belong to the world of subjects of pleasure and pain. That undeterminability also renders her a precarious ethical figure, one that challenges the thesis of transparency from without and from within.

As Du Bois was setting out to consider black interiority—in the figure of a double soul instead of a divided one—the Hegelian version of the modern ethical text was reconfiguring determinacy as the interior (self-propelling) contention of two moments of the same transcendental consciousness. Among other modifications,

---

15 For his rendering of free will, see Immanuel Kant, *Critique of Practical Reason* (Cambridge: Cambridge University Press, 2015). John Stuart Mill's version of utilitarianism is presented in particular in his writings on self-interest as self-determination; see Mill, *On Liberty* (New York: Penguin Classics, 2007).

this version of the *transcendental I* has consequences that delimit the trajectory of blackness in twentieth-century thought. For it is not only that blackness (as Nahum Chandler argues) challenges the core of the discourse on racial purity. More importantly, I find, as Chandler also considers, that as a referent (categorial or existential) of the wounded captive body in the scene of subjugation, blackness questions the ethical realization that emerges from the self-producing and self-revealing movement of Spirit. Blackness unsettles the themes of identity (as all becomes but a vanishing moment of the same), historicity (the *homo historicus*, the fundamental temporality/interior thing), and recognition, namely, the ethical concept that predicates the inseparability between the *I* and *world* only because it is itself grounded in the assumption that, in the post-Enlightenment era, the Human (self-consciousness) finally reaches the moment of transparency. As an account becomes possible in which necessity (figured as an effect of the relations that make up the dialectical movement that unfolds in time) comes to be attributed not only to the knowledge of (the) world but also to defining the (self-)knowledge that is self-consciousness itself, blackness—indexing an object among objects (as Fanon describes), and yet that which by definition does not signify in the text, ruled by the arche-form or *arkhé*-form of the subject (as Spillers suggests)—confronts the demand for transparency made by/for the object and subject alike. When doing so, however, she cannot be rushed to stand as, to mirror an otherwise that would be figured like the subjectum in the Market, as economically differentiated (labor and capitalist) traders, whose juridical (as parties in a contract) equality allows for the setting up of an opposition that recalls Hegel's famous passage. This is so because Marx's oppositional subject positions are described in an economic scene of equality—in this case, the Market—which does not differ from the one where Hegel locates the violent meeting of "pure self-consciousnesses."

The question "ain't I a woman?" does not announce a movement to occupy existence, rendering it always already an effect of knowledge, the unfolding of which is the comprehension of the world by the Understanding and Reason. The question, her question, resonates beyond Sense Perception and without (transcendental) Reason and the Understanding, that is, without the forces with which modern thought has moved to apprehend and comprehend the world, the movement that needed the body to serve as either an instrument (as the senses' role for knowledge) or a surface of inscription. Just as the (Kantian) Understanding's task, determinacy, which cannot but render objects, Reason's transparency (the Hegelian and the Husserlian version of it) has populated the planet with "Others" whose bodies and modes of existence fail to exhibit that which would characterize what Sylvia Wynter calls "Man2."[16] Though commenting primarily on language when noting that it maintains "its transparency and contain[s] the increasing opacity of the world within the limits," Glissant writes, "it would thus maintain its transparency and contain the increasing opacity of the world within the limits of a well-phrased classicism,"[17] he both describes and convokes a refusal to yield to the demand for transparency that consistently resolves what comes before it in the circuitry of the racial dialectic. For this reason, while opacity might hopelessly carry the meaning of not being understandable (or not understanding), I prefer to read in Glissant's more expansive approach a *refusal* that seeks to release both (Du Bois's) "the world" and (Husserl's) *world* to undeterminability, and not only this or that "linguistic" or "cultural" group. That, I advance, is the manner through which what had to be delimited in the assembling of a totality of reason haunts modern thought. Not as a constitutive outside, but as that which signifies nothing and everything because its appearance is not the result of the productive rules of a discursive formation in which it would become the figuring of an other (thinking of Foucault here). Nor does she figure abjection, as her opaqueness (absence) does not refer to what Judith Butler calls "unthinkable, abject, unlivable bodies," which inhabit "those 'unlivable' and 'uninhabitable' zones of social

16 Man2, in her analysis of the modern episteme, refers to the construction of the subject as an economic and biological entity. See generally Wynter, "Unsettling the Coloniality."

17 Édouard Glissant, *Poetics of Relation*, trans. Betsy Wing (Ann Arbor: University of Michigan Press, 1990), 111.

life which are nevertheless densely populated by those who do not enjoy the status of the subject." If that were the case, she would remain a signifier in the terms of modern thinking, but only because, as a referent to a "zone of uninhabitability,"[18] she would necessarily be comprehensible by the same conceptum that constitutes the subject within the totality from which she would have been excluded.

Not her. The wounded captive body in the scene of subjugation is not the Other of the proper figuring of the Subject produced in discourse, nor is she the abjection that exposes its forms and the formation of it. Why? Her position in modern signification is given by the juridical form—the title that renders her someone's use value (commodity and property) renders her and her offspring's labor uncountable in the calculations that expose the inner workings of capital as a totality. Her radical potential resides in how it is from within that she expands the scope for the appreciation and interrogation of the workings of the *transparent I* and the moments (juridic, economic, ethic, and symbolic) that compose its political architecture.[19] Blacklight shining from within, she de/composes the racial dialectic and irrupts through the (nonproductive of surplus value) terms of the equation of value not because she is claiming a place with/in them; the racial dialectic unravels precisely when she returns (as a high-frequency beam) the total violence (the overseer's and the whip's potential energy transduced into wounds) of the scene of subjugation to the white side of the image that renders her subjugation cause and effect of her physical and mental traits. The equation of value does not dissolve before a demand for a third position confronting wage laborer and capitalist. Bursting through the cotton and the spindle, she recalls a whole range of other contributors to the exchange value of the commodity that do not enter into the calculation because of a prior delimitation

---

18 Butler, *Bodies That Matter*, 3.

19 Terada captures this potential when she discusses Hegel's attribution of racial thinking and racialization to the racial subaltern. Rei Terada, "Hegel's Racism for Radicals," *Radical Philosophy* 2, no. 5 (Autumn 2019): 11–22.

that attributes the production of surplus value to the juridical form of the contract. Here, again, the challenge comes not from her labor (as an economic category) but from a distinction between kinds of labor that occur in a distinct register—the "social conditions" of production that play no role in the theorization of capital because, as with "the colonies" in regard to accumulation, it is a condition of possibility (for Labor and capitalist to meet in the market), not an element in production proper (which happens in the factory). Sneaking in from ancillary moments that only have an incidental role in accounts of value, she accomplishes something that only an insider can, which is to raise the question of whether that which holds everything together (in the case of capital, labor) stands on the firm ground required for the assembling of a totality.

When she appears as labor "pure and simple," without the properties and capacities it acquires as the conceptum that sustains the totality that is capital, the wounded captive body in the scene of subjugation undoes much more than the equivalence that balances Marx's equation. Because the excess (x) figured in the double occupation that is her last name and her cry has remained, as Douglass commented, beyond the temporal markers of slavery, as a physical mark, that is, in/as blackness as a referent of juridical domination, it authorizes total violence (of police killings) and indifference (of Jair Bolsonaro's and Donald Trump's decision to let people die in the COVID-19 pandemic). The work blackness does—and in doing so refuses its operations as a category—every time the black body is released from its grip (when mobilized as a simile) is to recall the wounds that signal the Owner's authority or the total violence that mapped the colonial context.

The wounded captive body in the scene of subjugation, as Spillers's *female flesh ungendered*, names the effect that precedes her apparition and renders her arrival an overturning (\X).[20] Certainly, as I said before, when assembling her as a reading tool,

20 For an activation of *female flesh ungendered* (\X), see Ferreira da Silva, "Hacking the Subject."

I am also repurposing Walter Benjamin's "dialectical image" as an anti-dialectical tool. What interests me is not the plot of the oppressor and the oppressed that the halting of history might stop or reverse. Her function troubles the very oppositional setup that does no more than model the political discourse on the forms/laws of thought (according to the principle of identity and law of noncontradiction). Because she stands with her lacerated back to the "brutal lash," the wounded captive body in the scene of subjugation's confrontational stance is best described as *refusal* rather than merely *oppositional*. For she does not face the Owner and seek his destruction or his recognition or to take his place. For her, the scene, its context, and its sole player, as Fanon explained, must come to an end.

"meanings that repeat the initiating moment?"

> We might well ask if this phenomenon of marking and branding actually "transfers" from one generation to another, finding its various symbolic substitutions in an efficacy of meanings that repeat the initiating moment?
>
> —Hortense J. Spillers, "Mama's Baby, Papa's Maybe"

> I was back at home—in my own house, in my own time. But I was still caught somehow, joined to the wall as though my arm were growing out of it—or growing into it. From the elbow to the ends of the fingers, my left arm had become a part of the wall. I looked at the spot where flesh joined with plaster, stared at it uncomprehending. It was the exact spot Rufus's fingers had grasped.
>
> —Octavia E. Butler, *Kindred*

Uncomprehending is perhaps the only possible descriptor for the intellectual maneuver capable of making sense of the materializations of the scene of subjugation. It makes sense that Dana's charge was lifted when Rufus tried to exercise his authority to deploy total violence and beat and rape her; it also makes sense that Dana's charge had to be met, because otherwise, had Rufus died, she would not have been born. What does not make sense is when these two statements are brought together: Dana had the obligation to keep alive someone who could at any moment kill and rape her, otherwise she would not exist. This does not make sense when one tries to comprehend Dana's predicament, when one approaches it through the terms and formulations that both make possible the assembling of and give sense to the racial dialectic and the equation of value, that is, as long as our image of existence only allows for existents and events comprehensible by/through the onto-epistemological descriptors and pillars of post-Enlightenment thought.

When commenting on Du Bois's deployment of the preposition "between," Chandler teases out the elements that, I find, refuse to delineate the position marked by the wounded captive body in the scene of subjugation. In a manner not dissimilar to Douglass's account of "the color line," Du Bois's articulation of "between" can also be read, as Chandler does, as a reference to how the juridico-economic moment mediates the encounter and prevents both the white and the black person facing each other from being read in terms of Husserl's natural attitude or phenomenological consciousness. This impossibility reverberates beyond that existential scene, as it goes to the core of the text within which that scene makes sense, in which Dana's charge makes and does not make sense, reaching its metaphysical basis and the onto-epistemological formations that express it. Expectedly, a similar shift occurs when the wounded captive body in the scene of subjugation is recalled in/as the raw material in Marx's formalization of his general law of value. At this level it is not only a shift that turns around the very conditions of knowledge (metaphysical and onto-epistemological) that render the equation (the deployment of equality) possible (Euclid's postulate) and necessary (the whole basis of modern claims to truth); it reaches the level of comprehension itself in terms of how one goes about knowing and how this knowing plays out in existence. Put differently, in addition to calling for an other image of existence and descriptors that do not presume, postulate, or facilitate its apprehension and comprehension, the wounded captive body in the scene of subjugation being read in the same position and performance of cotton in the equation of value is the enactment of a mode of knowing premised on undeterminability because it violates the basic pillar of separability (between the cotton and the slave laborer) and determinacy (wage labor and capital). How Dana's charge calls for such a deep troubling of the grounds of modern thinking begins to make sense when one considers how she "looked at the spot where flesh joined with plaster, stared at it uncomprehending. It was the exact spot Rufus's fingers had grasped."

Another way of embracing her charge is perhaps to consider how Dana's arm was cut into the wall of the house she just moved into, the house that marked her entrance into the world of those who own property. How it happened only once, when she decided to settle her charge and kill Rufus. How it happened the first time that Rufus treated her as his property, exercising his right to total violence. How, when it happened, a part of her body got stuck in the wall, exposing it as the line between her present and Rufus's. Doing so recalls how the spatiotemporal line exists in everything whose total value is yielded by slave labor under the threat of total violence. Everything of any (economic) value whatsoever. What Dana does is to question the questions that support and guide modern thinking: What happened? Why did it happen? By which means did it happen? For what happened to Dana—traversing the line of time—is not supposed to happen. When time traversal is the answer to the question of what happened, the other two questions do not follow. Because the *what* itself violates a metaphysical assumption of modern thought, namely the linearity that establishes the centrality of time. Though it might be possible, as there is no theory or proof—which is what matters for modern thinking—Dana's travels in time are not probable, because there is no evidence showing that it can or cannot be done.[21]

What if, I propose, one embraces the possible and the virtual and accepts Dana's recollection that it happened, all of it, everything, instead of questioning it? She found herself in antebellum Maryland saving her Owner's life, she lived as a

---

21 Einstein's equations for general relativity take into account time travel to the past but not to the future.

Slave and met her ancestors, she lost part of her body in the wall of her new house upon returning to 1976 Los Angeles after killing him when he attempted to rape her. Elementally, that could have happened, because what we call time is nothing other than the registry of what happens, in particular of those things that cannot unhappen—such as the transfer of internal kinetic energy (calor).[22] In sum, though not probable, Dana’s traversals are possible as something that can be imagined and that happens (actually, possibly, and virtually) when that which exists is approached elementally.

From this point of view, considered elementally—without the liberal “social [juridical and ethical] conditions” that hold capitalism as a totality from without—“slave labor” enters into Marx’s equation of value as/in the raw material. As a laborer, the wounded captive body in the scene of subjugation does not stand on the grounds of equality (in the Market) before either the capitalist or the wage laborer. Without a place to stand on the ethical grounds (liberty and equality as figured by private property and contract) of Marx’s original presentation of capital, her “social conditions” are ones he saw no need to theorize. Undetermined by what *is* relevant—as in his distinction between those who own the means of production (mp +) and those who do not (mp −)—by what provides the answer for the what, the why, and the by which means of capital, she does not enter the formalized presentation of labor’s efficacy (equation of value) as a subject predicated by (private) ownership and (public) authority. Being herself a means of production, a use value that yields no exchange value (to the Owner) or surplus value (to the Capitalist), except when compared to other means of production, a plow, a horse, or a spindle, which she operates nominally (qualitatively), she presents the difference between two types of labor—either productive of exchange value (pev +)

22 The perception of time passing, the arrow of time, is given by heat (calor), which is “the irreversible progress of heat in one direction,” or entropy, which is captured in the second law of thermodynamics. Carlo Rovelli, *The Order of Time*, trans. Simon Carnell and Erica Segre (New York: Riverhead Books, 2018), 23.

or nonproductive of exchange value (pev –). But that, as we know, is the delimitation of what belongs in the totality that is capital (because determined by universal labor), the one specified by labor (in the abstract, labor time) insofar as it is productive of surplus value (that is, price of labor – value of the product). What this reading of Marx's delimitative (qualitative) statements finds is neither negation nor affirmation of the *what* (the being or meaning) of her and her social conditions ("the colonies"). For in such statements, the distinction—which could have been determined (and was, anthropologically, by Luxemburg), but was not by Marx, with taxonomic procedures guided by the qualitative application of the principle of identity—that institutes a negative presents identity not as *what is not* (that from which it is distinguishable) but as *what is a non* (part of what has been determined). Put differently, I am highlighting here the distinction between (a) the Negative that is the Other (that which is Not) because it inhabits the same region, and (b) the Negative that is incommensurable (that which is Non) because it is defined by not resulting from the particular (determinative) effect of formal/efficient reason or by not being part of the relevant totality (the set) where oppositions make sense.[23]

This departs from all four dimensions that enter into considerations of both what happens and what is knowable. The most general and complex departure, because it is at the metaphysical level, offers *infinity* in lieu of *linearity* as the image of existence. While the exposition of infinity requires a thorough engagement with modern philosophy, the presentation of *corpus infinitum*, in contrast with the ordered universe, cannot be a conceptual exercise. Such procedure would reproduce the very

---

23 In other words, when I say that black is non-white, this is not a negative judgment that applies to that which belongs to the same region, to what has been defined and specified or determined. Nothing is said here about what black is, just that black is anything and everything else—the whole incomprehensible infinity that is existence, that is, that which does not enter into the determination of white, that which is not comprehended by that category.

onto-epistemological premises against which it is proposed—for many reasons that I cannot discuss here because it would require a framework for thinking (and therefore also for both the analysis and description) of existence, which must be carefully presented lest it become a mere rewriting of the Kantian program. Incidentally, a description of this departure relying on Kantian language would read like this: What I am calling delimitative statements are akin to Kant’s Infinite judgments. Marked by the particle *non-*, they index not *indetermination*, which refers to what is (still) unknown, but *undeterminability*, which is the quality of what is unknowable. Perhaps a more straightforward way of putting it is to say that the negative meaning here attaches to knowing and not to what is not known, which is not determinable, or which refers to the infinite. In the case of the particle *in-*, there is a sense of what is yet to be established, decided, fixed, that is, the indefinite. Put differently, the particle *in-* remains in the field of knowledge and presumes that it has or can obtain what is needed for a definition, explanation, or interpretation to arise. The particle *non-*, in contrast, opens up a whole range of unknowable im/possibilities and virtualities as well as actualities; it is not in the order of the form (concept, category, definition) but in the register of matter as *pars* (the plenitude of existence), namely, *corpus infinitum*. The implications of such a move are various and have different degrees of complexity. Ontological indeterminacy, as Barad proposes, does not only relate to the im/possibility of stating that there is a *what* there—a statement regarding the reality of something. More importantly, it is about not being able to assume that whatever is there is such or such a thing, because anything that is there is something with the addition of all that is possible and virtual. Here is the level at which the hacked female flesh ungendered (\X) does the unraveling, activating undetermination but turning attention from the something (let’s say, “1”) to the indeterminate (the possible and the virtual that always accompanies it, that is, $\infty - \infty$).

Also significant is something that does not necessarily follow from the impossibility of ascertaining identity, of determining, of setting boundaries and limits: $1 + \infty - \infty$ or

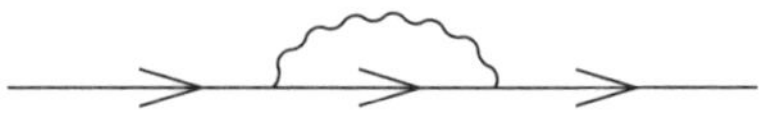

(electron self-energy)

Whether in mathematical or physics notation,[24] this image, which captures Barad's ontological indeterminacy, inspires the question of how to figure all that exists in a way that does not violate the basic configuration of existence, namely, that everything is itself + everything else (thing + non-itself, instead of thing-in-itself) that may or may not exist (actually and virtually), that is, an infinite composition. If any existent, regardless of its mode of appearance—solid, liquid, gas, or plasma—always has the indeterminate added to it, then it is also both *singular* and *similar*—as every quantic existent can be formally presented as $1 + \infty - \infty$.[25] That being the case, it may be worth trying to reverse the process Benjamin describes, that is, to take the consideration of *similar* back from within the core of what is language,[26] and to explore the meanings it gives in the usages in *anatomy*

24 This well-known diagram of electron self-energy is called a Feynman diagram. The quantum physicist Richard Feynman created several similar images for conveying complex and counterintuitive quantic events.

25 I have said it before, but it is good to recall how my proposal differs from Badiou's. This figure may make it more explicit, as I hope it indicates that I am not as much interested in 1 as I am in the fact that it is never found without $\infty - \infty$. A manner of reading his project is that he is interested in the 1 (both as "count-as-one, or structure" and "the one as effect." That interest is consistent with his proposal of an ontology informed by set theory that he calls a mathematical ontology or, similarly, his view that mathematics is ontology; see Badiou, *Being and Event*, 90. Incidentally, $1 + \infty - \infty$ is not a mere rewriting of Deleuze and Guattari's "$n - 1$." There are many different ways of naming the difference. Let me say here that, unlike them, I am not making a case for multiplicity; see Gilles Deleuze and Félix Guattari, *A Thousand Plateaus: Capitalism and Schizophrenia*, trans. Brian Massumi (Minneapolis: University of Minnesota Press, 2005), 6, 27. What interests me is the intrinsic complexity of the singular composition that also always includes the undetermined and the undeterminable.

26 Walter Benjamin, "The Doctrine of the Similar," trans. Knut Tarnowski, *New German Critique*, no. 17 (Spring 1979): 67.

(homogeneous parts of the body), *geometry* (forms with the same shape but different sizes or orientation), *music* (motions in which individual melodic lines move in the same direction), or *mathematics* (the square matrices Y and Z have the relationship $Y \rightarrow X^{-1} ZX$, where X is a third matrix). Each of these renderings of the *similar* refers to a materiality (that of which) that is given as content (that out of which), shape, direction, and transformation (matrix).

Though I think of this general description for the *singular composite* ($1 + \infty - \infty$) as one of the infinitely possible presentations of the elementa—namely, the existent or the *being of the world*[27]—it is also a point of departure for a tool capable of reading beyond the fixities created by modern thinking and the context it has designed and justifies. For this is precisely what the wounded captive body in the scene of subjugation does when she re/de/composes the racial dialectic as the racial event: in

27 This idea of a *being of the world* has been inspired by, as well as borrows and combines, two articulations I encountered in the past years. The first, which I would call ontological, I found suggested in Glissant's critique of transparency in general. In particular, I find its possibility indicated in a passage from *Poetic Intention* I have cited; see Denise Ferreira da Silva, "Toward a Black Feminist Poethics: The Quest(ion) of Blackness towards the End of the World," *Black Scholar* 44, no. 2 (2014): 81–97. The second, which I will call ontic, I found in Barad's articulation of her thesis of ontological indeterminacy, in which she says: "Questions of the nature of measurement—or, more broadly, intra-actions—are at the core of quantum physics. Intra-actions are practices of making a difference, of cutting together-apart, entangling-differentiating (one move) in the making of phenomena. Phenomena—entanglements of matter/ing across spacetimes—are not in the world, but *of* the world. Importantly, intra-actions are not limited to human-based measurement practices" (Barad, *What Is the Measure of Nothingness?*, 7–8). I am not aware of any other such indications. However, I would be surprised if no one else has thought of it. Incidentally, my distinction between an ontic and ontological rendering of it is meant to indicate the registers addressed by Glissant (philosophical/phenomenology) and Barad (scientific/physics). In my rendering of being of the world, this distinction makes no sense. The same is true for the related distinction between (the age-old philosophical theme of) existence and essence, being and becoming, etc.

the figuring of racial subjugation, where linearity rules and returns racial violence (the cause) and its effects by the side door of morality to those subjected to it, she exposes how the racial dialectic has the same form as the scene of the *transparent I* (the post-Enlightenment figuring of the Subject) and, by forcing them face to face, setting up a confrontation, she shows how they are not contradictory but complementary pieces of the whole play of subjugation, that is, the racial event. As an image, the racial event is not something that lies there as evidence waiting to be gathered and interpreted; it is what comes out of the reading, which Benjamin advises is always part of the image itself, in the instant when the pieces come together in a shape that violates the course of linear time and thinking. That is so, because insofar as *the image* is *a singular infinite re/de/composition of the fractal*, that which it exposes repeats from each of its points of approach (from how one approaches or reads an image).

***

For Douglass and Fanon, the total violence that visits the colonies did not indicate that the racial event is eternal but that it repeats both in time and in that which total violence produces. That to me is an insight into why and how any reading of what happens, what has happened, and what may come to happen is fundamentally poethical—namely, political (ethical), practical, poetical. This is so for two reasons. First, since the reader is always there in the reading as it takes place as an element in the re/de/composition—a reading is always also (as Barad would say) an "intra-action"—that reading is also her creation, something that is also constituted by her labor and calor. Second, when the elementum is the existential level of attention given, the cosmic and the quantic dimensions, where spacetime (as we know it) does not operate, become relevant. In any event, the capacity of the wounded captive body in the scene of subjugation to produce use values as well as producers of use value, if considered from labor's materiality (of the elementum) and not universality (of the conceptum), invites considerations of whether and how blackness, insofar as it is a referent of her juridico-economic condition, recalls the body as a re/de/composition of the land on which it is conceived and grows—whether and how the black body, like the bodies of persons who are born and grow on the expropriated Native lands of then and now consist in nothing other than re/de/composed elementa of their original owners and ancestors. That being the case, each and every person in North America holds an unpayable debt to the original inhabitants and ancestral guardians of these lands, which is also a debt that we own (even if through no decision of our ancestors) and that is ours to honor. Along the same lines, labor's materiality and the elemental implicancy of body and land raise questions of how blackness and Indigeneity may be jointly mobilized in confrontations with coloniality and raciality as a political (anticolonial) composite when each descriptor becomes singular/similar (one of the many possible figurings), a fractal referent of the total violence that allowed for the expropriated bodies and lands, and demands the attention of everyone who owes the colonial, unpayable debt that should no longer go unthought or unconfronted.

Past Perfect

If everything and any existing thing is but a re/de/composition, another mode of appearance of a combination of elementa, that is, a singular/similar composite, the follow-up question is: How does this come to be? How does what was remain in what has become? And if elementa are distinct but not different, if the leptons, quarks, gauge bosons, and Higgs bosons play distinct roles in the composite of matter energy, and if time no longer matters in this play (both the constitution and the composition of matter), how is this accounted for? Here is where I think imagination is at play.

We know that the constitution of matter, the coming together of the basic elements, is not something that happens in time, in the same way that we know that the transformation of protons into photons (expressed by $E = mc^2$) is something that happens with the addition of speed, that is, kinetic energy. We also know that phase transition depends on another kind of transfer of energy, through pressure and calor. Every significant, observable, and nonobservable re/composition or de/composition has occurred through the activation of matter's capacity (material capacity) in its presentation as energy. Every presentation of matter as energy has resulted from a process in which an excess is built up, forcing a release.

Unavoidably, one wonders whether such process was at work in Dana's movement from 1976 Los Angeles to 1830s Maryland. Not so much how did she travel but, except for the last time, when her arm gets stuck, it seems that she only disappeared and materialized in one spot inside of her home. She didn't travel. Dislocation in time and space played no role in her predicament. Dana did not travel, because 1830s Maryland was always right there, wherever she was. It had been there in/as her body. The DNA codes from both the white and the black branches of her family defined the elementa that entered her body, from when she was being gestated, throughout her mother's pregnancy, and later gathered from the food, air, and water she consumed as well as the calor, that invisible red glow happening to and between things all the time. Dana did not have to go anywhere, 1830s Maryland remains in/as the capital was expended in the creation of everything that entered into the building of her house and its acquisition, the money she and her partner paid or inherited, earned, and borrowed to buy it.

Everything, in each and every elementum that entered the composition of her context, mid-1970s Los Angeles, could have been part of the composition of the context of early 1800s Maryland. There is a point in the cosmos from which early 1800s Maryland and mid-1970s Los Angeles occur in the same instant, where one can see both as immediately connected. From there, there is no such thing as distance between her home and Rufus's farm. Dana never moves at all.[1]

1 Traveling as an event is a temporal probability, just as it is to be born and die; it is also just as temporal as the sequencing of what happens as events in a person's life (biography) or in a place's duration (history); the only difference, of course, Newton and Kant would remind me, is that in traveling we must account for space. But then again, space must only be taken into account if traveling is needed at all.

On June 25, 2012, Paula Chakravartty and I sent out the final draft of the introduction to our special issue of *American Quarterly* titled “Race, Empire, and the Crisis of the Subprime.” That happened nearly two years after we drafted the proposal, in the summer of 2010, while I was in residence at Stellenbosch Institute for Advanced Study as part of the Genres of Critique residential group (along with Mark Antaki, Stewart Motha, George Pavlich, Patricia Tuitt, Karin van Marle, and Jagath Weerasinghe), which explored connections between law, aesthetics, and literature. Though I was not aware of it at the time, the conversations (sometimes heated and always rich) held in that disturbing and confrontational embodiment of apartheid South Africa are also reflected in the argument unfolded here.

By the time we started working on the journal’s special issue, I was professor of (and held the inaugural chair in) ethics in the School of Business Management at Queen Mary University of London (QMUL). That was a significant intellectual move; I had left an associate professorship in the Department of Ethnic Studies at the University of California San Diego, where I had developed a new line of research in critical ethnic and critical racial studies on race, war, and violence, in collaboration with Yen Espiritu, Ross Frank, and Wayne Yang, and our remarkable graduate students (Maile Arvin, Long Bui, Ofelia Cuevas, José Fusté, Julietta Hua, Grace Kim, Rashné Limki, John Marquez, Angie Morrill, Kit Myers, and Ma Vang). At QMUL, I joined the notable group of faculty and graduate students that Stefano Harney and Gerry Hanlon gathered around the Centre for Ethics and Politics, which for many months embodied a critical agenda that combined the themes and concerns of critical racial, postcolonial, and Marxist feminist and autonomist scholarship.

At the University of British Columbia (UBC), I thank the faculty, staff, and students at the Institute for Gender, Race, Sexuality and Social Justice, as well as the members of the Critical Racial and Anti-Colonial Studies Research Network and the Critical + Creative Social Justice Studies Research Excellence Cluster. In 2019, UBC’s Peter Wall Institute for Advanced Studies, through the Wall Scholars Program, provided invaluable resources, including time released from teaching and administrative work and stimulating conversation with other Wall Scholars and visiting international scholars.

Unpayable Debt also benefited from conversations and responses to presentations I gave over these many years. A most important presentation and ensuing conversation was with the Apatride Society of the Political Others, a documenta 14 public program coordinated by Nelli Kambouri, Max Jorge Hinderer Cruz, and Margarita Tsomou. Thanks to their invitation to present in Athens, I revisited the writing and thinking around the term "unpayable debt" that did not make it into the introduction to the *American Quarterly* special issue in 2012, and thanks to Quinn Latimer, who invited me to publish the text in *The documenta 14 Reader*. This book is, for the most part, an expansion of that essay, which was published in 2017. Ana Teixeira Pinto's unrefusable invitation to be part of her On the Antipolitical series with Sternberg Press was instrumental in getting all of this on paper, and Max Bach carefully copyedited the manuscript. Michaeline Crichlow, Mark Harris, David Lloyd, Massimiliano Mollona, and Fred Moten offered invaluable comments on different drafts of the manuscript.

My thinking here has benefited from opportunities created by collectives such as the Critical Legal Conference, in particular Peter Fitzpatrick (in memoriam), Brenna Bhandar, Colin Perrin, and Véronique Voruz; the Anti-Colonial Machine (J. Kameron Carter, Colin Dayan, Sora Han, Laura Harris, David Lloyd, Fred Moten, Dylan Rodriguez, and Atef Said); Practicing Refusal (Rizvana Bradley, Dionne Brand, Tina Campt, Hazel Carby, Kaiama Glover, Saidiya Hartman, Arthur Jafa, Tavia Nyong'o, Darieck Scott, Christina Sharpe, Deborah Thomas, Alexander Weheliye, and Mabel O. Wilson); the Institute for Physical Sociality (Karen Barad, Gabriel Catren, Barry Esson, Bryony McIntyre, Fred Moten, Wu Tsang, Boychild, and Fernando Zalamea); and the artists, curators, activists, and scholars who have assembled as part of the Global Condition Workshop.

I have learned so much in my ongoing collaborations with Valentina Desideri and Arjuna Neuman and my recent ones with Daniel Ananias da Silva, muSa Michelle Mattiuzzi, Jota Mombaça, Amilcar Packer, Anti Ribeiro, and Joy Mariama Smith, as well as in conversations with Cash Ahenakew, Vanessa de Oliveira Andreotti, Phanuel Antwi, Gianpaolo Baiocchi, Boatema Boateng, Charles Briggs, Matt Browning, Camilla Rocha Campos, Silvana Carotenuto, Filipa César, Nahum D. Chandler, Sara Sejin Chang, Glen Coulthard, Pedro Gabriel S. Daher, Kodwo Eshun, Chiara Figone, Ruth Gilmore, Natasha Ginwala, Alyosha Goldstein, Avery Gordon, Ayesha Hameed, Louis Henderson, Stacey Ho, Hudda Khaireh, Léopold Lambert, Diane Lima, Ana Lira, Johnny Mack, Tayyab Mahmud, Clara Mantini-Briggs, Olivier Marboeuf, Renisa Mawani, Dory Nason, Elvira Dyangani Ose, Byron Peters, Emily Pethick, Nataša Petrešin-Bachelez, Manuel Piña, Elizabeth Povinelli, Sherene Razack, Ronald Rose-Antoinette, Denise Ryner, Anjalika Sagar, Sarita See, Lutze Segu, Paula M. Seniors, Ash Sharma, Thiago de Paula Souza, Hortense Spillers, Sharon Stein, Brett St Louis, Jean Tible, Massimiliano Tomba, Françoise Vergès, Tiffany Willoughby-Herard, Susanne Winterling, Marika Yeo, and Vivian Ziherl.

From far away, family has always been a source of love and courage, reminding me of the reason I do what I do: in Brazil, my parents José and Amélia, my brother Denis, my nephews Daniel and Lucas, and my niece Ilka Maria; in Australia, my parents Mal and Maureen, my sister Meaghan and her husband Cyrus, and my nieces and nephews: Shae, Cleon, Jackson, Georgie, Callie, Grace, Leilani, Aimai, Zarine, Harper, William, and baby Leshae.

For all these years, Mark has been home, gathering the intellectual, emotional, and material support that allowed me to venture into the kind of thinking that made possible the writing of these words. Thank you!

I am grateful to the hən̓q̓əmin̓əm̓ speaking xʷməθkʷəy̓əm (Musqueam) people, on whose traditional, ancestral, and unceded territory this book was written.

Agamben, Giorgio. *Homo Sacer: Sovereign Power and Bare Life*. Translated by Daniel Heller-Roazen. Stanford, CA: Stanford University Press, 1995.

Althusser, Louis. "Contradiction and Overdetermination." *New Left Review* 1, no. 41 (January/February 1967): 15–35.

Althusser, Louis, Étienne Balibar, Robert Establet, Pierre Macherey, and Jacques Rancière. *Reading Capital: The Complete Edition*. Translated by Ben Brewster and David Fernbach. London: Verso, 2016.

Arendt, Hannah. *The Human Condition*. Chicago: University of Chicago Press, 1958.

Bacon, Francis. *Advancement of Learning*. In *Selected Philosophical Works*, edited by Rose Mary Sargent. Indianapolis, IN: Hackett Publishing, 1999.

Badiou, Alain. *Being and Event*. Translated by Oliver Feltham. London: Continuum, 2007.

———. "A Philosophy for Militants: Alain Badiou Interviewed by Aaron Hess." *International Socialist Review* 95 (Winter 2014/15). https://isreview.org/issue/95/philosophy-militants.

Barad, Karen. *Meeting the Universe Halfway: Quantum Physics and the Entanglement of Matter and Meaning*. Durham, NC: Duke University Press, 2007.

———. *What Is the Measure of Nothingness? Infinity, Virtuality, Justice*. Berlin: Hatje Cantz, 2012.

Barrett, Lindon. *Blackness and Value: Seeing Double*. Cambridge: Cambridge University Press, 2009.

Beckert, Sven. *Empire of Cotton: A Global History*. New York: Alfred A. Knopf, 2014.

Benjamin, Walter. "The Doctrine of the Similar." Translated by Knut Tarnowski. *New German Critique*, no. 17 (Spring 1979): 66–69.

Bhandar, Brenna. *Colonial Lives of Property: Law, Land, and Racial Regimes of Ownership*. Durham, NC: Duke University Press, 2018.

Boas, Franz. *The Mind of Primitive Man*. New York: Free Press, 1963.

Brown v. Board of Education, 347 U.S. 483 (1954).

Bureau of Labor Statistics, U.S. Department of Labor. "Unemployment Rate Unchanged at 3.6 Percent in May 2019." *Economics Daily*, June 12, 2019. https://www.bls.gov/opub/ted/2019/unemployment-rate-unchanged-at-3-point-6-percent-in-may-2019.htm?view_full.

Butler, Judith. *Bodies That Matter: On the Discursive Limits of Sex*. New York: Routledge, 1993.

Butler, Octavia E. *Kindred*. Boston: Beacon Press, 1988.

Canguilhem, Georges. *A Vital Rationalist: Selected Writings from Georges Canguilhem*. Edited by François Delaporte. Translated by Arthur Goldhammer. New York: Zone Books, 2000.

Cardoso, Fernando Henrique, and Enzo Faletto. *Dependency and Development in Latin America*. Translated by Marjory Mattingly Urquidi. Berkeley: University of California Press, 1979.

Chandler, Nahum Dimitri. *X—The Problem of the Negro as a Problem for Thought*. New York: Fordham University Press, 2013.

Connelly, Roxanne, Vernon Gayle, and Paul S. Lambert. "Ethnicity and Ethnic Group Measures in Social Survey Research." *Methodological Innovations* (January 2016). https://doi.org/10.1177/2059799116642885.

The Constitution of the United States: A Transcription. National Archives, U.S. National Archives and Records Administration. Accessed July 1, 2020. https://www.archives.gov/founding-docs/constitution-transcript.

Coulthard, Glen Sean. *Red Skin, White Masks: Rejecting the Colonial Politics of Recognition*. Minneapolis: University of Minnesota Press, 2014.

Cox, Oliver C. *Caste, Class, and Race: A Study in Social Dynamics*. New York: Monthly Review Press, 1948.

Deleuze, Gilles, and Félix Guattari. *A Thousand Plateaus: Capitalism and Schizophrenia*. Translated by Brian Massumi. Minneapolis: University of Minnesota Press, 2005.

Derrida, Jacques. "Racism's Last Word." Translated by Peggy Kamuf. *Critical Inquiry* 12, no. 1 (1985): 290–99.

Douglass, Frederick. "The Color Line." *North American Review* 132, no. 295 (June 1881): 567–77.

Dred Scott v. Sanford, 60 U.S. 393 (1857). Our Documents. Accessed April 31, 2020. https://www.ourdocuments.gov/doc.php?flash=false&doc=29&page=transcript.

Du Bois, W. E. B. *The Autobiography of W. E. B. Du Bois*. Oxford: Oxford University Press, 2007.

——. *The Souls of Black Folk*. New York: Bantam Books, 1989.

Durkheim, Émile. *The Elementary Forms of the Religious Life*. Translated by Joseph Ward Swain. Mineola, New York: Dover, 2008.

Euclid. *The Thirteen Books of Euclid's Elements*. Vol. 1. Translated by Sir Thomas L. Heath. 2nd ed. New York: Dover, 1965.

Evaristo, Conceição. *Olhos d'água*. Rio de Janeiro: Pala Mini, 2018.

Fanon, Frantz. *The Wretched of the Earth*. Translated by Constance Farrington. New York: Grove Press, 1963.

Ferguson, Roderick A. *Aberrations in Black: Toward a Queer of Color Critique*. Minneapolis: University of Minnesota Press, 2004.

Ferreira da Silva, Denise. "1 (life) ÷ 0 (blackness) = ∞ − ∞ or ∞/∞: On Matter beyond the Equation of Value." *e-flux journal*, no. 79 (February 2017). https://www.e-flux.com/journal/79/94686/1-life-0-blackness-or-on-matter-beyond-the-equation-of-value/.

——. "Before Man: Sylvia Wynter's ReWriting of the Modern Episteme." In McKittrick, *Sylvia Wynter: On Being Human as Praxis*, 90–105.

——. "Blacklight." In *Otobong Nkanga: Luster and Lucre*, edited by Clare Molloy, Philippe Pirotte, and Fabian Schöneich, 245–52. Berlin: Sternberg Press, 2017.

——. "Fractal Thinking." *aCCeSsions*, no. 2, April 27, 2016, https://accessions.org/article2/fractal-thinking/.

——. "Hacking the Subject: Black Feminism and Refusal beyond the Limits of Critique." *philoSOPHIA: A Journal of Continental Feminism* 8, no. 1 (2018): 19–41.

———. "An Introduction: The Predicament of Brazilian Culture." *Social Identities* 10, no. 6 (2004): 719–34.

———. "No-Bodies: Law, Raciality and Violence." *Griffith Law Review* 18, no. 2 (2009): 212–36.

———. "On Difference without Separability." In *32nd Bienal de São Paulo: Incerteza Viva*, edited by Jochen Volz and Júlia Rebouças, 57–66. São Paulo: Fundação Bienal de São Paulo, 2016.

———. "The Racial Limits of Social Justice: The Ruse of Equality of Opportunity and the Global Affirmative Action Mandate." *Critical Ethnic Studies* 2, no. 2 (2016): 184–209.

———. "Reading the Dead: A Black Feminist Poethical Reading of Global Capital." In King et al., *Otherwise Worlds*, 38–51.

———. "Scene of Nature." In *Searching for Contemporary Legal Thought*, edited by Justin Desautels-Stein and Christopher Tomlins, 275–89. Cambridge: Cambridge University Press, 2017.

———. *Toward a Global Idea of Race*. Minneapolis: University of Minnesota Press, 2007.

———. "Unpayable Debt: Reading Scenes of Value against the Arrow of Time." In *The documenta 14 Reader*, edited by Quinn Latimer and Adam Szymczyk, 81–112. Munich: Prestel, 2017.

Fortunati, Leopoldina. *The Arcane of Reproduction: Housework, Prostitution, Labor and Capital*. Translated by Hilary Creek. Brooklyn, NY: Autonomedia, 1995.

Foucault, Michel. *The Order of Things: An Archaeology of the Human Sciences*. New York: Vintage, 1994.

———. *"Society Must Be Defended": Lectures at the Collège de France, 1975–1976*. Translated by David Macey. New York: Picador, 2003.

Frank, Andre Gunder. "The Development of Underdevelopment." *Monthly Review* 18, no. 4 (1966).

Galileo. *Dialogue Concerning the Two Chief World Systems*. Translated by Stillman Drake. New York: Modern Library, 2001.

——. *The Two New Sciences*. Translated by Stillman Drake. Toronto: Wall & Emerson, 2000.

Glazer, Nathan, and Daniel P. Moynihan. *Beyond the Melting Pot: The Negroes, Puerto Ricans, Jews, Italians, and Irish of New York City*. Cambridge, MA: MIT Press, 1970.

Glissant, Édouard. *Poetics of Relation*. Translated by Betsy Wing. Ann Arbor: University of Michigan Press, 1990.

Gould, Carol C. *Marx's Social Ontology: Individuality and Community in Marx's Theory of Social Reality*. Cambridge, MA: MIT Press, 1980.

Hall, Stuart. "Race, Articulation, and Societies Structured in Dominance." In *Black British Cultural Studies: A Reader*, edited by Houston A. Baker Jr., Manthia Diawara, and Ruth H. Lindeborg, 16–60. Chicago: University of Chicago Press, 1996.

Harris, Cheryl. "Whiteness and Property." *Harvard Law Review* 106, no. 8 (June 1993): 1707–91.

Hartman, Saidiya. *Scenes of Subjection: Terror, Slavery, and Self-Making in Nineteenth-Century America*. New York: Oxford University Press, 1997.

Harvey, David. "The 'New' Imperialism: Accumulation by Dispossession." In *Socialist Register 2004: The New Imperial Challenge*, edited by Leo Panitch and Colin Leys. London: Merlin Press, 2003.

Hegel, G. W. F. *Outline of the Philosophy of Right*. Translated by T. M. Knox, edited by Stephen Houlgate. Oxford: Oxford University Press, 2008.

——. *Phenomenology of Spirit*. Translated by A. V. Miller. Oxford: Oxford University Press, 1977.

——. *The Science of Logic*. Translated and edited by George di Giovanni. Cambridge: Cambridge University Press, 2010.

Husserl, Edmund. *The Crisis of European Sciences and Transcendental Phenomenology*. Translated by David Carr. Evanston, IL: Northwestern University Press, 1970.

——. *General Introduction to a Pure Phenomenology*. Translated by F. Kersten. Book 1 of *Ideas Pertaining to a Pure Phenomenology and to a Phenomenological Philosophy*. The Hague: Martinus Nijhoff, 1983.

James, Joy. "Captive Maternal Love: Octavia Butler and Sci-Fi Family Values." In *Literature and the Development of Feminist Theory*, edited by R. Goodman, 185–99. Cambridge: Cambridge University Press, 2015.

——. "The Womb of Western Theory: Trauma, Time, Theft, and the Captive Maternal." *Carceral Notebooks* 12 (2016): 253–96.

Judy, R. A. *Sentient Flesh: Thinking in Disorder, Poiesis in Black*. Durham, NC: Duke University Press, 2020.

Kant, Immanuel. *Critique of the Power of Judgment*. Edited by Paul Guyer, translated by Paul Guyer and Eric Matthews. Cambridge: Cambridge University Press, 2000.

——. *Critique of Practical Reason*. Translated by Mary Gregor. Cambridge: Cambridge University Press, 2015.

——. *Critique of Pure Reason*. Translated and edited by Paul Guyer and Allen W. Wood. Cambridge: Cambridge University Press, 1998.

King, Tiffany Lethabo, Jenell Navarro, and Andrea Smith, eds. *Otherwise Worlds: Against Settler Colonialism and Anti-Blackness*. Durham, NC: Duke University Press, 2020.

Levine, Sam, and Ankita Rao. "In 2013 the Supreme Court Gutted Voting Rights—How Has It Changed the US?" *Guardian*, June 25, 2020. https://www.theguardian.com/us-news/2020/jun/25/shelby-county-anniversary-voting-rights-act-consequences.

Lloyd, David. *Under Representation: The Racial Regime of Aesthetics*. New York: Fordham University Press, 2019.

Locke, John. *An Essay Concerning Human Understanding*. London: J. M. Dent, 1993.

——. *The Second Treatise on Civil Government*. Indianapolis, IN: Hackett Publishing, 1980.

Lorde, Audre. "The Master's Tools Will Never Dismantle the Master's House." In *Sister Outsider: Essays and Speeches*, 110–14. Berkeley, CA: Crossing Press, 2007.

Lukács, Georg. *History and Class Consciousness: Studies in Marxist Dialectics*. Translated by Rodney Livingstone. Cambridge, MA: MIT Press, 1972.

Luxemburg, Rosa. *The Accumulation of Capital*. Translated by Agnes Schwarzschild. London: Routledge Classics, 2003.

Marx, Karl. *Capital: A Critical Analysis of Capitalist Production*. Vol. 1. Translated by Samuel Moore and Edward Aveling, edited by Frederick Engels. London: Swan Sonnenschein, Lowrey, 1889.

——. *Capital: A Critique of Political Economy*. Vol. 3, *The Process of Capitalist Production as a Whole*. Edited by Friedrich Engels. New York: International Publishers, n.d. Accessed December 12, 2020. https://www.marxists.org/archive/marx/works/download/pdf/Capital-Volume-III.pdf.

——. *Grundrisse: Foundations of the Critique of Political Economy*. Translated by Martin Nicolaus. London: Penguin Books, 1993.

McKittrick, Katherine, ed. *Sylvia Wynter: On Being Human as Praxis*. Durham, NC: Duke University Press, 2015.

Mill, John Stuart. *On Liberty*. New York: Penguin Classics, 2007.

Montero, Roberto. "Love in the Flesh, Toni Morrison and Hortense Spillers 30 Years after Beloved and Mama's Baby, Papa's Maybe." *Alpenglow: Binghamton University Undergraduate Journal of Research and Creative Activity* 4, no. 1 (2018). https://orb.binghamton.edu/alpenglowjournal/vol4/iss1/4.

Moten, Fred. *In the Break: The Aesthetics of the Black Radical Tradition*. Minneapolis: University of Minnesota Press, 2003.

——. "The Subprime and the Beautiful." *African Identities* 11, no. 2 (2013): 237–45.

Moynihan, Daniel P. *The Negro Family: The Case for National Action*. Office of Policy Planning and Research, United States Department of Labor, March 1965. Accessed July 15, 2020. https://web.stanford.edu/~mrosenfe/Moynihan%27s%20The%20Negro%20Family.pdf.

Myrdal, Gunnar. *An American Dilemma: The Negro Problem and Modern Democracy*. New York: Harper & Row, 1962.

Park, Robert E. "The Nature of Race Relations." In *Theories of Race and Racism—A Reader*, edited by Les Black and John Solomos, 105–12. London: Routledge, 2000.

Peralta, Eyder, and Krishnadev Calamur. "Ferguson Documents: How the Grand Jury Reached a Decision," NPR, November 25, 2014. https://www.npr.org/sections/thetwo-way/2014/11/25/366507379/ferguson-docs-how-the-grand-jury-reached-a-decision.

Plessy v. Ferguson, 163 U.S. 537 (1896).

Quijano, Aníbal. "Coloniality of Power, Eurocentrism, and Latin America." *Nepantla: Views from South* 1, no. 3 (2000): 533–80.

Robinson, Cedric J. *Black Marxism: The Making of the Black Radical Tradition*. Chapel Hill: University of North Carolina Press, 2000.

——. "Capitalism, Marxism, and the Black Radical Tradition: An Interview with Cedric Robinson." Interview by Chuck Morse. *Perspectives on Anarchist Theory* 3, no. 1 (Spring 1999). http://www.hartford-hwp.com/archives/45a/568.html.

Rovelli, Carlo. *The Order of Time*. Translated by Simon Carnell and Erica Segre. New York: Riverhead Books, 2018.

SLAC National Accelerator Laboratory. "SuperCDMS | Super Cryogenic Dark Matter Search." Accessed August 10, 2020. https://supercdms.slac.stanford.edu/overview.

Spencer, Herbert. *First Principles*. 2nd ed. London: Williams and Norgate, 1867.

Spillers, Hortense J. "Mama's Baby, Papa's Maybe: An American Grammar Book." *Diacritics* 17, no. 2 (Summer 1987): 64–81.

Spillers, Hortense, Saidiya Hartman, Farah Jasmine Griffin, Shelly Eversley, and Jennifer L. Morgan. "'Whatcha Gonna Do?' Revisiting 'Mama's Baby, Papa's Maybe: An American Grammar Book,'" *Women's Studies Quarterly* 35, nos. 1/2 (Spring–Summer 2007): 299–309.

Spivak, Gayatri Chakravorty. *A Critique of Postcolonial Reason: Toward a History of the Vanishing Present*. Cambridge, MA: Harvard University Press, 1999.

Terada, Rei. "Hegel's Racism for Radicals." *Radical Philosophy* 2, no. 5 (Autumn 2019): 11–22.

——. "The Racial Grammar of Kantian Time." *European Romantic Review* 28, no. 3 (2017): 267–78.

Thompson, E. P. *The Making of the Working Class*. New York: Vintage, 1966.

Tomba, Massimiliano. *Marx's Temporalities*. Leiden: Brill, 2013.

Tomich, Dale W. *Through the Prism of Slavery: Labor, Capital, and World Economy*. Oxford: Roman & Littlefield, 2004.

Truth, Sojourner. "Ain't I a Woman?" National Park Service. Accessed May 19, 2019. https://www.nps.gov/articles/sojourner-truth.htm.

Ture, Kwame, and Charles V. Hamilton. *Black Power: The Politics of Liberation*. New York: Vintage, 1992.

UNESCO. *Four Statements on the Race Question*. Paris: UNESCO, 1969. https://unesdoc.unesco.org/ark:/48223/pf0000122962.

Vernon, Jeremy. "The Black Panthers' 10-Point Program." Black Power in American Memory, April 18, 2017. http://blackpower.web.unc.edu/2017/04/the-black-panthers-10-point-program/.

Vitale, Sarah. "Beyond *Homo Laborans*: Marx's Dialectical Account of Human Essence." *Social Theory and Practice* 46, no. 3 (July 2020): 633–55.

Wallerstein, Immanuel. *The Modern World-System: Capitalist Agriculture and the Origins of European World-Economy in the Sixteenth Century*. New York: Academic Press, 1974.

Weber, Max. *Economy and Society: An Outline of Interpretive Sociology*. Edited by Guenther Roth and Claus Wittich. Vol. 1. Berkeley: University of California Press, 1978.

Weheliye, Alexander G. *Habeas Viscus: Racializing Assemblages, Biopolitics, and Black Feminist Theories of the Human*. Durham, NC: Duke University Press, 2014.

Wilderson, Frank B., III. "The Prison Slave as Hegemony's (Silent) Scandal." In *Warfare in the American Homeland: Policing and Prison in a Penal Democracy*, edited by Joy James, 23–34. Durham, NC: Duke University Press, 2007.

Williams, Raymond. *Marxism and Literature*. Oxford: Oxford University Press, 2009.

Wolfe, Patrick. "Settler Colonialism and the Elimination of the Native." *Journal of Genocide Research* 8 no. 4 (2006): 387–409.

Wynter, Sylvia. "Unsettling the Coloniality of Being/Power/Truth/Freedom: Towards the Human, after Man, Its Overrepresentation—An Argument." *CR: The New Centennial Review* 3, no. 3 (2003): 257–337.

Wynter, Sylvia, and Katherine McKittrick. "Unparalleled Catastrophe for Our Species? or, To Give Humanness a Different Future: Conversations." In McKittrick, *Sylvia Wynter: On Being Human as Praxis*, 57–58.

Žižek, Slavoj. *The Fragile Absolute, or Why Is the Christian Legacy Worth Fighting For?* London: Verso, 2000.

——. "We Can't Address the EU Refugee Crisis without Confronting Global Capitalism." *In These Times*, November 2015. http://inthesetimes.com/article/18385/slavoj-zizek-european-refugee-crisis-and-global-capitalism.

Denise Ferreira da Silva
Unpayable Debt

Published by Sternberg Press

On the Antipolitical, volume 1
Series Editor: Ana Teixeira Pinto

Editor: Max Bach
Proofreading: Zoë Harris
Index: Dan Michael Fielding
Design: Joaquín Gáñez
Printer: Tallinn Book Printers, Estonia

ISBN 978-3-95679-542-8

First published 2022, reprinted 2025

Distributed by The MIT Press, Art Data, Idea Books and Les presses du réel

Sternberg Press
71–75 Shelton Street
London WC2H 9JQ
www.sternberg-press.com